A barely audible voice whispered over the radio, "Four-four, this is 3-5. We're at the same drop-off location from yesterday. Be advised, bad guys very close, but they don't know we're here."

I flew on a few more minutes until we were almost on station. The LRRP keyed his microphone and I could hear shooting in the background. There was no whispering now. "Four-four, 3-5. Need help! We've been detected. Had to pop our claymores already."

There was very little time to take action. Since I remembered the exact location where the LRRPs were to have dug in, I decided to risk shooting without having them identify their locations. "Three-five, where do you want rockets?"

"Four-four, 3-5. Put 'em ten meters north. Hurry. We're having trouble holding them back."

This was a dicey proposition. Ten meters was the theoretical kill radius for our rockets. The LRRPs were calling down fire virtually on top of themselves. "Three-five, confirm. Only ten meters north?"

"That's affirm. Do it now!"

CENTAUR FLIGHTS

A Cobra Pilot in the 4th Cav

Richard D. Spalding

IVY BOOKS • NEW YORK

This book contains an excerpt from the hardcover edition of *Reluctant Warrior* by Michael C. Hodgins. This excerpt has been set for this edition only and may not reflect the final content of the hardcover edition.

Ivy Books
Published by Ballantine Books
Copyright © 1996 by Richard D. Spalding

Excerpt from *Reluctant Warrior* copyright © 1997 by Michael C. Hodgins.

http://www.randomhouse.com

Library of Congress Catalog Card Number: 96-94816

ISBN: 0-8041-1560-5

Manufactured in the United States of America

First Edition: March 1997

10 9 8 7 6 5 4 3 2 1

Contents

LOCATIONS OF MAJOR U.S. AND ALLIED COMBAT UNITS IN VIETNAM (EXCEPT ARVN)
December 1968

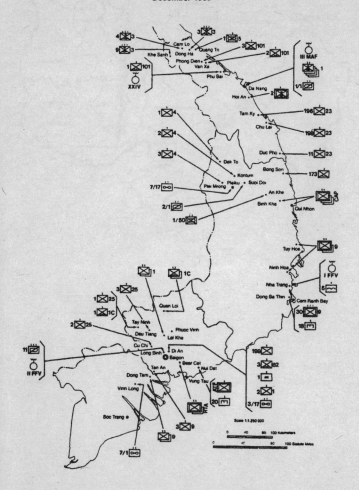

Cambodia

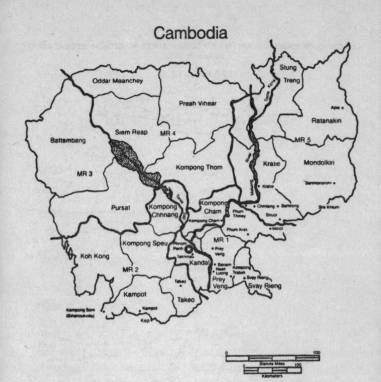

★ CHAPTER 1 ★

Something in the Blood

My blood line is German, Cherokee Indian, Irish, English, and French. Given the history of the French fighting the Germans and the English, the Irish fighting the English, and the Indians fighting everyone, maybe I had to be a soldier.

Or perhaps it was the three years of military high school that prepared me for Army aviation. The school, Miami Military Academy, was run like West Point. I remember listening, when I was only sixteen years old, to one of the military science instructors telling of his experience in the Pacific during World War II.

Captain Bartlett explained, "Before we tossed a grenade into a Jap hiding place we let the fuse burn for a while so they wouldn't have time to throw it back at us. Grenades had a five-second fuse. We'd count off seconds by saying 'One-Jap-dead, two-Jap-dead . . .' etc."

The school decided to offer flying as an extracurricular activity. The instruction was given in a Piper Cub seaplane on floats. I quickly discovered that, with only a seventy-five-horsepower engine, the plane came down a lot better than it went up.

At the end of my third flight lesson the instructor maneuvered the ship for the approach to landing. With reduced engine power, the ship silently glided down toward the glistening water of Biscayne Bay. Without the air blowing in through the open door, the tropical afternoon heat would have been extremely uncomfortable. The door was split horizontally at its midpoint and hinged at the top and bottom. The instructor had left the top opened upward and hooked to the underside of the wing while the door's bottom half was opened down and hooked to the lower edge of the fuselage. Effectively, there was no right side to the ship's small cockpit. We were gliding toward the bay from over the land. There was a row of tall palm trees at the edge of the bay that we had to clear before landing.

"In situations like this," said the instructor, "we can slip the plane. The slip increases our descent angle without increasing airspeed."

By kicking in the left rudder pedal and moving the joystick to the right, the instructor made the ship's nose yaw left and the wings roll to the right. We dropped like a stone! The wind burst into the cockpit, rustling the fabric sides of the little ship, and I looked straight down through the open door. It felt like I was going to fall out. I strained to lean left against the pull of gravity, grabbed a fuselage bar with my left hand, and held on for dear life until the instructor leveled the ship just before touching down to a perfect landing. While I taxied the ship back toward the docking ramp, I thought about quitting flight lessons. Why make myself scared? I thought. But something made me keep going.

Forced-landing practice took on added importance as I neared having the required flight time and skills necessary to fly solo. Forced landings were the first and most basic emergency procedure when flying single-engine airplanes. Even though my instructor was a pleasant enough person most of the time, he was beginning to get somewhat frustrated with me because I was having some difficulty in mastering forced-landing techniques. I began to dread each flight. I think my instructor knew this and tried to help. "Nice day to go flying, isn't it?" he said.

I looked up at the bright blue sky and saw only a very few

puffs of brilliant white cloud. "Yes it is. The ship's pre-flighted and ready to go. Are you ready?"

"Sure, let's do it."

We pushed the ship down the mossy wooden ramp into the water where it bobbed on Biscayne Bay's light chop. I kept hold of the wing strut and held the ship close to the ramp while the instructor climbed onto the float and into the rear seat. I pushed off the ramp and sprang up onto the float as the ship drifted away from the ramp. I hung on to the wing strut with my right hand, leaned forward, and gripped the little wooden prop with my left. I called to the instructor, "Contact."

"Contact," he answered, and turned on the magneto switches that would allow the engine's spark plugs to fire.

I spun the prop, and the little engine coughed to life. I carefully made my way back along the float to the open door and climbed into the front seat. The instructor told me to do the takeoff, which I did, and then he began to repeatedly ask a nagging question.

"Something's wrong. What is it?"

I scanned the instruments, what few there were, and otherwise looked around to see what the instructor might be talking about, but I didn't discover anything out of the ordinary. I made another practice takeoff. I had reached two hundred feet when the instructor abruptly pulled back the throttle to simulate an engine failure. I tentatively lowered the nose to try to retain flying speed.

"I've got the aircraft," said the instructor. He advanced the throttle and entered straight and level flight. "You idiot!" he said. "If you can't get the nose down any faster than that at low altitude then you may stall and spin in. That might not bother you, but I don't want to be with you when it happens. This is what I want you to do."

He entered a standard climb at full power, chopped the throttle, and pushed the stick abruptly forward. The nose of the small craft dropped precipitously while I was simultaneously thrown upward with my head aimed at a tubular steel fuselage bar. As I ducked and covered my head with my left arm, the instructor brought the plane back to straight and level flight and I crashed down onto my seat. Then came the disapproving scolding from the rear seat.

"Not only don't you get the nose down fast enough, you're even too dense to fasten your seat belt! *That's* what's been wrong all this time, dummy. Think you can remember to buckle up and to get the nose down if the engine quits now that you've seen the consequences of not doing both?"

There was no doubt about my remembering. I'd thought I was going right through the roof of the plane. I hadn't fully regained my composure, so I merely nodded my head yes. That was enough of an answer for the guru in the back seat. He knew the kind of lesson he'd given me wasn't easily forgotten. That's why he gave it to me in the first place.

I missed soloing on my sixteenth birthday by nine days. Solo-day drill has been the same for instructors for much of aviation history. They watch you make several successful takeoffs and landings and then pop the fateful question. "Are you ready to solo?"

When it became my turn, the question galvanized my senses. It was like I was outside my own body watching a play in which I was the star. Some uncontrolled force inside me automatically answered with the confidence of a novice, "Sure am."

"Okay, taxi over to that dock." The instructor climbed out onto the float, turned around, and gave me some last-minute instruction. "Take off, go around the pattern, land, and come back here to pick me up. Remember, with me not being in the plane it will tend to take off and climb a little faster than you're used to." He closed the door and climbed onto the dilapidated dock.

At last, I was alone in an airplane. There would be no one to save me if I screwed up. The thought was simultaneously exhilarating and scary. I lined up into the wind for takeoff, held the stick full back, and pushed the throttle forward. Spray pinged off the prop as the plane slowly accelerated. At forty miles per hour I leveled the nose and the plane skipped across the water. I reached takeoff speed and pulled back on the stick. The plane left the water and I was flying! Everything was happening just as I'd been taught. But wait. Something was amiss. The plane wasn't performing better than with the instructor aboard. In fact, it seemed quite a long time before I had enough altitude to make my first pattern turn. All the instrument indications were in their green arcs. I gave up trying to figure out what was wrong. I figured I was probably oversensing. When I got to the point in the pattern adjacent to where I wanted to land, I reached down to turn on the carburetor (carb) heat before retarding the throttle. It was already set to the full on position! I'd forgotten to turn it off after the last landing and hadn't checked it before takeoff. That's why the plane performed lousy during takeoff and climb!

The first thing I did after landing was to turn off the carb heat. I very carefully taxied up to the dock and picked up my instructor. He climbed in, slapped me on the shoulder good-naturedly, and said, "Congratulations, pilot. One thing, though, your pattern was a bit large, wasn't it?" This question was phrased in the timeless way of instructors probing for an answer that would cause the student to learn something new.

"Guess it was," I replied. I offered no further explanation. Better to not mention my lack of checklist discipline, I thought.

All through my junior and senior years I tried, but failed, to gain an appointment to the Air Force Academy. Going to the Air Force Academy had seemed like a natural extension of the path upon which I had set out in high school, but it was not to be. I did gain acceptance to Rutgers University and I looked forward to starting normal studies like all the other college-bound civilian students in the nation. It was 1966.

★ CHAPTER 2 ★

Storm Before the Calm

Rutgers was a no-nonsense place. I filed through the large gym doors with the rest of the freshmen for orientation. There were thousands of us. We all wore the required school tie.

A speaker approached the podium and waited for silence. "Everyone look at the person sitting on each side of you." He paused and looked over the audience for effect. "At the end of the first semester two out of the three of you won't be qualified to continue here. If you're not ready for the discipline of college studies then you can go grow up in the armed forces. Maybe you can return at a later date."

He wasn't kidding. There was a draft in effect. Student deferments were worth their weight in gold to some people. Being only seventeen, I wasn't yet too concerned.

My first-semester study load was heavy and included Air Force Reserve Officer Training Corp (ROTC). My plan was to complete college, do five years in the Air Force, preferably flying transports, and then get hired by the airlines. Planning and doing proved to be two different matters.

I tried out for the distinguished Air Force ROTC drill team, the Queen's Guard. I was very familiar with much of the drill, but the Guard didn't use oral commands. All movements were executed through silent counts. It was also strange to march without swinging my arms, as the Guard required. After a few weeks, we started to use rifles in our drills. We used the same kind of World War I–vintage Springfield '03 rifles I'd drilled with in high school. One dis-

6

tinct difference was that the Queen's Guard fixed thirteen-inch gleaming chrome bayonets to the rifles. Our rifle drills included twirls and exchanges. Twirls with fixed bayonets were spectacular for audiences; within the ranks they were downright sobering! A gleaming bayonet would be seen to whiz by out of the corner of each eye.

Even by studying all the time I couldn't keep up my grades. They were marginal except in Air Force ROTC, where I naturally excelled. I was "disinvited" to continue at Rutgers for the second semester. I could reapply the following year, but for spring 1967, studying was done. It was too late to get into some other school for that semester.

I was disappointed, but my dad, who was a pilot for Eastern Airlines, offered me a deal I couldn't refuse: "Well, Dan, I guess you can take one of a couple of options for this semester—you can either go to work or, if you want, I'll pay for you to get your commercial pilot's license."

Finishing work on my license sure sounded good, and it worked out even better than it sounded! It was January in New Jersey. When the weather was bad, I studied for my ground tests or went snow skiing. When the weather was good, I went flying. I rolled up flight hours like mad, and the day came to take my commercial pilot's license flight exam.

I had completed all the required air work maneuvers and we were heading back to the hometown airport, in Somer-ville, New Jersey. The FAA-designated examiner was an okay guy, but hadn't said very much during the check ride. His talk had been all to the point.

"When you get there, demonstrate a high overhead approach to a landing," he commanded.

Arriving over the airport at 3,000 feet, I positioned myself over the touchdown point, turned on the carb heat, pulled off all the power, and spiraled down in a tight sixty-degree banked left turn. At 1,200 feet I rolled right, headed for the pattern key position, and completed the approach to touch down gently at precisely the spot intended. No power adjustments had been necessary for the entire sequence. The examiner looked at me and somehow knew I was pleased with myself. Maybe I was smiling. We taxied over to the tie-down spot, and I shut off the engine. We sat for a moment, listening to the gyro's whine.

"Well, what do you think?" I said.

The examiner grumbled, trying hard not to acknowledge my capability. "Guess I'll have to sign off your commercial ticket. Then you can go get your Certified Flight Instructor (CFI) rating and learn how to fly," he said.

Pursuing the CFI was a lot like getting the commercial license except it was necessary to learn how to tell and show a student what to do. The examiner had been right. It was a lot easier to do the flying than to tell someone how to do it. Of course, airplane instructors fly from the right seat, and all the controls are designed to be operated from the left. This complicated things a bit, and added to the different visual perspective from the right seat, it took a few flight hours to get used to. One additional maneuver was added to the commercial pilot repertoire—spins. Spins are those maneuvers one sees in the movies, when the airplane is pointed straight at the ground and is twirling "out of control" around its nose. In the movies the velocity noise steadily increases until the fatal crash and fireball. Knowing I was going to do spins, even on purpose, was disconcerting. My dad volunteered to show me how to do them.

I rented a plane for the purpose. Dad and I climbed to 3,000 feet and went to the practice area. The cloudless sky was baby blue. Looking to the east we could see the smog barrier encircling New York City. Small trails of black Boeing 707 and DC-8 jet exhaust poked out from the smog in all directions. To avoid collisions, we made sure no jet exhaust trail was headed for our own little part of the sky.

"Okay, I've got the aircraft," Dad said. "First we'll do a couple of clearing turns."

The plane broke into a thirty-degree bank and turned through a half circle to the left and then back to the right. We scanned the area for conflicting traffic and saw none.

"Here we go," Dad said.

I grabbed the edge of the instrument panel with my right hand. With my left hand I held on to the front lower edge of the seat. Dad pulled off the power and pulled back on the stick to raise the nose. The stall warning horn blared with increasing intensity as we neared minimum flying speed. Air burbled over the top of the wing, causing a bass-sounding rumble that could be felt as well as heard. As the wing stalled (quit making lift), Dad kicked in full right rudder and goosed the engine with a shot of throttle. The plane's nose snapped right and down. It seemed to me we were going straight for the ground, which was now twirling madly in the windshield. The sensation was like riding in an airborne front-loading clothes dryer with its window pointed at the ground. Dad stopped the spin by applying full left rudder, pushing the nose even farther toward the vertical, and then pulling out firmly, but smoothly, before the airspeed climbed past redline. The pullout stress was two "g's." I noticed the g's most in my arms. Effectively, I weighed twice as much as normal.

Dad did a few more spins for demonstration. He talked me through each one, and I followed through on the controls.

"You ready to do one now, Dan?"

I wasn't ready. It was too scary. I had only begun to be able to keep my orientation a little during the maneuver. "I don't think so," I tentatively answered. "I think I've had enough for one day. I'll try again some other time."

It was a relief to hear Dad say, "It's your choice."

After we landed and shut down the ship, we walked across the parking area toward the operations building to pay for the rental. Although I hadn't done much of the flying, my clothes were wet from nervous sweat and I felt exhausted. Dad slapped me on the back good-naturedly.

"Just like they taught me in Army Air Corps primary flight training back in 1941. Flying is simple. If you want to go up, pull back. If you want to go down, pull back—hard."

I went up solo and tried to do a spin. I was too chicken to get into the maneuver. I either gave up and recovered normally from the incipient stall, or I ended up in a steep spiral dive. How could I get myself to do the job right? I had an idea that wasn't in any books.

I reduced power to idle and pulled the nose up slowly. The stall warning sounded and the air rumbling started. Then I closed my eyes while simultaneously jerking back on the wheel, kicking full right rudder, and goosing the engine.

I counted out loud to ten. Only then did I open my eyes. Voilà! The ground was spinning around nicely underneath my nose. I tried to count the turns, but I was disoriented and gave up. After what I thought was two turns, I added left rudder until the spinning stopped and lowered the nose by relaxing back pressure to break the stall. The airspeed built up rapidly! Before I knew it, the wind noise increased to a scream and the airspeed was into the yellow caution arc. I pulled back on the wheel gently, but firmly. By the time the ship reached the bottom of the pullout, the airspeed indicator was at redline. Trying to ignore the wind noise, I looked out at the left wing. It was bowed upward due to the g's, and it looked to me like it might break. While I climbed back up to altitude, I resolved not to look at the wings on my pullouts. After several more practices, I was able to get the ship in and out of the spin at will.

Next in line for a budding professional pilot was the instrument rating. I was taught to ignore my own senses and to trust the airplane instruments as to attitude, altitude, speed, and other parameters. Once this was mastered, it was possible to take off, navigate, and land without ever seeing much of the ground or sky. Of course, flying inside clouds means you don't see their physical form. This proved to be a distinct disadvantage.

It was summer. A mild warm front was moving through the area. My instrument instructor walked into operations after having flown a short air taxi flight to Connecticut.

"Hey, John, I know we're supposed to fly, but the weather doesn't look too hot. What do you think?"

"I just got back. It isn't too bad, and the forecasts are acceptable. We ought to be able to get some actual instrument time. Let's give it a try. File a flight plan to Philadelphia International and back. I'll meet you out at the plane."

The trip to Philly was a challenge for me. I was on instruments all the way. I'd gotten plenty of big-airport, high-density air traffic control flying and navigation practice. After landing, we went in to grab a Coke and check the weather for the return trip. The Flight Service Station weather briefer was not optimistic.

"We're getting some pilot reports of small embedded thunderstorms and turbulence along your return route," he said. "The ceiling and visibility aren't bad, though, and the forecast calls for improving conditions during your time of flight. Still . . . those storms could be a real problem for a small ship."

"Thanks a lot," said John. "We'll give it a try and see how it goes. We can always come back if it gets too interesting."

The plane we were flying was a two-place Cessna 150 trainer in which we sat side by side. Other than the seating arrangement, this plane was only a bit more sophisticated than the Cub in which I first soloed. It was legal for instrument flying, but had only the bare necessities.

As we climbed out and made contact with Air Traffic Control, John asked for the hand-held mike.

"Departure Control, this is Cessna 2-4-3-8 Charlie," he called.

"Three-eight Charlie go ahead," replied the controller.

"Ah . . . 3-8 Charlie has no radar," John said. "Could you keep us out of the large cells?"

The controller answered reassuringly: "Three-eight Charlie, wilco [will comply]."

Since we had no radar, it was not possible to see embedded thunderstorms that might be in our path. The controller's radar, although not specifically designed to do it, usually showed such storms. By the controller's "wilcoing" our request we could hope to be steered clear of any really big cells. We flew on for another five or ten minutes, receiving radar vector headings from Departure Control. As we reached 2,000 feet on our way up to our cruising altitude of 4,000 feet, it got dark and then the bottom fell out from under the plane, leaving my stomach somewhere in the dark clouds above us. The vertical speed indicator was pegged down. We were losing altitude fast! Suddenly, it felt as if I'd been hit in the butt with a brick. Now we were going up fast! We shot through 4,000 feet on our way to whatever altitude the storm might have in store for us. The wings were buffeted back and forth, making it very difficult to keep control.

Fighting a thunderstorm by trying to hold airspeed, altitude, or precise headings is one of the ways to cause an airplane to break up in midair. John sincerely hoped to avoid such an occurrence.

"Keep power constant and try to fly a level attitude," he cautioned.

No lightning flashed, but it sounded like there had been an explosion. The hard-driving rain was pelting our tiny aluminum craft without mercy. It was like being inside a snare drum. Drowned into submission by the intense rain entering the pitot tube, the airspeed indicator rapidly fell all the way to zero! The cockpit radio speaker was just above my left ear. The radio volume was turned full on, but I could barely make out the controller's asking us what our altitude was. If I could have taken my hand from the controls to pick up the mike I still couldn't have told him. Altitude was constantly changing, and, because of the turbulence, I couldn't read the altimeter very well anyway.

John leaned over a little and almost yelled to be heard over the din, "Can you hear what they're saying? I can't."

"Just barely," I replied while struggling to control the plane.

Taking the mike in hand, John proceeded to tell, not ask, the controller what we were going to do.

"Departure Control, this is Cessna 3-8 Charlie. Unable to hold altitude. Unable to hear your transmission. Proceeding direct to the VOR approach at North Philly. 3-8 Charlie, out."

To my surprise, John allowed me to continue to fly while he obtained the proper instrument approach plate and tuned the radios. North Philadelphia Airport was somewhere off to our right rear, and I headed for it while trying to lose some altitude in a semicontrolled manner. As we got within about ten miles of the airport, everything smoothed out and I made a reasonably normal instrument approach. Even the driving rain let up as we flew out of the cell. After landing, I taxied the little ship to a tie-down area, shut off the engine, got out, and stood under the wing. It was good to be on solid ground. My senses were keen to all the sights, sounds, and smells around me. A steady but light rain pelted the top side of the wing, making the same sound it does on a car roof. It was as if I was newly put on the earth and I was experiencing things for the first time. Everything seemed clean and fresh, especially the rain.

Armed with my new licenses, I wanted to get to work. Going back to college didn't seem like a very exciting thing to do when I could be a pilot earning my own money. I canvassed all the local airports. Because of all the hype that was then current about pilot shortages, I was surprised no jobs were available. A good example of the typical reaction I got came from one local airport manager.

As a slight smile crossed his weather-beaten face, he said, "Gee, son, I really don't have anything available. Besides, even if I did have an opening I couldn't hire you. No one would want to learn to fly with an eighteen-year-old. Sure do wish I'd been in your shoes when I was your age, though."

By the time I began to see the problem it was too late to reapply to Rutgers—or to any other major university, for that matter. I was, however, entitled to be admitted into the Florida regional college system because I'd graduated from a Florida high school. Miami-Dade Junior College had a special aviation curriculum. I looked forward to getting back to warm beautiful days with aviation as a central activity.

★ CHAPTER 3 ★

Mixed Directions

Compared to the rigor of Rutgers, the classes at Miami-Dade were easy. Of course, already being a licensed flight instructor and taking flight-related academics stacked the deck in my favor. One of my classmates told me about an operator at Homestead Airport who was giving aerobatic instruction. That sounded like something I'd like and that would keep up my flying proficiency. The school was using Citabria airplanes. Citabria is Airbatic spelled backward. The name was a neat marketing gimmick for jazzing up what was essentially an old design for airplanes.

The Homestead field was located close to the Everglades, away from most signs of civilization. I drove around looking for the field; but there were no road signs. Finally, I homed in on the airport by watching light aircraft flying in the traffic pattern. I found the appropriate operator when I spotted the Citabrias. Since the Citabria was a tailwheel airplane, their noses pointed up in an almost snooty attitude, and they stood out from the rest of the general aviation aircraft, which had nosewheels.

The Citabria was a modernized, beefed-up version of a 1930s-vintage Champion airplane, which was much like a Piper Cub. The Citabria had a 115-horsepower engine, rather than the Cub's 75, and could safely pull six g's positive and 3 g's negative. Later in my career one flight student cut through the technical jargon about positive and negative g's quite nicely: "Positive g smashes your head into your butt while blood pools in your feet. Negative g stretches your spine and bursts your eye capillaries." It was a crude but accurate description.

I walked through some beat-up double doors into the small operations building. There was no one else in the room except for one man behind the counter.

"Hi, I'm Dan Spalding."

The man lifted his arm across the counter and offered his hand for me to shake. "My name's Frank. Glad to meet you. What can we do for you today?"

"I'm a CFI. I heard you guys give aerobatic instruction. I'd like to get an intro so I can practice on my own a little. Any problems with that approach?" I asked hopefully.

"You got any tailwheel time?" he asked.

"No, but I'm well studied on them."

"Well, they're not all that different," he said. "If you're reasonably sharp it shouldn't take too long to check out. If you want, we can go up right now and see how it goes."

Frank came out from behind the counter and led the way. As we walked across the thirty feet of ramp area to a red-and-white sunburst-striped ship, Frank cautioned me, "Things can happen very fast when we're throwing the ship around. If anything goes wrong and I say I've got the ship, please let go of the controls. I'm getting kind of old and I'm not that strong anymore."

I guessed Frank to be in his mid-thirties, and he didn't look all that frail to me. Nevertheless, his line was a lot friendlier than "Look, asshole, if you fight me for the controls we can die."

Taxiing out, I found myself dancing back and forth on the rudder pedals to keep the plane straight. Although the Citabria's forward visibility was not as good as in a nose-wheel aircraft, it was okay since I sat in the front seat. Sometimes a little brake was needed on one wheel to keep the ship headed straight. The brakes were awkward. Unlike modern aircraft, the brake pedals were applied with the heels. It was necessary to rotate both heels inward to reach the pedals.

Frank talked me through takeoff procedures as we taxied. I lined up on the runway center line for takeoff and pushed the throttle forward cautiously. I was wary of the infamous tendency of tailwheel aircraft to be pulled off direction by "torque." I fed in lots of right pedal and was able to keep the plane reasonably on the runway center line. At the proper speed I pushed the stick forward to lift the tail. The torque changed abruptly. The plane veered to the right; I corrected left, but too much. The left side of the runway loomed in the windshield. I was about to initiate a right swerve to keep from exiting the runway when we reached takeoff speed. A little back pressure on the stick popped us into the air. With its bigger engine, the little ship climbed briskly even in the heat.

"Do some chandelles to get some altitude," Frank directed.

I lowered the nose into a shallow dive and let the speed build up. At entry speed I banked thirty degrees, pulled the ship's nose up to trade airspeed for altitude, and simultaneously added full power. Wind noise got progressively quieter and that made the engine seem progressively louder. After turning through ninety degrees, I gradually and continuously reduced my bank. The airspeed was just above stall when we had reversed direction, and we'd gained almost 1,000 feet. I did two more chandelles.

Frank said, "I have the airplane," and gave the stick a slight wiggle to signal me to let go. In a very short time, with me following through on the controls, Frank demonstrated loops, snap rolls, and barrel rolls. Then he rolled the ship upside down and held it there. I immediately wished I'd tightened my seat belt more. The belt stretched, and my head seemed close to the top of the cockpit. If I hadn't concentrated on pushing my feet up to the floor my knees would have dropped and hit my chin. Dust and crap fell up (I mean down) into my face. Frank kept the ship inverted and did a few gentle turns, then he rolled us upright.

"You want to do some loops?" asked Frank.

"That'd be great."

"Okay, you've got the airplane."

I took the stick in my right hand and gave it a wiggle while I placed my left hand on the throttle. I lowered the nose into a shallow dive and added power to gain airspeed. Then I pulled back on the stick and, as the nose came up through the horizon, I added full power. The engine noise increased and airspeed began to fall off rapidly. I kept pulling back on the stick, but not enough. I reached the top of the loop without enough airspeed, got disoriented, and allowed the ship to fall out of the maneuver. It careened crazily, simultaneously spinning ninety degrees and heading for the ground. I managed to regain control and pulled out to straight and level flight.

Understating the obvious, Frank said, "That wasn't too great. Try a few more. You need to use more back pressure on the stick sooner."

I did a few more loops, and the last one was actually pretty good. Then Frank got bored. "Now for some real fun!" he said with enthusiasm. Frank took control, rolled over into inverted flight, and lowered the nose into a dive. He rolled right side up and pulled up into a loop. At the top of the loop he jerked the stick back and kicked in full left rudder. The ship snapped abruptly into a left spin. Frank had done most of the flying, and I thought I should do something to get my money's worth from the lesson. Besides, I thought Frank might be trying to intimidate me to see how I'd react. "Do you want me to recover?" I inquired.

"Sure, go ahead. You've got it."

I jammed in full right rudder. Unlike the Cessnas I was used to, the ship didn't stop spinning instantly, but finally, after another quarter turn, it did stop. I released back pressure on the stick but that didn't break the stall.

"You need more forward pressure than in a normal trainer," Frank instructed.

I pushed the stick farther forward and that did it. The airspeed didn't build up as fast as I was used to, but the pullout was otherwise normal.

"Do you know where you are?" asked Frank.

"Yeah, we're right over the field."

"Okay, let's enter the pattern and shoot some landings."

My first couple of landings in the tailwheel airplane with spring-steel main landing gear were a matter of bouncing and veering almost, but not quite, out of control. Frank never touched the controls, though. His nerve was amazing! The last three landings weren't smooth and, to me, bordered on being dangerous. However, each landing was a little better than the last, and I never quit trying to make the airplane do what I wanted it to.

"Let's taxi in," Frank said.

As we walked to operations I wondered how much dual instruction time I was going to be required to take.

"So what do you think?"

"You're not too bad," he said. "A couple of hundred more flight hours and you might make a pretty good pilot. Right now I'll sign you off as a qualified renter. Just be cautious. Let me know when you want to get some more dual aerobatics."

I was astounded at the brevity of the check ride, but pleased to not have to foot the bill for a lot more dual instruction.

I'd checked out a library book on aerobatics, and my routine for teaching myself aerobatics consisted of two parts. First I'd study one or two maneuvers during the week. Then on the weekend I'd go flying. I'd practice until I either successfully executed the maneuvers or I scared myself, whichever came first. Not a conventional way to learn, but it worked as long as I wasn't too picky about precision.

I told one of my classmates about my endeavors and he was wild to go with me. Jim had never flown before and I was wary of his reactions.

"You can come along next time if you like, but it's not my fault if you're ruined for flying," I cautioned.

Up we went. The blind leading the blindest. Before each maneuver I'd tell Jim what I was going to do. After I completed each maneuver I looked back over my shoulder and asked if he was ready for some more. I did a loop. All was well. A snap roll, no problem. Then I did a falling leaf.

"That one was fun, let's do it again!" said Jim.

I did some chandelles to gain altitude and entered a three-turn spin. This time when I looked back, Jim was literally green! I'd never seen anyone that color before. I didn't ask if he was okay, but quickly entered the traffic pattern, landed on the grass, braked as hard as I could, and threw the door open. Jim heaved mightily. The vomit shot out of his mouth as if propelled by some invisible pressure tank.

"Guess that's enough for one day," I said.

"Yeah, that's enough for me," Jim said with a quavering voice.

I taxied the ship over to its tie-down and pulled the fuel/air mixture control to the idle cutoff position to shut down the engine. Jim got out of the airplane, turned around to face it, put his arm on the engine cowling, and rested his head on his arm. He stayed that way until I had secured the tie-downs.

"You okay to go now?" I asked.

"I guess so. It must've been something I ate."

"Like hell. Unless you want to claim to have been eating spins."

"Well, maybe you're right. Guess I'll wait until I get some normal flying under my belt before we do this again."

I was getting bored with school. It was too easy. I took out a classified ad to give flight instruction, but the only call I got was from a female who invited me to a party in a pretty posh part of town. The conversation turned real strange. "Do you wear one of those skimpy brief bathing suits?" she asked. Then in the background I heard a door open and some guy yelled, "What the hell are you doing on the phone?" There was a crash, and the phone went dead at the other end. Four hours ahead of "party time," I drove to the address I'd been given. I was worried about the girl and just plain curious as well. The party address sat between two beautiful and quite large houses, but the only thing at the party address was an empty lot. I decided not to show up after dark.

In the fall of 1967, my draft board in New Jersey finally figured out I was no longer at Rutgers and changed my draft status to 1-A (prime meat)—no student deferment. I figured I could fight the classification by showing I was in college full-time, but it didn't seem to be the right thing to do. Every night the war news from Vietnam was on the television. It looked like things were heating up into a larger conflict. I began to think it would be proper to enlist in the armed forces. It was time to do my bit, and by enlisting at least I could get a choice of what I did.

Of course, already being a pilot, I wanted to fly. I checked with every recruiter—Air Force, Navy, Coast Guard, Marines, and Army. All except the Army required a college degree to enter flight training. None of the branches gave any "credit" for already being a pilot. The Coast Guard recruiter told me they required their pilots to be graduates of the Coast Guard Academy! The Army recruiter told me that since I was already an airplane pilot it was likely I'd get sent to fixed-wing school. A heavy-duty written test was given to weed out recruits with little potential for success in flying. I had bought a book that had the basics of helicopter flight theory in it, and I studied it in preparation for the exam. I was quite surprised to find out I scored better in the helicopter portion of the exam than in the fixed-wing portion. The only answer to this curiosity was that grades must have been awarded on the curve. Apparently, most people knew even less about helicopters than I did.

It was only October, and I wanted to finish the school semester before joining up, so I took advantage of a delayed enlistment option. My date to report for active duty was January 8, 1968. I would be nineteen years old.

★ CHAPTER 4 ★

First a Soldier

Through happenstance, I missed my flight to Fort Polk, where I was to go through basic training. With my military school background, I knew this was not a good way to start out. A call to the processing center got me assigned to other transportation.

The flight I was supposed to be on would have connected with a Trans Texas Airways flight into Fort Polk.

Trans Texas Airways (TTA) flew vintage DC-3 airplanes and was disparagingly known as "Tree Top Airways." Now, however, I had the dubious honor of taking a bus. It was a long ride across the Louisiana swamps. I would have preferred TTA.

I arrived at Fort Polk about three A.M. A light but steady rain was falling. A drill instructor (DI) got into the doorway of the bus to give directions.

"You guys fall out of the bus and beat feet to the supply building over there. When you get there, stand on one of the yellow squares. Now, *move out!*"

We rushed into the downpour, running the twenty yards to the building pointed to by the DI. There were some painted yellow squares on the pavement. Each one was two feet square, and each of us made sure he found one to stand on. There was some pushing and shoving, full-contact musical chairs played in the rain.

The DI was displeased to be up so early in the morning in the rain. Unlike us, at least he was wearing a poncho to keep off the rain. "Everyone quit moving around," the DI barked over the noise of the rain. "Face the building. Put your heels together with your toes angled out at forty-five degrees. Cup your hands at your sides with your thumb along your pant seam. Look straight ahead. *Don't move!* This, gentlemen, is called attention. We will now wait for Supply to open so you can be issued your bedding."

The DI ambled over to the supply shed, turned to face us, and sat down under a small overhang covering the supply building steps. We waited, at attention, in the rain, for about an hour. Around four A.M. the door opened and we were given sheets, blankets, and pillowcases. We ran individually over to a barracks. Inside, another DI insisted that we make up our bunks. At 4:30 we fell out and walked to breakfast as a group.

I had thought there would be some sort of special basic training for future pilots, but I was wrong. The way the

Army figured it, any one of its people might find himself on the ground in a battle. Basic training was going to be the same for everyone.

We assembled outside the barracks and our DI introduced himself. "At ease, flatdicks," he said. "My name is Sergeant Riggs. *Never* call me 'sir.' I am a noncommissioned officer and I am to be called sergeant."

"Flatdicks" turned out to be the best thing he would call us all through basic.

Between training sessions a group of us talked with one of our marksmanship instructors, who had returned from Vietnam fairly recently. We knew he had received the Silver Star and were anxious to know what combat in Vietnam was like.

"I'll tell you one thing," he said. "Pay attention here. Some of what you learn will be useful, but combat has a way of being spontaneous and unpredictable. Sometimes you have to make up your own rules. In my case, our base camp was overrun. We ended up in hand-to-hand fighting, but things happened so fast there wasn't any time to fix bayonets. I took off my helmet and struck anything that moved. Hell, I killed more gooks with my steel pot than with anything else!"

I remember being very confused about one part of our dietary regimen. After a few weeks, we were allowed to go to the Post Exchange. We could buy 3.2 percent beer, but for some reason we weren't allowed to drink Coke or any other kind of soda. The Army must have had its reasons, but it seemed real weird to me.

There were lots of training movies. Two of them made an impression on me. When we first arrived we were marched into the auditorium, where a DI briefly introduced a film. "In case you haven't figured it out, the barracks you're living in have been around since the Second World War. They're older than a lot of you. The film you're going to see shows why there's no smoking in bed."

The lights dimmed as the film started. One of our barracks appeared on the screen. A GI walked in and started a small fire in the middle of the lower floor. A time-sequenced film showed the barracks burning to the ground. It took only ten minutes of real time until the barracks was nothing but a pile of ashes.

After viewing the second film, I hoped it had no relevance to me or my eventual duty destination. The film was about cold weather operations. It explained how to prevent frost-bite. Then the film showed what happens if bad frostbite isn't prevented. A time lapse was shown of a soldier's toes withering up into a set of blackened stubs. I cringed at the end when what was left of the toes was lifted off the foot with tissue goo streaming behind.

The *Pueblo* incident occurred while I was in basic training. The North Koreans surrounded and captured one of our intelligence-gathering Navy ships, which we claimed was in international waters. Boot camp gossip had it that Korea might be a new destination for us. The image of the frostbitten foot plagued me. Also, the massive Viet Cong Tet offensive of 1968 started about a month into my basic training. The way the news reported the Tet offensive, it sounded as if the United States was getting its ass kicked. Some people began to think going to Korea sounded good. Especially the draftees. Draftees and volunteers were inter-mixed in basic training. As the real consequences of our training began to hit home, some of the draftees began to think about getting out of the Army. This attitude reached its peak one day on the rifle range.

After firing a group of shots, I walked toward my target, as did the rest of the platoon. Strung out side by side, we car-ried our unloaded rifles. This safety precaution prevented a rifle's being accidentally fired from behind us. I came to a point a foot in front of my target, bent forward a little, and reached out to remove the target from its holder. There was a loud report from a rifle to my right. I, and everyone else, dove for the ground. As I was on my way down I looked right and saw something black flying up into the air. The DIs ran over to the commotion and helped someone limp back toward the firing line. Eventually the DIs told us to carry on. No explanations were made at that time. We finished shooting and marched the seven miles back to the barracks. The next day we heard that a recruit had been so overwhelmed by being in the Army that he had tried to blow off part of his foot to get himself out. The black object I'd seen flying was the toe of his combat boot. As we heard it, the recruit's ploy backfired; he didn't do enough damage. He was patched up, jailed for a few weeks, then "recycled." He got to start basic training all over again.

As a sort of finale to basic training we had to negotiate an infiltration course. The infiltration was supposed to simulate what it would be like to assault a fortified enemy position. Machine guns were set up at one end of the course to fire live ammunition over our heads. Starting from the far end of the course, we were to make our way past the machine guns. We had to traverse a maze of barbed wire, trenches, and sand-bagged areas containing explosives that could be set off at will by the DIs. Just to make the whole thing interesting, it had to be done at night. The course was covered with sand and dirt, as if we were preparing for the Normandy landings of World War II. During the day we got to do the course without any explosions or live fire. Of course, we had to low-crawl through the sand and dirt. Low-crawling on elbows and hips was an excruciatingly tiring thing to do, and the DIs were fond of using it for physical punishment when we screwed up. Our platoon lined up in single file along the side of the course. We were walking down an inclined ramp that led us into a trench from which we'd "go over the top" at the far end of the course. I looked off into the distance and noticed something.

"Hey, Joe, look at those trees out there. See anything odd?"

"No. What the hell are you worried about?"

"I'm not worried. At least, no more than the rest of the platoon. But it looks to me like those trees are chopped off from all the bullets going their way."

"Yeah, I see that. So what?"

"So . . . all the treetops are at least ten feet above the course. The DIs must make sure the machine guns are aimed high so the bullets are not so low to the ground. That means low-crawling isn't necessary. Hell, I bet we could stand up and walk the course and not get hit!"

"You do whatever you want," said Joe, "but as for me, I ain't going to be standing up with real bullets flying over my head."

That night, I waited my turn to climb out of the trench. The noise from the machine guns was continuous and thousands of orange tracers flew by over the trench. There were intermittent very loud explosions, and every once in a while a flare would go off over the course. The tension of the situation built up in all of us. Somehow, thinking about the height of the trees didn't work to break my own tension. It was scary.

A whistle blew and I climbed out of the trench into the sand. Of course, a whole group of us went over the top at the same time, but it was a pitch-black night and I couldn't see anyone else. I felt very alone. I couldn't even see the obstacles ahead of me. I started to low-crawl and soon my legs and arms began to ache from fatigue. I came upon a ditch before I knew it and kind of flopped three feet down into it, hitting the bottom hard. This really stinks, I thought. I'm going to get through this as fast as I can. No more low-crawling for me. I got out of the ditch and began to crawl on my hands and knees as fast as I could go. I couldn't bring

myself to stand up, though. Whenever I looked up at the
tracers, they didn't appear as high off the ground as my mind
told me they were. I was making good time when I hit my
head hard on a sandbag wall. I knew there were explosives
behind the sandbag, so I quickly moved to the right and
increased my pace, but the DIs must have been watching.
The noise and concussion of the subsequent explosion made
my ears ring and, dazed, I stopped dead in my tracks. I'd lost
my bearings and it took a moment to figure out which way to
go. Finally, I pointed myself in the direction of the machine
guns and proceeded full speed ahead past them. My only
thought as I stood up was that I hoped like hell I never had to
do anything like this for real. It would have been suicide.

As graduation time neared, I was anxious about my next
assignment. Of course, I was supposed to go to primary
flight school. According to my recruiter, fixed-wing flight
school. But, if the Army screwed up ... It was nerve-
wracking. When orders were finally posted I was only partly
relieved; I was going to primary flight training. Primary *helicopter* flight training.

★ CHAPTER 5 ★

Hover Happy

Primary helicopter school was conducted in Fort Wolters,
Texas. Fort Wolters was fifty miles west of Fort Worth. Fifty
miles west of Fort Worth was the middle of nowhere. There
was, of course, the ubiquitous military town—in this case,
Mineral Wells—located next to the base. Unlike Leesville,

the town outside the gate at Fort Polk, which had been nick-named "Fleasville," Mineral Wells had no Army nickname.

As a basic trainee I got used to being treated as a nothing. Upon graduation I became a "real" private and was treated like a soldier. Becoming a warrant officer candidate (WOC, sounds like "rock") I became less than nothing. The first several weeks of WOC schooling were military leadership training. The hazing, physical exercise, harassment, and mental games were like those of any officer candidate school.

The olive drab Army bus pulled up in front of the head-quarters building in Fort Wolters. The brakes squealed as the driver brought the bus to a halt. I looked out my window and saw we were being greeted by several upper-classmen who, judging by their actions, hadn't eaten their ration of meat that week. The bus door opened and one of the upperclassmen bounded onto its steps to usher us out. "Fall out and form up beside the bus!" he yelled. We gathered into platoon-size elements and stood at attention. The upperclassmen worked their way down every rank yelling questions in our faces. An incorrect answer earned one the privilege of push-ups. One tall and imposing upper-classman was particularly unpleasant. "What's a WOC?" he boomed as he came face-to-face with each rigid candidate. No one answered satisfactorily. I, like everyone else, got to do twenty push-ups. Arriving at the last person in the ranks, the upperclassman seemed to have grown weary of the game.

"Let's see if you're any smarter than these other morons," he said. "What's a WOC, candidate?"

"Sir. I don't know, sir," answered the candidate. All possible answers had already been exhausted by the men before him.

"Give me twenty push-ups—*now*," the upperclassman screamed. He walked out in front of the platoon, looked us over with disdain, and began to elaborate on how pitiful we were. "You guys aren't going to make it. You're all too dumb." In the best Elmer Fudd imitation I'd ever heard, he said, "Everyone here knows a WOC is what you throw at a wabbit. All of you, give me twenty more push-ups for being so dumb."

At the first opportunity, I searched out an authority to discuss my assignment. I stood square in the open doorway of the TAC officer's office and knocked on the doorsill to get his attention. The TAC looked up from his paperwork and motioned me into his inner sanctum. I took three steps forward, centered myself in front of the TAC's desk, and snapped a salute that he promptly returned.

"At ease, candidate," he said. "What do you want?"

"Sir, I'm a civilian fixed-wing flight instructor. How can I go about getting transferred into fixed-wing school? It seems to me they could give me some short transition training to qualify me as a fixed-wing Army aviator."

The counselor chuckled under his breath. "You've got to be kidding," he said. "Everyone wants fixed-wing school. Trouble is, there's no need for new fixed-wing pilots in the Army. As far as I know, the fixed-wing school is shut down. Hope you like choppers, candidate."

So did I.

Our entire time at Fort Wolters, clothes, personal hygiene, shoes, and facilities all had to remain inspection-spotless. The concrete barracks floors were spit-shined by hand. You could literally see your reflection in them! Anyone who dared wear shoes to walk on one of these marvels was grossly abused by his compatriots.

I got to be friends with Joe Klecko. Joe had been in the Air Force as an enlisted-man flight engineer. Joe was the "old" guy in our outfit. He was thirty. Joe's background was a lot different from that of the rest of us, and I was curious.

"How come you signed up to be a WOC, Joe?" I asked. "Didn't you have a pretty good career going in the Air Force?"

"It's kind of a long story, but I can sum up the reasons with one incident. When I was working in C-124s we had to have periodic crew check rides. On one check ride the flight-check captain decided it was time for some engine-out procedures. He reached over and pulled back the throttle on one of our four engines. The check ride was normally kind of a formality because we were flying a lot all the time. I was feeling feisty. Instead of going into the required engine-out emergency procedures, I calmly reached over, took another one of the four throttles in my hand, pulled off the power, looked the check captain in the eye, and said, 'Your turn.' This guy was a hard-ass. He took offense at my levity and wrote me up. It was kind of the straw that broke the camel's back. That's when I decided to get out of the Air Force. I had no college, and the Army was the only branch that would let me be a pilot. So, here I am."

Another prior-service convert was Glenn Fredricks. Glenn had been a bosun's mate in the Navy. When Glenn was the CQ (charge of quarters), we'd be blasted awake from sound sleep by the piping of a bosun's whistle. This was almost a sacrilege on an Army base. Glenn caught hell for it from the TACs, but they couldn't stop him no matter how many push-ups and extra duties they heaped on him. I think Glenn believed he was upholding the honor of the Navy or something. The bosun's whistle was a minor irritant compared to another habit of Glenn's. He'd suck up a mouthful of lighter fluid and spit it out while setting it on fire. The scorch marks on the barracks ceiling were hard to remove.

Every morning we would stand at attention in formation while the post flag was raised. Shortly after the flag reached the top of its mast a distinct buzzing approached from our left. A small training helicopter would come into view, and I'd watch as the base commander flew his personal TH-55 to the helipad in front of his office. It made me anxious to start flight training and added to the frustration of doing only classroom work.

Finally, the day came to start flying. I was glad to have been assigned to train in the TH-55. The other trainers, the OH-13 and the OH-23, were birds dating back to the Korean War. I walked into the flight briefing room. There were lots of tables with cardboard nameplates on them. I located the table having a nameplate with my last name on it. There were three students to an instructor. My instructor was a Captain Graham. Graham was five foot six, had a flat-top haircut, and was built like a boxer. Like all our instructors, he was a Vietnam veteran.

"So, Spalding. I see from your paperwork that you're a civilian rated fixed-wing pilot."

"Yes sir, that's right."

"Where did you train for your licenses?"

"Mostly out of Morristown, New Jersey, sir."

"No kidding? Did you ever get into Somerville?"

"Yes sir. That was my hometown airport."

"Well, I'll be damned," said Graham. "I trained there myself as part of ROTC with Rutgers University. Looks like it really is a small world, huh?"

"Yes sir, it sure does."

Graham's somewhat loose manner was a welcome change from all the spit and polish. After a little more introductory chitchat with his other two candidates, Graham took us out to the flight line and showed us how to preflight the little helicopter. On the way, Graham explained a deviation from military protocol.

"You don't salute anyone when you're on the flight line," he said. "The idea is to be alert to turning rotor blades. Saluting could be an unsafe distraction. Of course, if being decapitated doesn't worry you, salute all you want."

There must have been three hundred of the two-place ships sitting on the flight line. They were positioned on individual painted squares, like the ones my basic training class had started out on, except these were helicoptor size. People or aircraft, the Army approach was the same.

Like all helicopters, the TH-55 had some unique characteristics. The main rotor transmission was driven by a set of five automobile-type V-belts. The three main rotor blades were fully articulated. That is, they were hinged so that they could flap up and down and move fore and aft at the rotor hub. The TH-55 had two tubular skids for landing gear. The design combination of skids and a fully articulated rotor could lead to a condition known as ground resonance. Ground resonance could occur as the the ship began to alight on its gear for landing. A little bounce from the skids could be transmitted into the rotor system and in short order the ship would vibrate itself apart. Shock absorbers were supposed to stop this, but I did see it happen once. Luckily the pilot, a solo student, shut the ship down quickly—and he walked away from the pile of junk that had once been a helicopter. The TH-55 had other curious characteristics. For instance, we weren't to fly it in the rain. The tail rotor was balanced with a special tape. Rain would cause the tape to come off, the tail rotor to get out of balance, and the resulting high-frequency vibration could cause loss of control. Furthermore, on the outside top of the two-person cabin bubble was an airfoil. Without this airfoil the ship had a tendency to nose over uncontrollably when in autorotation.

As I absorbed all this information about the machines I was going to spend hundreds of flying hours in I began to realize that my first thoughts about helicopters had been correct: They're kind of an accident looking for a place to happen.

Unlike airplanes, helicopters couldn't spin, but they made up for that lack of stimulation with a unique one of their own—autorotation. Autorotation occurs when a helicopter engine stops but the air passing up through the rotor keeps it spinning. The idea was to cushion the forced landing by using the rotational energy in the rotor just before touching the ground. Like engine failure practice before my first airplane solo, autorotation took on special importance as my training got more advanced. The whole maneuver took only twenty seconds from 500 feet. Quick reactions and positive control were a necessity. To practice autorotations, the instructor would chop the motorcycle grip throttle. The correct reaction was to immediately bottom the collective pitch-control lever held in your left hand. Otherwise the rotor would not autorotate. Falling with a stopped rotor, out of control and ultimately crashing, was not one of the instructor pilots' favorite maneuvers. They were emphatic and forceful about making us get the collective down quickly. When the collective was quickly bottomed it gave you the same sensation as jumping off a cliff. You began to go down rather fast but still kept some forward speed. Simultaneously with bottoming the collective, full right pedal had to be added so as to stop the ship from spinning around the rotor, but in the opposite direction.

Helicopters don't really glide. The descent angle in an autorating TH-55 was forty-five degrees. When the ship got down to fifty feet above the ground a backward pull on the cyclic control stick, located between the legs and held in the right hand, would make the ship rear back like a bronco. This stopped forward motion. Landing slightly sideways, on skids, with forward motion could cause the ship to roll over. Before the tail rotor contacted the ground, which would also be a nasty experience, the cyclic was pushed forward to level the ship and the rotor pitch was increased by pulling up on the collective. This stopped the downward momentum and cushioned the landing. Done right, everything was cool. Done wrong, consequences could be very serious. There was only one try. In civilian training they didn't even practice autorotations all the way to a ground touchdown.

*   *   *

On my presolo check ride, with a different instructor, I had completed all maneuvers but autorotations. Making a series of normal approaches to landings, I was flying in a rectangular traffic pattern. I'd noticed a great field for an emergency landing to the side of the heliport. It was on the instructor's (the left) side of the ship, so it wasn't too easy for me to see. Being an instructor myself, I knew that one instructional technique was to wait for a student to be preoccupied with something else and then give him a forced landing. While flying the normal traffic pattern, we came into position beside the field. I looked away to my right with a deliberate and exaggerated head movement. Sure enough, the instructor pilot (IP) cut the throttle. I bottomed the pitch and banked hard to the IP's side. I rolled out, and my selected field appeared in view through the chin bubble. It was in perfect position. I continued the approach, making small corrections until the IP saw that I had the maneuver nailed. Then he took over to recover from the approach.

"Nice job, candidate," said the IP.

"Thanks, sir."

"I'm going to sign off this ride as an A, but you realize it's up to your own IP as to when or if you solo, right?"

"Yes, sir. That's perfectly clear."

The next day, Graham had me working on steep takeoffs and landings. After the third landing, the intercom clicked on. "Hover over there and set her down," he said as he pointed to the side of the heliport.

As I gently lowered the ship onto its skids, Graham looked over at me and asked the required question, "Are you ready to solo?"

I knew I was flying okay, but I also knew I wasn't really the master of the machine. I looked over at Graham and said, "Sure I am—as long as nothing goes wrong."

Graham laughed, disconnected his helmet from the radio system, got out of the ship, and sent me on my way. After returning to the main heliport, we boarded the bus for the trip back to our barracks. Now it was my turn to get thrown in the motel pool, used to christen newly soloed pilots. The fact that my first solo had really occurred several years before didn't rate me any mercy with my classmates. Four guys, one on each leg and arm, swung me back and forth, letting me fly up six feet in the air. I came down on my back, hitting the cold water hard. The cotton flight suit was very clammy as I climbed out.

After the class had a requisite amount of solo flying, we got introduced to the buddy system. No counterpart to this system exists in civilian flight training. They'd pair two soloed candidates into a ship. Students flying with students! Sometimes the guys would talk each other into unwise activities. In one such incident two candidates were killed as they flew at a very low level, in defiance of standing orders, and hit some high-tension wires.

For primary phase two we were assigned to a new IP. The one I drew sat at the table reviewing our records from phase one.

"Spalding, do you know what your grade out of phase one was?"

"Yes sir, I do."

Graham and I had gotten along fine. Except for hovering and autorotations, most of what we did in phase one was similar to airplane flying, so I'd naturally gotten good grades.

"Well, you can bet that during the next phase with me as your IP that grade is going to come way down."

Oh boy, just what I needed, a vengeful IP to teach me about landing on sloped ground, pinnacles, and confined areas. These were all things one doesn't do in airplanes. One flight certainly proved this.

"Spalding, do you see that practice slope landing area at our eleven o'clock?"

"You mean the one marked with the red tires?"

"Yeah, that's it. Go ahead and make a normal approach into it. We'll be doing some slope operations there."

The red tires indicated the slope was maximum difficulty for training and it wasn't to be used by solo students. This was the first red tire slope for me. I hovered over to what looked like a suitable place and began to land by lowering the collective pitch. As the right, uphill, skid touched I gradually added right cyclic, keeping the rotor level, just as we'd been taught. This technique kept the rotor thrust at an angle that precluded the chopper's slipping down the slope while it was light on the skids. I alternately watched the rotor tip on the uphill side, to see that it didn't contact the ground, and the right skid footing. The left skid touched the ground lightly. We were leaning over to the left about fifteen degrees. The rear of the right skid was sitting on a six-inch-diameter rock, but it looked solid.

"Left side's okay," said the IP while he watched the left skid footing and I gradually lowered the collective farther to put more weight on the skids. The chopper suddenly lurched down the hill. The right skid had slipped off the rock. I immediately pulled in a bunch of collective, too much really, and we popped up ten feet into the air. I heard the IP gasp even before he pushed the intercom button.

"What the hell do you think you're doing?" he bellowed.

"My skid slipped off a rock, sir. I terminated the landing."

The IP lifted his right arm and banged on my helmet with his open hand. My helmet twisted, and I thought my ears were going to be ripped off. It was difficult to hold the ship still. The IP kept yelling, "Are you trying to kill me with a heart attack? Don't you ever make a move that fast again. The lesson's over for today. I've got the aircraft."

The IP flew back to the base, landed, and marched into the operations room without saying another word to me. The entry he made in my training log was an understatement: "slope operations."

* * *

My flying buddy had completed his hour of solo air maneuvers. He was walking toward me across the cow pasture that was serving as our landing area for the day. The foot-thick grass swished against his boots and flight suit as he came near.

"It's all yours, Dan," he said.

Suddenly, and for no known reason, an overwhelming feeling swept over me that if I flew this particular ship at this particular time I would die.

"Anything wrong with the ship?" I asked, trying not to show how I was feeling.

"Nothing I know of."

"Okay. See you later."

I walked past my buddy toward the ship and hoped my parting comment was not an idle boast.

The heat waves from the pasture made my view of the little chopper waver, ghost-like, in the afternoon sun. I walked to the ship, barely feeling the ground underfoot. The fear in the pit of my stomach was gaining intensity with every step. I debated about not going, but decided that if I didn't lick my fear right then, I might not get over it. I spent twice the normal time on the preflight and checked the canopy airfoil three times. I couldn't find anything wrong, so I went flying. I didn't do any maneuvers. I treated the ship very gently in the hope that it would reciprocate. I was tense for the whole hour, and by the time I landed safely at the field my mouth was so dry I could barely swallow. But I had faced down something that had seemed like certain doom. It was good practice.

As graduation neared, I began to think I wanted to fly gunships as opposed to troop carriers. The idea of landing in the jungle to drop off troops and merely sitting there while the bad guys shot at me wasn't appealing. If I was going to have to fly helicopters that got shot at, I at least wanted to be able to shoot back. We had to select a preference for our advanced training location. Dothan, Alabama, and Savannah, Georgia, were the choices. I went to see the TAC officer, who was in charge of the company, to discuss the choice. I entered the TAC's office, snapped to attention, and saluted. The TAC lazily returned the salute.

"At ease, candidate," he said. "What's up?"

"Sir, I've decided I'd like to fly gunships. Would my advanced training base selection make any difference for getting into Cobra school?"

"Well, all I can tell you is that if you want to go on panty raids you don't go to an all-male college."

"Sir?"

"Being dense today aren't you, Spalding? Cobra school is conducted at Hunter Army Airfield in Savannah. There's no way to tell if being there would help, but it's my guess it couldn't hurt. Now, get out of my office and quit asking dumb questions."

I opted to volunteer for Hunter.

After one of our last flying days, our TAC officer entered our barracks right behind us as we filed off the buses. Two other officers I'd never seen before were with him.

"A-ten-shun!" someone called.

The whole company came out from our three-man rooms and braced at attention in the long hallway outside our doors.

The TAC commanded, "Prepare for inspection."

This seemed a little out of place. As we'd gotten to be the senior class, snap inspections had become a thing of the past. I scampered into my room, opened my locker, and stood by my bed at attention. The three officers worked individually, each covering rooms exclusively from the other two. There seemed to be more talking than was normal for an inspection. One of the unknown officers entered my room. He carried a clipboard. He walked over to my roommates and asked each of them a single question. When an answer had been given, the officer made notes on the clipboard. Then it was my turn.

"Assume you're flying a gunship in Vietnam," he began. "A ground platoon is engaged with the enemy a thousand meters from your location. You see a pregnant Vietnamese woman with a child strapped on her back walking along a rice paddy dike. The woman is carrying two mortar rounds. What do you do?"

The whole time you're in military flight training you're in competition. The competition is set up on purpose, and it comes naturally to most guys anyway. I figured this was some kind of psychological competition and gave the answer I thought they'd want to hear from a future gunship pilot. Without hesitation or blinking an eye, I said, "Sir, I'd immediately roll in and kill the woman."

Unexpectedly, the officer offered a further observation. "That's good, candidate. Anytime you can get more than one with a single attack it's very efficient." The officer scribbled on his clipboard and walked out of the room. The idea of "efficiency" in war had never entered my mind. There was no feedback on this questioning session. I wondered if this was an official part of training or just some ad hoc exercise cooked up by the TACs. I also wondered if I could do what I had said.

I'd done well enough in training to be the Honor Graduate for graduation. The Honor Graduate for each class was the person who held the best combined academic and flying grades. There was an Honor Graduate for the WOC class and one for the parallel regular officer class. At Fort Wolters, it was customary for the base commander to have the two Honor Graduates to lunch in the officers' club. Until then, the highest ranking person I'd talked with was Captain Graham. The idea of being so close to a full colonel was simultaneously exciting and worrisome. What if I said something stupid? I met the Lieutenant Honor Graduate at the curb where we were to be picked up for lunch. A government car pulled up and the left rear window was lowered to expose the colonel's smiling face.

"Good morning, gentlemen. Mr. Spalding, come around and get in the right side of the car. That way I can sit next to each of you for our discussion on the way to the club."

I started around the back of the car and said, "Yes, sir." I opened the door and slid in beside the colonel, who was starting a conversation with my companion.

"Well, Lieutenant, what do you think it is that allowed you to be the Honor Graduate?"

"Sir, I think I had some really good instructors and that had a lot to do with it," replied the lieutenant.

What a nice safe answer, I thought. Compliment the "principal" about his staff. How could you go wrong with an approach like that?

"What about you, Candidate Spalding?" asked the colonel.

"Well, sir, before I enlisted I was a civilian flight instructor in fixed-wing airplanes. I also went to a military high school. The majority of the training here was redundant to my previous experience."

"Oh, I see," said the colonel.

I don't recall the colonel saying much else to me for the rest of the luncheon. Maybe it was just my imagination.

★ CHAPTER 6 ★

Bigger and Faster

I drove another candidate's car, a Chevelle Super Sport, from Fort Wolters to Hunter Army Airfield in Savannah, Georgia. I crossed the country at outrageous speeds, but somehow avoided getting a ticket. Hunter seemed a great improvement over Fort Wolters. It was a lot newer, and I later found out that it had once been a Strategic Air Command base. The Air Force did things first class.

On a bright August day, I formed up with the rest of my class in the parking lot across from our new barracks. The barracks were cinder block construction with large windows, three floors, and large shade trees in front. Gray Spanish moss dangled from every limb of the trees. A concrete sidewalk led up to the double-door barracks entrance. Two UH-1, Huey, rotor blades were anchored in the ground on each side of the sidewalk. They were tilted to form an inverted V over the sidewalk. A pair of Army aviator wings was suspended between the rotor blades. The sight of the larger-than-life wings brought the Army aviation motto to mind. I wondered, did "Above the Best" mean that Army aviators flew over the best ground forces, or did it mean that Army aviators were the best pilots? While I was lost in my own thoughts the men of our unorganized group started to grumble about the heat and humidity.

A tall, very tan, man exited the barracks doors and started toward us. He had taps on his shoe heels, and they clicked loudly as he purposefully strode toward us. The guy's trousers had a very sharp crease in them and his shoes glistened in the sun. I warned the group, "I think the TAC is on his way over here, guys. Better get ready."

The TAC wasted no time. He bellowed "A-ten-shun!" at us from across the street. We stood rigidly, baking in the hot Savannah sun, while the TAC gave us our first in-processing lecture. The sweat soaked through my uniform. Mercifully, the briefing was short. Even at that, one guy passed out. We ran into the barracks to set up housekeeping. I marveled at the comparative luxury. Only two guys were assigned to a room. Better yet, there was a bathroom that was shared with only the room next door instead of the typical serve-all latrines we'd grown used to.

* * *

Our first advanced training was in instrument flying. The result of Army helicopter instrument training was a "tactical" instrument rating. The main difference between this rating and a "full" instrument rating was that only low-frequency radio aids were used for navigation. Low-frequency aids had been one of the first ways to navigate by radio and were suited to Army aviation because the transmitters were relatively small, and hence portable. They could be installed virtually anywhere. Basic low-frequency radio navigation involved following a needle that pointed at the radio aid. One ground school class instructor made a point we all took to heart.

"Make sure you identify the radio transmitter by its Morse code ID before you use it," he began. "As an extra precaution, try to cross-reference other transmitter locations if there are any. Charlie [the Viet Cong] could set up a transmitter in the jungle and surround it with antiaircraft batteries."

We were taught three types of instrument approaches: ground-controlled approach (GCA); automatic direction finder (ADF); and tactical. Only the tactical approach was new to me. The tactical approach was made by flying a figure-eight pattern over the ground with the single radio aid used as the eight's crossing point. The idea was to let down slowly on one of the eight's straight legs. The minimum descent altitude was calculated by the pilot starting with terrain elevation. We were scheduled to first practice these approaches in flight simulators. When the time arrived, I marched over to a large hangar with the rest of the class and was startled to see rows of World War II–vintage Link trainers as our simulators. The devices were still painted in old Army Air Corps colors—dark blue fuselages and yellow stub wings. Inside, the only change that had been added was a pretend collective pitch lever. It was a dummy and didn't affect the trainer's behavior in the least.

In-flight instrument training was conducted in specially

outfitted OH-13s, the kind of helicopter used in the movie *M*A*S*H*. With its large cockpit bubble and truss tail boom structure, the OH-13 seemed somewhat more substantial than the TH-55. It was an older aircraft, though, and its design reflected its age. We weren't required to qualify in the OH-13; we just flew them for dual instrument instruction.

The day came to practice instrument takeoffs. My IP had landed us in a medium-size confined area surrounded on all sides by thirty- to fifty-feet-tall pine trees.

"Remember, you can't hover on instruments," the IP said as he briefed me. "Therefore, the instrument takeoff procedure calls for simultaneously establishing a positive rate of climb and forward motion right from the ground."

I'd been trained in airplane instrument takeoffs, and in the classroom, the idea of not being able to hover before takeoff had not seemed to be any big deal. Somehow the image of taking off blind from an area surrounded by trees hadn't connected. Now, looking out at the tall Georgia pine trees in front of me, it was greatly disturbing. I was very glad that, unlike me, the IP could see outside.

I pulled down the vision-limiting hood on my helmet and commenced the takeoff by pulling on the collective. As the ship left the ground it shook and yawed a little to the right. I added left pedal and moved the cyclic forward to gain speed, but kept the collective coming up to the desired engine power setting. I scanned the instruments anxiously. The altimeter showed fifty feet. The intercom clicked on and the IP let out a sigh. He must have been holding his breath. "I've got the aircraft," he said. He flew a tight traffic pattern and again landed in the practice area.

"Let's try that again. You only cleared the trees by about five feet. You need to get the collective set to proper power a lot sooner, and don't worry so much about getting forward speed too fast."

It was nice to fly with someone who didn't yell and hit.

*   *   *

Checkout in the Huey was our next training step. The Huey was a lot larger and flew considerably faster. The biggest learning challenge was the different and more complex systems. That included learning to start the jet engine. The first Hueys I flew had a manual start sequence that, if not performed properly, could cause a "hot start." This would be detected when the temperature rose too quickly for the percent of engine rpm achieved. Hot starts could range from a relatively mild event all the way up to melting off the back end of the engine. Every start was fraught with tension until repetition wore off the rough edges.

Of course, we practiced working out of confined areas, on slopes, and on pinnacles. Pinnacles and slopes were hard to find in the Georgia flatlands, so the Army made some by bulldozing hills of earth, but the effect was not intimidating after having used the real buttes and hills of Texas.

I'd returned from practicing some slope landings. My buddy and I had shut off the engine and waited for the rotor to stop before we got out of the ship. Then we exited, tied down the main rotor blade, and started to walk across the hot asphalt to the operations shack. Across the flight line, a hundred feet away, another Huey was cranking up to go for practice. I waved to my compatriots and heard the familiar increasing whine of the jet. The more distinct whopping sound of the main rotor overpowered that of the engine as the bird began to lift itself to a hover. There was a loud noise to my left. I turned my head in time to see the Huey rolling over on its right side. The main rotor touched the ground and the Huey beat itself to death like a dying insect. Pieces of the rotor blade flew by me a foot over my head. I dropped to the ground, but crap was skidding across the pavement, too. Miraculously, none of the debris hit me or my companion. It was all over in the blink of an eye. The dead chopper's two pilots exited out the left (now upper) door faster than I'd ever seen two people move. They ran across the flight line in case the aircraft's remains blew up, but it just lay there.

Whenever an accident like this occurred, all us other pilots wanted to know everything that happened. This was true even when someone died in a crash. It wasn't a morbid curiosity that drove us to seek all the details behind accidents. Our motivations were more like that of the religious person seeking "the truth." Obviously, by knowing about a particular pattern of events that led to an accident, we could hope to better know how to cope with them. This was the scientific part of our quest for knowledge. The psychological part was, perhaps, even more important to our well-being. As we'd find out about how a crash happened, every one of us would rationalize how he would have been able to prevent or cope with the sometimes fatal sequence of events better than the guys who got hurt or died. It was the "it can't happen to me" syndrome in spades, but it helped keep us going. It turned out that this particular accident investigation showed that a main rotor pitch-control link had failed. The pilot lost control of the ship because the controls were completely gone! Beyond inspecting the pitch-control links carefully during preflight, none of us could figure a way we could have done better. It wasn't a comforting realization.

After our Huey checkout, we entered the phase of training known as tactical training. We got practice doing some things we would have to do in combat as Huey pilots. One of the first things we learned about was carrying sling loads under the ship. This set of maneuvers and techniques would be crucial to resupplying troops in the field.

I watched the ground guide through my chin bubble. He motioned me forward. I tried to keep the Huey moving very slowly forward, but being twenty feet over the ground made for imprecise perceptions. Finally, the ground guide, who was being blasted by my rotor wash, motioned me to stop. I held the ship as steady as I could while the ground crew attached cargo cable from a fifty-five-gallon drum onto my cargo hook. The hook was right under the transmission, and I couldn't see the ground crew, but I could feel some bumps through the floorboard. If the engine quit now, there'd be some squashed ground crewmen. Eventually, the guide motioned me to pick up the load. I raised the collective and the ship moved up steadily until the weight of the concrete-filled drum came to bear. Then I had to add more power. I had the Huey at a thirty-foot hover when the guide motioned me to take off. I moved the cyclic gently forward. It was weird having the Huey feel so heavy and sluggish without any load visible from the cockpit.

"Remember the first rule they taught us," my flying buddy cautioned.

"You mean, 'Don't fly over anything you don't want to squash'?"

"Yeah. I wouldn't want to kill some Georgia cracker's cow or something."

"I'm not so concerned about that. What bothers me is the chance of maneuvering too fast and setting up an uncontrollable oscillation. The tail wagging the dog thing, you know?"

"I know, all right. You be real gentle on the controls. Don't forget I'm over here watching after my own ass. If you're not gentle, I may have to kill you and take over myself."

"Yeah, yeah. Big-talking slick driver you are," I said.

I flew us to the designated load drop-off point and easily deposited the load for the receiving ground crew. The little finger of my right hand was strained. I guessed I'd been holding it in position out from the red button on the cyclic grip that would have released the load when pressed. That's the first thing I'd have had to do, along with bottoming the collective, if the ship's engine had quit. Some things about flying choppers were beginning to be ingrained in my habit patterns.

*   *   *

We navigated using the same charts as ground troops. Apparently, flight charts were something for pilots, not Army aviators. Low-level flying was especially fun. Normally, at altitude, flying gave very little, if any, perception of speed. Down low, things flew past the ship at amazing speed. It was exhilarating. Actually, we practiced nap-of-the-earth flying. That is, we stayed as close to the terrain as possible, following its contour. If there was a hill we climbed up one side and pushed over the back side, never getting higher than three feet off the ground. Flying the fuselage between and below the tops of trees, with the main rotor blade just clearing them, was one way of not giving potential enemy gunners time to get you in their sights. One of the problems with low-level flying was that, because we couldn't see much of the surroundings, it was easy to get disoriented. The person not flying did the navigation while the pilot on the controls concentrated on not hitting things.

One day Roy Smith and I were on a buddy system low-level training flight. Roy was navigating.

"You need to turn left at the creek line, which should be coming up in about two minutes," Roy announced.

Three minutes passed. No creek bed came into view.

I asked, "Roy, you sure about that creek?"

"I'm sure it's on the map."

Another five minutes went by and still no creek.

"Let's turn north. We ought to come to a road running east-west. Then we can get our bearings," suggested Roy.

I rolled the ship to the right and headed north. The wind had picked up a little and there was some light turbulence, but otherwise the weather was good. After another ten minutes of flying no road came into view.

"I think we're lost," I said.

"Hate to admit it, but maybe you're right."

I climbed the ship to 2,000 feet and we tried to locate something on the map that we could recognize on the ground. Georgia farmland, marsh, and forests stretched to the horizon. In the distance I saw what looked like a water tower. I flew toward it. As we got closer the object became unmistakably a water tower. I dropped down to 100 feet and circled the tower. Not only was there a town, but the tower had the town's name painted on it. The town wasn't on our map. We'd flown off the edge of the chart!

"You know," said Roy, "I've heard of this town before. I think it's located somewhere roughly northwest of the base."

"Okay, we'll head southeast. I hope you're right. Fuel's getting a little low."

Roy's guess was right on. I flew for fifteen minutes, turned on the ADF, and homed in on the base. Ours was the last ship to arrive. As I brought the ship to a hover, the twenty-minute fuel warning light glowed. I was glad to be close to the ground. Roy and I took quite a ribbing for using our unconventional navigation aid. No one thought the Viet Cong would be kind enough to paint names on their town landmarks.

Survival school was another high point in our training. We had to learn how to forage for ourselves in case we went down behind enemy lines. The Air Force conducted a two-week survival training course. Army chopper pilots got one day and one night. I wasn't sure if the difference in emphasis was a good or a bad omen.

"Okay. Listen up, you mugs," said the instructor. "There's a can of grub worms being passed around. Everyone take one and examine it closely. You can find these under rotten logs and leaves in almost every forest in the world. They're full of protein. Everybody ready?"

We screamed in unison, "Yes, sir!"

"On my command, then. Ready, eat!"

I popped the small round worm into my mouth. The guy next to me finished his.

"What do you think it tastes like?" he said.

"Hell if I know. I swallowed mine whole. I'd have to be a lot hungrier than I am now to enjoy the taste."

The instructor reached into a bag and pulled out a common brown rabbit. "Guess where the term 'rabbit punch' came from?" he said. With that, he held the live rabbit upside down by its hind legs and gave it the gentlest karate chop to the base of its head. The rabbit was instantly dead. We ate it as part of a rabbit-and-rattlesnake luncheon stew.

After daytime lectures, we paired up into escape and evasion teams of one officer and one WOC. We were driven to the edge of some Georgia swampland just before dark.

My partner was Jim Granger. Jim wasn't a commissioned officer. He was a warrant officer who had started out as a supply sergeant and worked his way up. Now he was in flight training. We were supposed to be preparing a meal, but Jim and I were plotting our trek to evade the "hostiles" who were going to be trying to catch us.

"Jim, do you have any outdoors experience?" I asked.

"Not really. I'm basically a city boy."

"Unfortunately, I am, too. I've done a little camping out and hiking when I was a kid, but compared with this stuff I don't think it counts for anything. I guess we're equally inept."

"Reckon so. Let's collaborate on our moves instead of electing one of us the leader. Does that sound right to you?"

"I guess it's the only thing that makes sense," I said.

Our discussion was interrupted by the noise of several heavy vehicles screeching to a halt. "Hostiles" came pouring out of the backs of trucks and began capturing our compatriots. Jim and I ducked and ran ten yards, then peered through the heavy brush to see what was happening. The hostiles were between us and our objective. The map showed a swamp on our right flank.

"What do you think about trying the swamp, Spalding?"

"We'll be going backwards for a while, but what the hell. That's the kind of thing they told us to do."

We headed for the swamp. When we got into it we turned

to our left and made a straight line for our objective. The swamp got denser and denser the farther into it we got. The brush became so thick we almost couldn't push through it. There was a heavy overcast ceiling at 500 feet. There was no sign of the moon or the stars. It was black as the inside of a chimney. After four hours we figured we'd only made 200 meters of progress and still had a long way to go. We'd been alternating who led the way so as to not completely exhaust ourselves. I'd found the technique that worked best was to face opposite the direction I wanted to go, put my back up against the vines, and push as hard as I could. When Jim was leading I could tell where he was by his luminous watch dial. Sometimes he'd get too far out in front of me, only about four feet, and I'd have to tell him I'd lost his location. We didn't use a light or talk very much. Better not to give ourselves away, we thought. We stopped to catch our breath. The only noise was from the swamp animals—mostly frogs, I hoped.

"You know, I don't think anyone else is dumb enough to be in the middle of this damn swamp, Jim."

"You're probably right. Let's turn on a flashlight. Maybe if we can see we can make better time."

"Okay," I said as I fumbled for my flashlight.

Finally, I took the light out of my flight suit pocket and turned it on. To our horror there were thorn bushes, leaves, vines, fallen trees, and brambles all around us. It was like we were in the belly of a giant plant-eating beast.

"Turn out the light," Jim said. "It won't help, and in this mess we may be better off not seeing what we're up against."

I agreed and doused the light. The rest of our trek was accomplished in total darkness.

We made our objective without getting caught. Fifty yards to our front we could see a fire and lots of people moving around.

"Think those are the 'partisans' we're looking for?" asked Jim.

"According to where we think we are, they should be. There's really no way to tell, is there?"

"Nope. I'm sure glad this isn't the real thing. Tell you what. One of us should go in and see if these are friendlies. If not, maybe the other can get away."

We drew straws. I "won." I watched Jim go forward very cautiously. Fifteen minutes later he motioned me in. I had a gnawing worry, knowing that if this had been the real thing, I wouldn't have known whether or not to trust him.

The dawn broke with a brilliant sunrise. Everyone else showed up except three teams. Two teams were lost, and we had to wait until the TACs found them before we got to go back to the warm, dry barracks. The third team had been taken out during the exercise because one man had been bitten by a snake.

At graduation I was once again the WOC Honor Graduate. I beat out the second-place guy by only about half of a percentage point. New-assignment request forms—"dream sheets"—had previously been provided to us. Being at the top of the class, I figured I had at least some chance of getting what I wanted. My first choice was fixed-wing transition; second, Germany; third, "AH-1G Cobra transition."

I got my third choice.

★ CHAPTER 7 ★

The Snake

The AH-1G (attack helicopter, model 1, version G) was the first production helicopter designed specifically for the attack role. It was built, like the Huey, by Bell Helicopters. It was named the Cobra. Bell had produced another Cobra, the P-39 fixed-wing attack aircraft, during World War II. The World War II craft, nicknamed the Aircobra, had the unconventional arrangement of a nosewheel and a mid-fuselage engine. The driveshaft from the engine to the propeller ran under the pilot's seat, between his legs. I recalled my dad's saying that it was sobering to think of the nose gear's breaking, causing the prop to dig into the ground and the driveshaft to snap and, perhaps, castrate the pilot. I hoped the similarity between the Aircobra and the Cobra stopped with their names.

The Cobra did have many unconventional characteristics. The silhouette of the Cobra was unique. From the side, the fuselage looked sharkish. The nose was pointed. The enclosed canopy line stretched rearward and upward to its pinnacle at the main rotor transmission housing. The canopy was tinted blue. The main rotor transmission housing could have been a dorsal fin. Only three feet wide at its widest point, the Cobra was a tight squeeze to get into. I never saw a truly fat Cobra pilot. The crew sat one behind the other with the rear seat slightly higher than the front seat. A copilot/gunner sat up front, and the pilot in command sat in back. The skids were closer together than on the Huey, and the craft seemed to sit higher off the ground. Stub wings on each side served as armament mounting points. Overall, if you ignored the rotor blades, the Cobra looked more like a weird airplane than a helicopter.

Discounting armament, the biggest internal differences between the Cobra and the Huey were the front seat controls, the engine, and the stabilization system.

The front seat pilot controls were side mounted and wrist controlled. Behind the copilot, the pilot in command had a four-to-one leverage advantage over the front-seater, which meant that when we checked out in the rear seat, the IPs reminded us before each flight not to fight them for the controls if they said they had the aircraft. There was a little

rearview mirror mounted on the right front canopy windshield frame. It was used by the front-seater to observe the
rear seat occupant. Actually, all that could be seen was the
person's head and shoulders, but even that proved reassuring sometimes.

The Cobra engine developed 300 more horsepower than
the Huey for a total of 1,400 horsepower. That was great for
carrying armament, but there was a drawback. The same
transmission was used in the Cobra and the Huey. There was
a cute term for the mechanism used to preclude stripping
the gears in the transmission by unwisely using all of the
Cobra's engine power. It was called "pilot-derating." The
Cobra, like the Huey, was equipped with a transmission
torque meter. As more power was added, by increasing the
collective pitch and taking a bigger bite of air, the torque
meter would register the increase in resistance on the transmission. The meter's dial was calibrated in pounds of
torque. Pilot-derating for the Cobra transmission was a
fancy way of saying we watched the torque meter and didn't
pull in more than forty pounds of torque—or we suffered the
consequences. Pilot-derating could have been restated as
"Be careful."

The automatic stabilization (SAS) was a way of making
the Cobra a better gun platform so that it was more accurate.
This had a drawback, too. If the engine failed at speeds over
150 knots, the stabilization system would misinterpret the
naturally occurring nose pitch up as being unwanted. The
SAS would try to put the nose down by moving the main
rotor down in front. The canopy top and the main rotor could
come too close for comfort, possibly colliding. The solution
to this idiosyncrasy, like the solution to overtorquing, was
also pilot controlled. If we were in the middle of an attack
run, headed straight for the ground, with people shooting at
us, and the engine quit, we had to remember to give a slight
pull back on the cyclic control to signal the SAS not to over-
correct. In this manner we avoided decapitation. Helicopter

flying was getting more and more "fun" as I progressed through the individual types.

The Cobra was faster and heavier than the Huey. We could cruise at 150 knots (173 miles per hour) with no armament. In a dive we could get up to 190 knots (219 miles per hour). In ground school our instructor emphasized the 190-knot limit.

"There are two theories about what happens if you get past a hundred and ninety knots," he said. "One theory holds that the nose pitches up and left while the main rotor disintegrates. The other theory holds that the main rotor merely disintegrates without warning. I keep waiting for one of you hotshots to try flying outside the envelope so you can tell me which theory is correct. By the way, did any of you take time to figure out your sink rate fully armed on a hot humid day like you'll have in Nam? No? Well, this bird ain't no Huey in this respect. You'll have to carry about a quarter of your collective on the way down to keep the rotor from over-speeding. Start your flare at a hundred and fifty feet instead of a hundred feet because your sink rate will be close to five thousand feet per minute. This is great fun at night since the landing light only shows objects about two hundred feet away. The best rule for night autorotations is: When you get to two hundred feet, turn on the landing light. If you don't like what you see, turn the light off."

One of the first new maneuvers we had to master was the steep dive. The steeper the dive the more accurate our rockets would be. Steep dives were defined as those with a nose-down angle greater than thirty degrees. First, I'd practiced shallow and medium dives. They had been reasonably routine.

Then my IP had me climb to 3,000 feet. "I've got the aircraft," he said. He began to talk me through his demonstration of a steep dive. "First set the power at about ninety percent."

I watched as he moved the collective down smoothly and the rpm indicator showed exactly ninety percent.

"Now pull the nose up slowly."

The airspeed started to bleed off from our cruise speed at a steady rate. Altitude held rock steady. The IP's mastery of the machine was awe-inspiring.

"As you reach forty knots, push the nose over until you're pointed at the target."

The sensation of the nose rolling over from the 40-knot nose-high attitude was like being in the front car of a roller coaster on the first hill. The nose went lower and lower until I had to look up to see the horizon. Quickly, we were pointed at an angle that I felt was straight down. Even through the closed canopy and my helmet I could hear the rush of the wind as the airspeed increased. The attitude was alarming, and I unconsciously strained to press myself back (up) in my seat in an effort to not be pointed down.

"Hold this attitude until reaching fifteen hundred feet or your limiting dive speed, whichever comes first."

We went screaming by 150 knots, and the airspeed's rate of increase was accelerating. At 170 knots the ship started to vibrate and the IP began the recovery by pulling back on the cyclic and up on the collective.

"You need to pull about two and a half g's to recover smoothly without losing excess altitude. Remember to watch the torque. Okay, you try one."

In spite of my fixed-wing aerobatic experience, this maneuver was initially frightening. Heading for the ground in a spin at roughly 50 miles per hour, or being pointed briefly at it on the back side of a loop, was not the same as racing straight toward it at lower altitudes. It took me three tries to get the nose over far enough and fast enough to satisfy the IP.

Learning to use the weapons was a real kick. Of course, no one was shooting back. We practiced from both the front gunner position and the pilot-in-command position. The gunner fired either a minigun or a grenade launcher.

The minigun was a gattling-like machine gun that fired 7.62mm (.30-caliber) rifle ammunition at 4,000 rounds per minute. A regular machine gun fired only around 600 rounds per minute. The Cobra carried only one minute's worth of ammo, but oh what a minute it was for anyone on the receiving end.

Before my first firing of the minigun my IP cautioned me, "Only use the sight to get an initial firing point. Then walk the tracers to where you want 'em."

We were at 1,500 feet. I took the movable hinged sight in both hands and squeezed the two levers on the front of the sight handles with my three lower fingers to activate the turret. The whirring of the electrohydraulic turret could be felt through the floorboards as it slewed to where I had pointed the sight. I pulled the two triggers with my index fingers.

A *braaaaaaaap* sound filled the cockpit, and I could feel a very high frequency vibration in the floorboards. Tracers seemed to speed out from the ship's nose. By moving the sight around, I could walk bullets to almost wherever I liked. It was like moving the water stream from a garden hose with a high-pressure nozzle on it. Bullets bounced off the remains of an armored personnel carrier (APC) that was the target.

"Not too shabby, Spalding," said the IP. "This time around let's try the grenade launcher."

I pointed the sight at the APC and, with my thumbs, pressed the two red buttons at the top of the sight handles. I heard a deep-throated *poomp, poomp, poomp* and felt several solid jolts. It took a relatively long time for the grenades, each shaped like a stubby bullet about the size of a large four-speed gearshift knob, to reach the ground. The rounds were so big and slow that I could see them move through the air. One grenade after the other impacted and gave off a small black puff of an explosion. Each grenade had a five-meter kill radius, which wasn't nearly large enough for a person with my limited skill level. All the grenades were way past the target.

"Leaves something to be desired, don't it?" the IP growled. "Don't forget. With the grenades having such a slow speed they travel farther along our flight path before reaching the ground. You have to lead the target a lot."

After I was rear-seat qualified, it was time to try out the main armament—rockets. The rockets were 2.75 inches in diameter and were propelled at 1,800 miles per hour by a solid fuel motor. Each warhead had the same explosive force as a 105-millimeter artillery round.

I climbed to altitude and rolled into a medium dive. I checked the slip/skid indicator to make sure the ball was centered and maneuvered the ship with the cyclic until the pinpoint of light in the center of the orange sight circle was right on the target. With the lower side of my right thumb I pressed down on the red round button on the left side of the cyclic handle.

Swoooosh. White smoke streaked past as one rocket on each side fired. The smoke trails reached out like tentacles until the rockets hit the ground and burst into fireballs surrounded by dirty black smoke. My aim was low. Pulling back a little on the cyclic, I fired a second pair. Now I was high. I pushed forward on the stick and fired again. This was the right range, but the rockets were left of target. I was out of trim, holding too much right pedal. I was also out of altitude. I recovered from the dive and banked left into a two-g climbing turn.

"Hittin' things with these newfangled arrows ain't so easy, is it, Spalding?"

"Guess not. Got any suggestions?"

"Yeah. Practice makes perfect. Go back and do it again."

For me, there wasn't enough practice during the transition program to get very good with rockets.

I didn't graduate first in Cobra transition school. Maybe I'd been distracted. I'd met a girl, fallen in love, and gotten married—all in four months. The last month of the four was Cobra school. We had the wedding on a Sunday, rather than a Saturday, because I didn't want to interrupt my important flying with something as inconsequential as getting married.

★ CHAPTER 8 ★

Short-lived Rest

I was given a thirty-day leave after Cobra school. I didn't have much money. I had been married about one week. Up until then the honeymoon had been spent in a not-too-great local motel. Of course, I had flown every day. It was late January. The idea of going north, where my parents lived, wasn't all that appealing. Besides, we didn't really have enough money to make long trips. My wife's idea of going to Florida, relaxing, and having a long honeymoon sounded great to me.

It occurred to me that I could get a commercial helicopter rating added to my civilian pilot's license since I was a fully rated Army aviator. We made a mini-getaway out of the task and drove to St. Petersburg in our American Motors Javelin with a 390-cubic-inch engine. I glanced at the fuel gauge as we sped along the interstate highway at eighty miles per hour. I was astounded!

"Look at this," I exclaimed to my wife. I reached down and tapped at the gauge. "We're sucking up so much high-test gas you can see the fuel gauge's needle move."

"I don't believe it."

"Look at it a while. You'll see."

My wife stared for a minute. "Yeah, I can see some small movement. So what's the big deal?"

She was obviously unimpressed. Of course, those were the days of seventy mile-per-hour speed limits and before anyone ever heard of a fuel shortage. Unless you were a pilot who was trained to be constantly concerned about fuel status, there was no real reason to be impressed.

I filled out the required forms at the FAA office and showed them my Army flight records. That's all it took. When I got out of the Army I'd be able to fly commercially as either an airplane or a helicopter pilot.

Thirty days whizzed by. The tension of the coming departure was real but somehow not tangible. We drove back to Savannah so my wife could stay with her parents while I was gone. The fateful day came, and we went to the airport so I could catch my flight. My wife was very emotional and crying. There was lots of hugging and kissing. It was hard to stop, but I finally pulled away from my wife's arms, climbed up the air-stairs, turned around, and waved good-bye. I found my seat next to a window and settled into it. I continued to look at my wife until the plane taxied. She was waving. I looked away from the window and was enveloped by a resignation that manifested itself in a conscious thought: "It was a good life while it lasted. I'm a dead man now." The thought wasn't scary. It was just there.

★ CHAPTER 9 ★

A Big Pond

The Military Air Transport Service (MATS) used a chartered World Airways stretched DC-8 for the trip to the country known to us Army guys as "Disneyland East." I left the "real world" from Travis Air Force Base. I was surprised there were stewardesses on the trip. I thought that was a plush way to go to war. On the other hand, we were packed on the plane, six seats across from front to back. The plane held close to three hundred troops.

We flew, and flew, and flew. Every time I looked out the window there was nothing. Nothing, that is, but water! Flying across the Pacific made transcontinental trips seem trivial. We made an intermediate stop at Okinawa, where we got off the plane to stretch.

I went into the terminal and walked around, bought some magazines, relieved myself in the bathroom, and returned to the gate ready for the last leg of the trek. When I got back to the gate there was a MATS spokesman there.

"Gentlemen, may I have your attention please?" he said. "You will be spending the night here. The aircraft has a mechanical problem which will be fixed overnight. Buses are waiting outside to take you to your accommodations. Don't get into any trouble with the locals. The buses will bring you back here at zero-seven-hundred [seven A.M.] tomorrow."

I was curious about the mechanical problem. On the walk out to the buses I wandered over to the spokesman.

"What's the problem with the plane?" I said.

He turned and looked at me impatiently, but then he saw my wings and answered. "They tell me one of the artificial horizons isn't working right, sir. Sometimes they don't tell me everything, though. Your guess can be as good as my information lots of times. The best thing about the problem, whatever it is, is that you spend one more day outside the Nam."

"Sounds like you've been there."

"Yep. I got this duty two months ago. Believe me, you'll like it here a lot better."

The officers' overnight accommodations were in an old, but clean, small motel. We were put up two to a room. At dinner I ordered a Coke from the waitress. She spoke pidgin English. A few minutes later the waitress returned and served me something like a Seven-Up, but not as good. She was completely silent. Apparently, "Coke" wasn't as universal a word as I'd expected.

The approach into Tan Son Nhut airport in Saigon was uneventful. It was Tet 1969. The doors opened and an almost visible wave of heat flooded into the plane. I walked down the stairs and into a covered briefing area. As soon as our group was off the plane, a bunch of other troops got on for their trip home. Some looked at us and shook their heads from side to side. Some jeered. Most were headed purposefully for the stairs to what I'm sure they considered their personal freedom bird.

After a while we were called to board buses to the 90th Replacement Battalion at Bien Hoa. I entered, turned down the aisle, and almost tripped over a piece of quarter-inch-thick steel plate in the middle of the aisle.

"What's this for?" I asked the driver.

"Oh, that's nothing," he said. "Some gook rolled a homemade grenade under us about a week ago. That plate covers up the hole it made."

I was skeptical. After everyone was on board and the bus started to move, I lifted a corner of the plate and looked underneath. There sure was a hole. It was about two feet in diameter. The edge was turned upward slightly and it had scorch marks around it. Maybe the driver hadn't been pulling my leg. I leaned forward to ask about another curiosity.

"How come the windows are all covered with wire mesh?"

"You sure are curious for a new guy, sir. Most people don't say anything. They just sit in their seats in a kind of shock. Anyway, the wire stops the gooks from tossing grenades into the bus through the windows. Nice town, Saigon, ain't it?"

"Whatever you say, Sarge."

The driver guided the big olive-drab Army bus through the overcongested streets with an accuracy and aplomb that were wondrous. How hundreds of bicycle-riding Vietnamese weren't run over every day was an intriguing question. The horn seemed to be a necessary piece of survival equipment. The surrounding buildings were just shacks.

"When are we going to be out of the slums?" I asked the driver.

"What are you talking about, sir?"

"This part of the town is what I'm talking about."

"This ain't no slum, sir. In fact, this is a pretty nice part of town. There are some office buildings and things over on the other side, but this is about what most of the city looks like."

The first briefing at the 90th Replacement told us we'd be there for three days to undergo orientation, equipment issue, and assignment processing. The barracks I was assigned to held fifty people. It was a rectangular wood-frame structure on top of a concrete pad. There were double doors at both ends. Seven feet up the wall there was an open screened window that ran all the way along both sides. The roof was made of corrugated sheet metal. There were no inside walls. The east end of the barracks was only twenty feet from a main road. A barbed-wire fence, like those used in the States to fence in animals, ran between the barracks and the road. Between each two barracks stood an aboveground sandbag bunker that was open at both ends.

After dinner I walked with some of the other guys to the officers' club to see what was going on. It was 100 or so yards from the barracks. The place was filled to capacity. There was a small Vietnamese rock-and-roll band playing American tunes, although the words coming from the band weren't exactly English. I pushed my way through the crowd to the bar and ordered a seven-and-seven. I turned to a guy on my right to start a conversation.

"You been here long?" I asked.

"Not really. Been here four days. This is my last night. I ship out to my unit tomorrow."

"I would have been here last night, but our plane had a mechanical problem in Okinawa."

"You sure about the mechanical problem?"

"No. Like everyone else, I only know what they told me. Why do you ask?"

"Tan Son Nhut came under attack last night. I'm just a skeptical kind of guy. I figure the charter pilots don't sign up to work under fire. Maybe the mechanical fault was a convenience. That's all."

I took a sip of my drink.

Whoomp! Whoomp! Whoomp!

The battle-experienced guys dove for the floor at the sound of the first explosion. It took me until the third report to get the picture.

"Incoming!" screamed several voices simultaneously.

People pushed through the door and ran for their assigned bunkers. I reached mine, crouched down, worked my way to the center, and sat down on the bench. More "new guys" streamed in both ends after me. The bunker filled up rapidly. We huddled in the dark. No one said anything for a while. There were some other explosions, but they seemed farther away. The open ends of the bunker, and especially the one pointed at the road, made me feel unprotected. "You guys feel safe here?" I asked. Someone in the dark answered sarcastically, "Hell, if we're not safe here, we're in for a rough time. Haven't you heard? This is a secured part of the country." There was some nervous laughter. The explosions stopped, and we exited the bunker to look in the direction of distant gunfire. I heard the droning of two big radial-piston engines on an AC-47 "Spooky" overhead and some distance away. The AC-47 was a DC-3 that had three miniguns pointing out of the ship's left side. It could concentrate 18,000 rounds per minute on a target while orbiting overhead. The ship dropped some flares then and the night sky was split by a stream of bright orange tracers heading for the ground. A single burst of larger blue-green tracers arced up at the ship from the ground.

"That's .51-caliber stuff," remarked a combat veteran in our midst.

The tracers from the ground seemed to hit their mark. There was a small explosion on the Spooky. He turned away to his right and began to descend out of sight. We stood there, wanting to say or do something, but not knowing what. The rest of the night was quiet, but I still didn't sleep very well.

The next day, George Gilder, one of the guys who was with me the night I literally chased down my wife's girlfriend with my car to get an introduction, came up to see me and Bob Corbit. Bob had been in our primary and advanced training classes as well as my Cobra class. Bob and I met up at the replacement center. George had been in-country for sixty days before our arrival. When he came up to talk to us I didn't recognize him at first. Somehow he was different. We chatted awhile, and then George had to leave. He was flying mostly up north in the Pleiku area and was down in Saigon to pick up some supplies.

"Did George seem different to you?" I asked Bob.

"I think it was the handlebar mustache he's grown, but there was something else."

"He seemed real nervous to me. It was like he vibrated with anticipation. He was keyed up."

"Now that you mention it, I think you're right. Maybe combat flying does that to you. Guess we'll find out soon enough."

That night I didn't go to the officers' club. The club wasn't far from the perimeter, and it seemed to me that the enemy probably knew where it was. In my mind it made a juicy target. I read some magazines until about nine o'clock and then went to sleep. The siren wailed and I awoke with a start. Another attack began with the characteristic *whoomp*. There was a mad rush of half-naked men crushing through the doors as everyone in the barracks headed for the bunkers. When we'd settled into our spots in the bunker someone asked, "What time is it?"

I looked at my watch with its large luminous dial. It gleamed brightly in the pitch black of the bunker. "It's oh-three-hundred," I said.

"Guess they don't want us to get a good night's rest," someone else said.

We got back to bed an hour later. The adrenaline rush hadn't worn off. I lay in my bunk staring at the ceiling and waited for daybreak.

The next night was virtually a repeat of the last two. I was tired. At my last breakfast in the 90th Replacement I asked one of the serving guys if this was normal enemy activity: 365 days of fitful sleep was a troublesome prospect even if it hadn't included the possibility of being blown up.

"No, sir. I've been here for three months and this is the first time we've been attacked. I guess it has something to do with Tet."

Sarcastically I reflected, "Guess I picked a perfect time to come over. Didn't I?"

The server shrugged and said, "There's no good time to come to this shithole country."

I moved on down the chow line.

★ CHAPTER 10 ★

No Rest for the Weary

Bob and I were bused out to the airport to catch our flight to Cu Chi. We had been coincidentally assigned to the same base. "I wonder what the chance of our being assigned to the same unit is?" I asked Bob.

"Not very good, from what I hear. They don't do much of that in this war for some reason. One rumor even has it that they split people up on purpose."

"We could be unlucky in a couple of other ways, too. Remember we heard there was a shortage of both Cobras and Cobra pilots. It wouldn't be too neat to have to fly an old C-model Huey gunship and, on the other hand, I sure wouldn't want to be assigned as a Cobra aircraft commander without getting any combat experience."

"Holy shit! I never thought about that. I'll sure be glad to get my assignment. I think all this waiting and speculation is more nerve-wracking than doing the work."

"You may be right. Oh well, we'll soon find out."

We loaded into an Air Force Caribou for the trip. The high-wing aircraft had two large radial-piston engines set close to the fuselage. It was a short-takeoff-and-landing aircraft. We sat in webbed seats that hung from the sides and faced in toward the center of the airplane. The roar from the engines made it impossible to talk. It was curious to me that the two-man flight crew was wearing gloves but had their flight suit sleeves rolled halfway up their forearms. We leveled off for only about two minutes and then we began our descent into Cu Chi. Steep climbs and descents were the operational rule to minimize exposure to enemy fire. It wasn't a bit like being on an airline in the real world.

From the air, Cu Chi could be seen to be a rather large facility. I was glad to note fixed buildings rather than tents. The overall impression I had as we landed was of "dust city."

Bob and I were picked up by a jeep and driven over to the base commander's office. We reported for duty.

"Boy, am I glad to see you two," said the colonel. "We're short of Cobra pilots all over the place. I'm going to assign one of you to the Diamond Heads and one to the Centaurs. You got any preference?"

Bob and I exchanged glances. How would we have had a preference? Neither of us knew anything about either unit.

"Bob, I know you're married. Do you have any children?" I asked.

"Yes I do. A little girl. She's two months old."

It seemed to me it would be best if I took the most risk. At least I didn't have any kids. I turned to the colonel and asked, "Sir, which of the two units sees the most action?"

"I think the Centaurs do. They're an air troop of an armored cavalry squadron. The Diamond Heads are part of an air assault battalion. They mostly escort flights of Hueys into and out of landing zones."

"Okay. Bob, unless you object, I'll take the Centaurs," I said.

"That's fine with me," Bob replied.

A phone call was made to each unit. Fifteen minutes later, a jeep pulled up and the driver motioned to Bob and me. "Whichever one of you is Mr. Spalding, I'm your ride to the Centaurs."

That was the last time I saw Bob during my tour.

*   *   *

The driver took off down a dirt road. The jeep was beat up and the windshield on my side had a bullet hole in it.

"What happened here?" I said while pointing at the hole.

"A sniper put that there a couple of months ago. Had a captain sitting where you are. He wasn't hit, but it got real exciting for a minute. Some of the other officers refuse to sit up front. They ride in the back. Not as likely to be a target that way."

We rode around the perimeter road of the base camp immediately inside the defensive bunker line. There wasn't anything substantial between us and the "badlands" outside the camp. I tried not to think of snipers. We pulled up in front of a proper building.

"That's Flight Operations," said the driver. "Go inside and report to Captain Tagget. He's waiting for you."

Inside the operations building I saw a captain leaning on the counter and talking about something with a lieutenant. The man was the only captain in sight and had to be Tagget. He was over six feet tall and slightly overweight. He was losing some of his hair and had a large symmetrical bald spot on the back of his head.

"Are you Captain Tagget?"

The captain stopped talking and crooked his head in my direction. "That's what my name tag says," he said as he offered me his hand to shake. "You must be Spalding."

"That's right, sir."

"Well, welcome to D troop, 3rd Squadron, 4th Cavalry, of the 25th Infantry Division. Buffalo Bill was part of this outfit. If you make it through your tour we'll give you an 'old Bill' poster to remind you of all the fun. Let me tell you what you're getting into in the 3/4 cavalry. We have four platoons in the troop," Tagget said. "There's the aerorifles [light infantry], the LOHs [pronounced "loach" and short for Light Observation Helicopter], the slicks [Hueys], and the snakes [Cobras]. Snake main missions are visual reconnaissance, close air support, and LRRP support."

"Sir, what's a 'LRRP'?"

"Long-Range Reconnaissance Patrols—LRRP. We dump five or ten guys in the jungle so they can observe enemy troop movements. Walk with me around to the other side of this wall."

A large map of the area hung on the other side of the wall. It formed the front of a crude briefing room that could seat fifty people on steel card-table-type folding chairs. Tagget pointed at the map with his right index finger.

"Our area of operation is from the Mekong River just east of the camp, west to the Cambodian border, and north to War Zone C." Pointing at the Cambodian border, Tagget continued by showing distinctly shaped parts of rivers and the border. "This area is the Parrot's Beak, this one is the Angel's Wing, and this one is the Elephant Ear. Moving eastward toward the Vam Co Dong River, you should note the cities of Tay Ninh and Trang Bang. This city east of the Mekong is Dau Teang. Coming south down the river, this bend is known as the Mushroom, and this one is the Top Hat. Do you have any questions?"

We'd heard a lot of stuff about rules of engagement back in the States. I figured this was a good time to ask. "If we're shot at can we automatically shoot back without asking for permission?"

"Damn straight. Anything else?"

I was relieved. "Not for now, I guess."

"Okay, let's see if we can find you a place to bed down."

We walked out of the building and headed east toward several rows of barracks just like the ones at the 90th Replacement. There were two major differences in these buildings, though: No bunkers were visible between the barracks and each barracks was surrounded by a four-foot-high sandbag wall.

"Do you get attacked here very often?" I asked.

"Not really. It used to be a lot worse, but things have quieted down. We haven't had any incoming in about a month."

"That's good to hear. I spent the last three nights under mortar attack at the replacement center."

"No joke? That's really strange. They almost never have any battles down that way."

I opened the barracks screen door and entered with Tagget following. There was a hallway. Real walls greeted me! Well, they weren't exactly like walls at home. They were built out of rocket container planks and were unpainted, but they were walls nevertheless. Each guy had his own little room. Not too bad a deal, I thought.

Sitting at the end of the hall on the floor was someone with his shirt off. As I got closer, I was surprised to see that the man was playing the kids' game of jacks. He was good, too.

"Hi ya, Conners," said Tagget. "Spalding here is a new Cobra pilot. You guys got any room for him here?"

"Sure do. The Scrounge is in Saigon and won't be back for a couple of weeks. It's that room right beside you. Go ahead and stow your gear in there."

I opened the door of the room Conners had motioned to and found that the room had plywood-paneled walls. There was a sink, without running water, and even a little closet. They didn't call whoever owned this room the Scrounge for nothing. I could hear Tagget and Conners talking as I put my stuff away.

"Spalding will be going through in-country orientation for the next week, but get him his daytime check ride right after that, okay?" said Tagget.

"Will do, Cap."

I got situated and went exploring. Immediately to the right of my room was a little common lounge area with a TV, a light-blue vinyl couch, a couple of chairs, and a table. The wall over the couch was covered by last year's *Playboy* playmates of the month. A large peace sign was constructed of Christmas garland and overlay the set of beautiful naked women in the center of the wall. The easternmost barracks door led outside to pathways covered with wooden walkways that had drainage ditches under them. I searched the area until I located a bunker. The bunkers were between the barracks where I'd expected them, but they had been dug into the ground. Only the layered-sandbag tops showed aboveground. The bunkers were much more substantial than those at the replacement center and there was a steep-slope entrance at each end. I peered in and then ventured down into the barren hole. Even though it was a very bright day it was dark in the bunker. I didn't spend much time there, but I felt more comfortable knowing where there was cover.

I watched some TV after dinner with a couple of the other tenants. We watched Armed Forces TV. "Combat" was the show that was playing. "Combat" and "Star Trek" were the two shows that were favorites all across the country. Out of the corner of my left eye a pointy snout stuck from between the ammo boxes of the wall. An animal's eyes looked straight at me. It was two feet from me at eye level.

"What the hell is that?" I said.

"Oh, that's just Charlie," answered Conners. "He's mostly harmless. Charlie's a mongoose. Not a pet, but he's semi-tame. We let him alone so he keeps down the rat and snake population. We call him Charlie because, like the VC, he has a tendency to sneak up on us."

Conners went into his room and came back with a survival knife that he put on the table in front of him. We watched some more of the show. Then, with what appeared to be one smooth motion, Conners grabbed the knife and leapt up over the table into the corner of the room.

"I'll get you, you son of a bitch!" he growled.

I had no idea what was going on, and I stared at the spectacle in a state of disbelief. Conners repeatedly thrust the knife in the direction of the corner, screaming all the while. He stopped abruptly, reached down, stood up straight, turned to face me, and held out a four-inch-long rat.

"Welcome to Nam," Conners said as he teasingly swung the rat toward me.

We all headed for the sack around nine-thirty. I slept very soundly as the intensity of the past few days had mounted up on me.

Kaboom!

The thunderous explosion shook the whole building and instantaneously woke me fully. *Kaboom! Kaboom!*

These explosions were at least ten times the size of those I'd experienced in Bien Hoa. My adrenaline pumped. I burst out of the barracks east door, ran like hell down the pathway, and flung myself into the bunker. No one else was there. I was barefoot, in my undershorts, and had no shirt, but just then the trappings of civilization mattered to me not at all.

A Klaxon horn let out a single *Ahoooga*. Sirens began to announce the attack. *Kaboom! Kaboom! Kaboom! Kaboom!* I felt the concussions through the ground. A couple of other guys piled into the bunker. "Damn gooks are using 122s tonight," one of them exclaimed. We waited for five minutes, and there were no more explosions close by, though we heard some farther away.

"I'm going to take a look," said the second person sharing this quite large bunker.

He went up the ramp and looked around by lifting his eyes only a little above the sandbags. There was another large explosion, but it was different and very close. Our observer came tumbling back down into the bunker. His eyes were big with excitement.

"They blew up the supply shed across the street, and I can see gooks running around the other side of the road."

This wasn't good news. The road was only about fifty yards from our location. The staccato burst of a submachine gun split the night air. "That's an AK," said the first guy. The sound of two Cobras taking off over our heads was welcome news to my bunker companions. "About damn time!" one of them exclaimed.

The Cobras began to strafe the area 100 yards from our position. The tracers from the miniguns cut through the dark and bounced up off the ground in an eerie fireworks display. The fire team set up a racetrack pattern and started using rockets. I'd never thought I'd be on the receiving end of rockets. The awesome noise from their explosions made me jump but was comforting. The flames from the rockets looked like brilliant comets falling onto our little piece of earth. After fifteen minutes of pounding the target, the gun team returned over our heads and into the parking area we called the Corral. Immediately, another fire team took off and repeated the exhibition. After that there were no more explosions, and in short order even the small arms firing stopped. I and my companions of necessity stayed in the bunker until daybreak, when the all-clear sounded. I climbed out of the bunker into the dawn of a new day. The very first thing I did after getting into my fatigues was to walk to what was left of the supply building. An armed sergeant stood guard over the blown-up south end of the building, which was collapsed onto itself.

"Hey, Sarge, can I get a weapon here?"

"You new?" he asked.

"Yeah, I got here yesterday and spent last night down in a bunker with no weapon. I felt very naked."

"You been through in-country training yet?"

"No."

"Well, I'm not supposed to issue you your assigned arms until you're officially processed, but I can give you a grease gun if it'll make you feel better."

"That'd be fine. I'll take anything as long as it shoots."

The sergeant went inside and came out with a World War II–vintage .45-caliber M3A1 submachine gun and five magazines with a couple of boxes of ammo. I'd only seen grease guns in the movies, but I happily took it back to my room and loaded the magazines. It was reassuring to be armed.

At breakfast Conners sat down next to me. "Where were you last night?" he said.

"I went to the bunker south of our barracks. I'd like to know where all you guys were. There were only two other guys in there with me, and none of us were armed."

"You were in the enlisted bunker. Our bunker is the one north of the barracks. The reason there were so few people in the bunker with you is that you made a basic error. When we take incoming, don't get up and start running around. Just roll under your bunk and stay there. If a round hits close by, it's more likely to get you if you're standing up. The sand-bags around the hootch will protect you from almost everything except a direct hit. You're even more protected in the Scrounger's room. There's a hole cut out from the wall under your bunk. It leads directly into his own personal bunker. Take a look."

I found the entrance to the private bunker right where Conners had said it was. There was even a set of bedsprings in case sleeping in the bunker was in order. While I examined the inside of this newfound refuge, the effect of my first week's malaria pill took hold and I felt an increasingly painful gnawing deep in my bowels. I quickly headed for the outhouse latrine. Conners and another person in a jeep spotted me and called to me from across the walkway.

"Come with us, Spalding. We're going to the perimeter to get some pictures of the dead gooks they nailed in the wire last night."

The grinding in my stomach told me I had other priorities. Besides, I figured there'd be plenty of time to see dead men during the next year. "That's okay," I replied. "Go ahead without me. I'll skip it for now. Thanks anyway, though."

Fortunately, I got to keep the Scrounger's room for my whole tour of duty. Unfortunately, because we got mortared and rocketed frequently, I used Conners's lesson and the Scrounger's bunker many times during the next 362 days.

★ **CHAPTER 11** ★

New Guy

In addition to my unit's damage, the aftermath of the first night's incursion included eleven destroyed choppers, on the other side of the base, and the ammo dump was set on fire. The ammo dump burned for a number of days, giving us an unwanted intermittent but spectacular fireworks display. We had to get some rockets and ammo from another base and set up our own miniature reloading point for the Cobras in the Corral.

Ken Franklin, my only LOH-pilot hootchmate, came in from a mission and plopped down on a chair across from me.

"You heard about all the commotion in the next hootch?" he asked.

"No," I said. "What's the story?"

"The investigation into how we got overrun determined that the gooks sold dope to some of our perimeter defense guards. The sappers worked their way through the perimeter defenses and into the bunker where the guards were stoned. They slit the guards' throats and then used satchel charges to blow up the choppers. When our first sergeant heard about this he called a formation of all the people who pull guard duty in our sector. The way I heard it, the sarge told the assemblage that if he caught anyone using dope on the bunker line they wouldn't have to worry about the gooks because he was going to kill them himself. The sergeant returned to his room after work and discovered four pounds of C-4 plastic explosive wired to his bunk. EOD [explosive ordinance disposal] came over and defused the setup."

"Damn, my room's right across from the sergeant's! If that stuff had gone off it might have got me as well. I would have had at least one hell of a headache. Do they know who did it?"

"Yeah, someone snitched on him. The guy is in custody already. He was kind of a misfit. Most of our people are pretty straight. This fellow was new to the troop. He'd transferred in from another unit up north somewhere."

I began a one-week in-country orientation. The training goal was to get us acclimated and ready to go into the field. Surprisingly, there were a lot of National Guard guys in my classes. In the States, enlisting in the National Guard was looked at as one of the ways to avoid getting drafted and being sent to Vietnam. But here were a couple of units that had been mobilized and sent over. I talked with a couple of the Guardsmen before the class started, and they were even more surprised to be there than I was to see them! Our introduction to the indoctrination was not typical.

"Welcome to in-country orientation," said the chief instructor. "Normally, one of the reasons for these classes is to convince you people that there is a real war on. Since you were greeted last night by an honest-to-God attack, I imagine you have that part figured out."

A muffled, nervous laughter emanated from the crowd.

"Okay, okay. Calm down." The instructor waited for the talking to subside and then began his canned pitch. "First off, let me give you some simple lessons to help you make it through the year. Don't drink bottled beverages. The bad guys have a habit of putting battery acid, ground glass, and/or poison into bottled drinks. When you drink canned beverages, make sure you inspect them first. There's a rumor that someone's been puncturing the cans with hypodermic needles and injecting naughty stuff into them. Likewise, for the same kinds of reasons, don't eat the local food."

Nam was one great place all right. As long as you didn't have to eat or drink you'd be just fine.

On one training session we were marched out of the camp. We trod down a road covered by six inches of fine dust and soon my boots and the lower half of my trousers were permeated with it. This was our first time outside the protection of the base camp. We loaded the weapons we were temporarily issued and walked down the road. This was a far cry from what one would call the heart of enemy territory, but my senses were very alert. It was not a comfortable feeling. So that we could recognize our being shot at, the instructors fired AK-47s over our heads. The sound of bullets flying overhead wasn't like anything else I'd ever heard. If someone hadn't told me what it was beforehand I might not have known what the sound was. The sound was faint, like an ultrafast insect buzzing by.

Cu Chi had once been a VC stronghold, so it was honeycombed with tunnels. Part of our orientation was to go through some of the tunnels. Being a pilot, I didn't see much point in this. I talked to some other pilots about it. A couple of the guys were keen to go, but the rest of us went to talk to the head instructor and argued our case. To our surprise the instructor agreed with us and we didn't have to pretend to be tunnel rats. We tried the same tactic with the booby trap course, but on that training the instructor had a different view.

"You people are not thinking straight. People do get shot down, you know. A whole lot of this country is boobytrapped. We lose more guys to booby traps than to any other cause. If you have to hike out of the badlands you'll be glad to have had this training. Rejoin the class and pay attention."

We did both.

After lectures about the different types of booby traps, we

individually negotiated an area that was booby-trapped with small explosive charges. My turn came, and I entered the area very cautiously. Before long, I set off one of the traps. The explosion was quite near, and it scared the crap out of me. A small piece of splintered wood got embedded in my right arm. The medic who patched me up noticed my wings.

"Well, sir, are you ready to be a grunt?" he asked.

"I don't think so," I said. "I'll take my chances in the air."

"I know a lot of grunts who wouldn't trade with you, sir. They think you rotor heads are nuts."

Maybe there were some grunts who didn't want to fly, but in-country orientation helped instill in me a protective instinct for the ground troopers. I sure as hell didn't want their jobs.

The day after my orientation was complete I was to get my daytime check ride. I got up early and took my grease gun over to the supply shack.

"Hey, Sarge, remember me?"

"No, but I remember signing out that grease gun."

"Well, I finished orientation and I'm ready for my assigned weapon issue. Can we do it now?"

"Sure, step up to the counter and let me have that relic you're holding."

I handed over the grease gun and the sergeant went into the back. A few minutes later he returned with a pistol and a rifle. The rifle looked like an M-16, but it wasn't.

"You get a .45 and a CAR-15. The CAR-15 is a carbine version of the M-16. All the parts are the same except it has a short barrel and a telescoping stock, which makes it short enough to fit in the Cobra."

He pushed a form and a standard government-issue black ballpoint pen to me said, "Sign here."

I met Conners at the appointed time in the briefing room. "Let's go around the corner to Flight Ops and get the rest of your gear," he said.

We walked around the wall map and to the counter, behind which was a flight operations officer and a noncom.

"We need to get Spalding here outfitted," said Conners.

"Looks like he takes a medium chicken plate," the noncom said.

He reached under the counter, fumbled around for a few seconds, and then hefted a piece of body armor up onto the counter. The heavy armor plate hit the counter with a clunk. The chicken plate was a slightly curved, torso shaped, 3/4-inch-thick, twenty-pound piece of steel and composite material that would stop an AK-47 round at point-blank range. It was used as a chest protector. The Cobra had armored seats and strips of armor on the floor to help protect the legs, but there was no armor in the front of the ship. The chicken plate filled that role.

Conners led me out of Operations. We turned right on the walkway. I saw a little shack that looked somewhat like a covered bridge straddling the walkway. On top of the shack's peaked roof sat a man-size dummy of the Peanuts comic strip character Snoopy. He had a cyclic in his right hand and a collective stick in his left. A World War I flying helmet and goggles graced his head, and a white silk scarf hung from his neck. Inside the shack were the troop bulletin boards. We continued past the 50-by-100-foot corrugated steel maintenance hangar on our left. The Corral was an area 200 feet wide and 500 feet long. Helicopters were evenly spaced down both sides. The choppers sat between five-feet-high, two-feet-thick, revetment walls. This helped protect them from incoming mortar or rocket fire. We came to the Cobras first. They were stationed closest to Operations to better support quick-reaction (scramble) takeoffs.

"Our ship is 727," said Conners.

We found the ship by its tail number.

"Where does the CAR-16 go?" I asked.

Conners took the weapon from me, lifted himself up on the entry step, leaned in, and, with some difficulty, wedged the short rifle behind the right rear corner of the armored seat. There wasn't any room to spare, and the rifle stood straight up. If it had been of normal length there would have been no place it could have fit.

"Think you got that?" said Conners.

"Yes, but it looks kind of tricky. What do you do if you have to get out in a hurry?"

"That, my boy, is where your pistol comes in. You wear it. It goes where you go."

"Okay, but there's no way to wear this sidearm hip holster in there. There's no room."

"Another trick they don't teach in flight school. Slide the holster around to the front so that the pistol rides between your legs when you sit. This also gives you extra added ball protection."

I always doubted that the barrel of the .45 would be very effective as ball protection. This was especially true since the pistol was loaded. If it had been hit by a round it might have exploded itself. Nevertheless, later in my tour when they issued us shoulder-holstered .38 revolvers I missed the security blanket feel of the hefty .45.

I climbed into the front of the Cobra and squeezed into the armored seat. Our training ships hadn't had armor. The cockpit seemed a lot more cramped than usual.

Conners cranked the ship's engine. While the rotor was coming up to speed, I noticed that we had only 1,000 pounds of fuel rather than the full capacity 1,600 pounds. With my right foot I pressed the floor button (like an automobile dimmer switch) so I could talk over the intercom.

"We've only got a thousand pounds of fuel," I said.

"That's exactly right," said Conner. "With the weapon load we carry plus the ship's armor plus the extra heat and humidity, that's about all we can carry without being seriously over our gross weight operating limit. Even at that we're real close to the edge."

Conners pulled in a lot of collective pitch and the ship

slowly rose to a one-foot hover. Stateside, the standard hover height was three feet. Conners nursed the ship forward out from between the revetment walls, pedal-turned into the wind, got clearance from the tower, and began the takeoff. At twenty knots, translational lift speed, the ship naturally descended a little. Conners didn't try to stop the descent by adding more power because there was precious little more left. The fronts of the skids gently grazed the ground, and the natural rebound seemed to spring us into full flight.

Conners let me fly while he pointed out the operational area features I needed to know. Afterward, we returned to Cu Chi, where I was to make some normal approaches and landings to the main runway. My first approach was normal, but as I slowed through translational lift I had a difficult time stopping my forward momentum. I had to pull and hold a lot more rear cyclic than I was used to. At hover, the ship's nose had a distinct downward angle due to all the armor and armament. It took a little getting used to. After a few more practice landings, Conners told me to fly over to the POL (petroleum, oil, and lubricants) for refueling. The POL was on the southwest side of the camp immediately on the inside of the perimeter road. That way, if it blew up it didn't take out part of the base.

I made the approach into the POL, hovered over to an empty ten-foot-square concrete pad, and set the ship down. There were lots of other ships arriving, refueling, and departing.

"You get the fuel," said Conners. "Use the nozzle closest to our tank." It was standard practice to leave the engine running while we refueled. This was called hot refueling. On the Cobra, the fuel tank filler cap was located between the jet engine air intake and the rear seat canopy hatch. Later in my tour, after there'd been a couple of hot refueling explosions, we received directions that only the pilot in command, who sat in the rear seat, was to get out and put in fuel. The logic behind the new directive was that in an explosion he'd be cooked even if he were in the aircraft; the front-seater might stand a chance. Of course, when we were flying a lot, refueling was a chance to stretch and get rid of the ass-numbs. We normally alternated refuelings between the front- and rear-seaters. Even with the "rear-guy-only" rule, we sometimes alternated. After vibrating around in the sky for extended periods we figured the risk was worth the break.

I finished putting in the fuel, walked around the nose, and climbed into my seat. I buckled my seat belt and shoulder harness while a C-model Huey gunship started its takeoff out of the POL. The intercom clicked on.

"If you think we're underpowered, take a look at that C-model," said Conners.

The two side gunners were running alongside! Immediately before translational lift was achieved, the two gunners jumped onboard. The whole time it looked like the skids were never more than an inch or two above the asphalt.

"Guess I won't complain," I said.

It had seemed to me that the in-country orientation would never end. It was a relief to know that I was now qualified for daytime missions. That night I was sitting in the hootch lounge, where a group of my hootchmates were cooking a Chef Boyardee pizza one of their wives had sent over in a "Care package." The pizza sizzled in the electric frying pan being used to cook it. This wasn't the way the pizza was supposed to be cooked, but it worked well enough.

The troop Klaxon horn blared once, the signal for the number-one gun team to scramble. A door slammed behind someone running from the hootch next door. Two minutes later we heard the sound of Cobra jets starting, but there was no takeoff. A loudspeaker announced the problem.

"Mr. Samuels, report to your ship!"

"Sounds like they're missing a copilot," I said to Mike Crist, the Cobra platoon leader.

"Don't worry. Samuels will show up. I think he went across the street to get a Coke."

More precious time went by. The loudspeaker reiterated its plea. I looked at Mike inquisitively. "Do you think I ought to go, Mike?"

"You really aren't supposed to. You're not night-qualified in-country yet."

We waited another couple of minutes, and there was no change in the sound coming from the Corral. The Cobra fire team was sitting on the ground wasting precious fuel and—more important to the ground troops—time.

"Any Cobra pilot, report to Operations," boomed the loudspeaker.

I stood up and ran down the hallway, headed for Operations. I didn't take time to change into my flight suit from the civilian shorts and T-shirt that I'd donned for the evening. I ran into Operations, where there was an operations officer I didn't recognize.

"I'm a Cobra pilot," I said. "What do you need me to do?"

The operations officer looked disapprovingly at my civvies. "Who the hell are you?" he asked incredulously.

"Name's Spalding. I've been here for a week."

"Okay, report to the Cobra team lead out in the Corral. The assigned copilot still hasn't shown up."

I sprinted out of Operations and ran full speed into the Corral. The two Cobras were sitting in the middle with their position lights and red rotating beacons on. The warm billowing breeze from the rotors buffeted me as I approached the lead Cobra. I opened the canopy door and heaved myself up and into the seat. The ship took off before I could even close the hatch. The wind made it difficult to close the hatch, but I finally got it secured. I buckled myself in and then put on the helmet.

"Who in blazes are you?" asked the pilot in back.

"I'm Dan Spalding."

"Big deal! That doesn't tell me anything. Are you a Cobra pilot?"

"Yes, sir. I've just finished orientation and daytime checkout."

"Oh, great!" said the pilot, somewhat exasperated. He called to the fire team wingman behind us.

"Four-one, this is 4-2. Get arty for us. I've got a green copilot."

"Four-two, this is 4-1. Roger that."

There were artillery fire support bases all over the country, and they fired lots of different places. The possibility of being hit by friendly artillery shells on their way to get bad guys was always present. We would call a central artillery control unit and they'd tell us what bases were firing, what azimuth they were firing on, the maximum altitude of the shells, and the impact location. Then we'd plot our routes to go under, over, or around the artillery. Of course, I wasn't yet familiar with the drill.

"Four-two, this is 4-1. Cu Chi arty advises we're clear to our destination."

I tapped the intercom. "Where are we going?"

"Head for that flame up to our north. You've got the aircraft."

The night was black. There were absolutely no lights where we were going except for those flames. The flame was a brilliant orange skyscraper that seemed to lick at the earth's roof. Something was sure burning like hell. I glanced around the rest of the countryside to see what it looked like, but the blue-tinted canopy made it very difficult to see any ground reference. I made sure I kept up my instrument scan.

When we arrived on station, the pilot took the controls, contacted the ground troops, had them mark their positions with railroad flares, and found out what they needed. While one of our sister armored-cavalry troops had engaged the enemy, a Sheridan tank had been hit by an antitank RPG (rocket-propelled grenade). The tank still burned intensely.

"Centaur 4-2, this is Fox 2-6," radioed the ground troops. "We've got half our guys on each side of the stream and we're taking fire from its banks. Do your stuff."

We could see short bright-white muzzle flashes along the barely discernible stream. It was like looking at twinkling Christmas tree lights. My pilot swore under his breath, "Damn! These guys are too close together to use rockets. You think you're up to putting some minigun fire down there without killing good guys, Spalding?"

"Yes, sir," I said.

"Four-one, this is 4-2; runs will be racetrack along the stream line. Left breaks. Use minigun only."

"Four-one, roger."

We descended to 1,500 feet and rolled in along the stream. I sighted on the stream and pulled the minigun triggers. Tracers spewed out and disappeared into the darkness. The pilot didn't pull out of the dive until we reached 500 feet. Our own tracers were starting to ricochet off the ground and up toward us. The wingman started his run as we broke hard left out of ours. We made two passes.

"Fox 2-6, this is Centaur 4-2; how you doing?"

"Okay, now. Incoming has stopped. Can you hang around for dustoff escort?"

"Is the dustoff en route?"

"That's affirm," answered the ground trooper.

We had enough fuel, and we stayed in the area to provide an escort for the medical evacuation (medevac, a.k.a. dustoff) chopper. Then we headed for home. I got to fly back to the camp and made what I hoped was a cautious approach into the POL. It was awkward that the angle of the movable belly landing light was controlled by the pilot in back. I had to ask for light to be put where I needed it. Sitting in the POL with our lights on while we refueled made me feel like the bull's-eye on a target.

After rearming the pilot flew us into the Corral, slipped the Cobra into its revetment, and shut down the aircraft. I climbed out and walked with the pilot toward Operations to fill out an after-action report. He looked at me and grinned.

"You done good, Spalding."

"Thanks, sir."

"Knock off the 'sir' crap. One other thing, too—I never ever want to hear about you getting in an aircraft while wearing civvies again!"

Mike allowed that, just to be legal, this mission had to serve as my night qualification ride. For the next month I flew more nights than days.

★ CHAPTER 12 ★

Visual Reconnaissance

We referred to visual reconnaissance by its initials, VR. There was another type of mission referred to by its two initials, RF, for "rat fuck." A rat-fuck mission was one that had no point to it. Some VRs were RFs, but not all of them. VR could locate the bad guys. Then they could be either attacked or defended against, as appropriate. The operative component of VR was a LOH flying at ground level. A Cobra orbited around the LOH at 1,500 feet. The Cobra provided destructive firepower when something worth attacking was discovered, or it provided covering fire if the LOH came under attack. The LOH/Cobra teams were known as hunter/killer teams. Basically, VR meant going into the badlands and looking for trouble.

LOH drivers were a different breed of pilot. They frequently flew at ground level, in some cases following blood trails from a battle area to locate an enemy force. Besides Charlie, the LOHs had bird and tree strikes as common hazards. One LOH was damaged when a kid threw a Coke bottle into its flight path.

Air Force observation plane pilots liked to fly in our LOHs to "get closer to the action." Of course, the Air Force hitchhikers were accustomed to airplane, not helicopter, maneuvers, and LOH pilots used unusual tactics to avoid being hit by enemy fire. Not only was there a continuous up and down movement to avoid flying into the terrain, but whenever they turned, by banking left or right, they'd kick in opposite pedal to purposefully skid around the turn. Charlie was taught to shoot in front of helicopters. The LOH maneuvers resulted in the aircraft not going in the direction it was pointed. Sometimes ol' Chuck would miss because he aimed where the LOH wasn't going. At least that was the theory. Ten minutes into a VR, my conversation with a hitchhiker-carrying LOH would go something like this:

"Centaur 1-3, this is 4-4."

"This is 1-3. Go ahead."

"How's he doing?" I'd ask.

"Starting to get a little green. Now he's . . . oops . . . there he goes. Oh, man, that's gross."

"Thanks for the update."

The Air Force guys took quite a ribbing from us Army pukes. Of course, we never told them that everyone, including new VR pilots and observers, threw up for several missions until they got used to it.

One of the tallest Cobra pilots in the outfit was Oscar Popov. Popov was at least six-two. When he sat in the front seat of the Cobra his knees seemed to touch his chest. Popov was of Russian heritage and looked it. If he was captured, we figured Charlie might think Popov was some kind of special adviser and maybe they'd treat him pretty good. As for the rest of us gunship pilots, it was common knowledge that there was a bounty for us. My first VR was with Popov.

"You got the ship preflighted, Spalding?"

"Yeah, it's ready to go."

"Okay. Listen up. Before we go out, you need to understand your duties. You're the navigator. While we're flying circles around the LOH, I'm busy keeping him in sight and simultaneously watching out for other aircraft. Make sure you know where we are all the time. When the LOH reports he's spotted something, write down the map-grid coordinates with grease pencil on the inside of the canopy. When we get back from the mission we'll transfer them to paper. Lastly, but perhaps most important, if the LOH gets shot at, you're the first reaction. Use the minigun to hose down the area behind the LOH. I'll roll in with rockets as fast as I can get the ship lined up for a shot. Got it?"

"Navigate, locate, and react. I got it," I said.

"So, let's go fly."

Our hunter/killer team formed up and took off out of the Corral. We arrived at the area we were supposed to look over, and the LOH pilot announced he was going to start the VR.

"Four-three, this is 1-1. We're heading for the deck."

"Roger, got you covered," said Popov matter-of-factly.

The little ship rolled into a tight left-hand spiral and descended rapidly toward the terrain below. The rate of descent seemed fast enough that the LOH could have been in autorotation. The altitudes between 100 and 500 feet above the ground were known as the dead-man zone. Flying in the dead-man zone made it easy for ground gunners to hit an aircraft. We spent as little time as possible at these altitudes. The LOH leveled off a few feet above the terrain and began its visual reconnaissance. The LOH was painted olive drab, but the VR crews painted the top of the fuselage aft of the main rotor, as well as the tips of the main rotor blades, white. From altitude the LOH looked like a white speck surrounded by a white halo. The rest of the body blended into the foliage. After several minutes, the lack of any information from the LOH made it obvious there wasn't much recent enemy activity where we were.

Over the international distress frequency, which we monitored continuously, we heard, "Hunter/killer team in grid

253476, this is FAC three niner, on guard. Come up two two zero point two five."

Popov tuned in the ultrahigh-frequency (UHF) radio and called back.

"FAC 3-9, this is Centaur 4-3. What can we do for you?"

"Uh . . . I'm running a strike over here northeast of the mushroom. Can you do some bomb damage assessment [BDA] for us?"

"Sure can. Nothing much is happening here anyway. One-one, this is 4-3. Fly heading zero four zero. We're going to do some BDA."

Two clicks on the microphone indicated to us that 1-1 had received our directions. We flew to an area immediately to the southwest of where the air strike was being delivered. A flight of two F-4 Phantoms was dropping 500-pound bombs into an area that was 100 meters square. Smoke rose from the heavily wooded area. When the strike was over there was a lot of cratered bare ground where trees and shrubs had once stood.

"FAC 3-9, this is Centaur 4-3. What was your target down there?"

"I saw bunkers and maybe some personnel as I was flying over."

"Okay, 1-1, you got the area for BDA in sight?"

"Roger that."

The LOH headed for the bombed-out clearing.

"Spalding, follow 1-1 with the minigun sight."

I picked up the sight and located the pipper to the rear of the LOH as it entered the area. There was a discernible tension in the air, and no one spoke for a few seconds.

"I got three fresh bunkers, destroyed," reported the LOH. The word *fresh* threw an automatic switch in Popov's battle-conditioned mind. He told me, "Slew the turret and track behind him."

"Receiving fire! Receiving fire!" yelled the excited LOH pilot in a voice an octave higher than normal.

I squeezed the triggers and a line of minigun tracers arced

out to meet the ground behind the LOH. The LOH's nose rolled over as it accelerated and headed straight out of the area to our right. Popov rolled the Cobra left and pointed the nose at a smoke grenade that had been dropped by the LOH. No rockets were fired. I continued to squeeze the triggers, raking the ground with what I hoped was death from above. Popov pulled out and broke left. I kept spraying the area. Soon I was sighting backward and down. The turret reached its travel limit and I stopped firing.

Popov called the LOH. "One-one, you okay?"

"Yeah. We didn't get hit."

"I've lost you. What's your location?"

"We're orbiting two klicks [kilometers] due south."

"Be with you in a minute."

We headed for 1-1's location and soon found him running irregular circles in both directions.

"One-one, 4-3 has you in sight. FAC 3-9, did you copy our action?"

"Roger that. Understand fresh bunkers and you got shot at. I've got another flight coming in. Hold your position where you are."

The FAC rolled his twin engine, twin-tail boom OV-10 Bronco to the right and pointed the nose at the LOH's smoke. Two white phosphorous smoke rockets hit within ten meters of where the LOH had taken fire. The rockets exploded, leaving a brilliant white puff of smoke. The FAC pulled up, rolled left, and climbed to higher altitude. Using the white smoke as a target, another flight of F-4s pounded the area. There was nothing left except bomb craters.

"Four-three, this is FAC 3-9. You're clear for re-entry into the area."

The LOH made a beeline for the area, and we followed. As the LOH came within 100 meters of the target, I slewed the turret, but figured it was an unneeded precaution. I didn't believe anything could be left alive in that decimated plot of land. Ten seconds of VR time ticked away.

"Receiving fire! Receiving fire!" cried the LOH pilot.

Once again I squeezed the triggers and hosed the area with minigun fire while Popov rolled in on the target. This time Popov launched many pairs of rockets. To avoid detonating the rockets right in front of us, my minigun fire was automatically interrupted as each rocket pair left the ship. We broke right out of the attack in the same direction 1-1 had exited.

"One-one, this is 4-3. You okay?"

"Everything seems normal, but I took a round through the windshield. Besides, I'm bingo on fuel. Let's head for Dau Teang."

"Roger that. FAC 3-9, this is Centaur 4-3. You still got bad guys on the ground and they're really pissed. We're bingo on fuel and heading for Dau Teang."

"Okay, guys. Thanks for the help. I think I'll put another flight in here for good measure. Out."

A couple of minutes later, when we were well clear of the area, the LOH called to us, "Four-three, this is 1-1. We're coming up."

"Roger. Got you covered."

The LOH nosed over, picking up as much speed as possible. The pilot pulled the nose up and added as much collective pitch as available power allowed. The LOH seemed to jump through the dead-man zone on its way to altitude.

I stowed the turret sight on its pedestal, located in the right front of the cockpit.

"You've got the aircraft," Popov said.

I flew to Dau Teang and made an approach to the rearming point. Twenty feet from touchdown, a tremendous *boom* reverberated through the aircraft. I jumped instinctively, and the ship reacted to my involuntary control inputs by oscillating back and forth. I regained control and completed the landing.

"What the hell was that?" I asked Popov.

"Oh, I should have warned you. They fire eight-inch guns

from here. They're the biggest things we've got in this area and they make a hell of a concussion. Even when you know about them, they can scare the devil out of you. My first thought when they catch me off guard is that the engine has exploded."

We shut down and walked around to start reloading. As the front-seater, I took care of the minigun. I opened the ammo bay and turret side door, disconnected the ammo belt at the gun entrance, and rotated the minigun barrels counter-clockwise to make sure the gun was clear. A latent round fired, scaring the shit out of me and hitting the revetment in front of us. This was normal practice. The trick was to make sure no one was in front of the gun when you cleared it. Later in my tour, a new device called a "bullet catcher" was used. It had to be attached over the front of the barrels. If a round went off, the bullet would hit inside the catcher. Hot gas and minute bullet fragments would spray back into the hand that was rotating the barrels. I liked shooting the round off into space better.

I walked past the revetment into the ammo dump, grabbed a heavy case of 7.62mm linked machine-gun ammunition, and hauled it to the Cobra. I slid the ship's ammo container out onto the ammo bay door and removed the top. I connected the first link from the new ammo to the first link of the remaining ammunition in the ship's container and then layered the ammo into the container, working first from one end and then the other. I left some of the ammo hanging out of the container, closed the top, routed the start of the belt into the reconnected ammo feed line, pushed the container into the ammo bay, fed ammo up to the minigun through the feed line, and closed the ammo bay door.

After servicing the minigun, I helped Popov, who was loading rockets. None were assembled. The warheads had threads at their bases and screwed onto the rocket bodies. The warheads were supposed to be tightened with a torque wrench to make sure they didn't unscrew in flight.

"Where's a torque wrench?" I asked.

"I've been here four months and I've never even seen a torque wrench," said Popov. "Let me show you how to do this."

Popov screwed a warhead into a rocket motor until there was a quarter turn left to go. Holding the assembly slightly off vertical, with the warhead in his right hand and the rocket in his left, he bent his arms and wrists inward toward his body. He simultaneously snapped his arms outward and straightened his wrists. The warhead seated into the rocket motor with a satisfying clunk.

"That's all there is to it," Popov said.

A warm tropical downpour started to fall on us. After the heat inside the Cobra, getting wet was a relief. We ignored the rain and kept working. I assembled two rockets, put one on each shoulder, and walked to the ship. With the seventeen-pound warheads, the assembled rockets weighed twenty-seven pounds. Not too much, but it was clear I was carrying a load. As I approached the ship I saw Popov sliding the last of two rockets he'd most recently carried out into its firing tube. A caution flashed through my mind. The rockets were fired by electric current.

"Aren't we supposed to ground the pods before loading rockets?"

"Yeah, but there's no grounding straps anywhere I've been. Be careful to stand to one side of the rocket pods as much as you can."

I slid my rockets into their tubes. The procedure was repeated until all the tubes were filled.

"Get the break-out knife and come around to the rear of the pods," said Popov.

The break-out knife was a two-pound, thick, stubby-bladed "knife" that was used to break out of a canopy in case a hatch was jammed shut. The rear hatch opened on the right and the front hatch opened on the left. In the event the Cobra rolled over, one or the other of the hatches was sure to be obstructed. The break-out knife handle fit in the palm of the hand like an overly thick roll of coins and had a wide flange at its base that rested against the knife edge of the hand when the fingers were curled around the handle. I retrieved the knife and walked around to the right side of the ship, where Popov was standing.

"We need to make sure the electrical firing pins are snug against the base of each rocket," said Popov. "Let me have the break-out knife."

We were standing behind the rocket pods.

"Do the inside pod first," said Popov.

Popov took the break-out knife and tapped the metal lever inside each tube that served as the electrical firing circuit end.

"See how I'm standing to the side," Popov said. "If one of these things fires by accident maybe I'll only lose my arm." Popov finished all the right inside tubes and handed me the break-out knife.

"You do the outside pod."

Popov watched as I tapped home all seven of the outside pod's contacts.

"Nothing to it, right?"

"Guess not. Have you ever heard of these things firing by accident?" I asked.

"Not when rearming, but sometimes a rocket will cook off while a ship is sitting in its revetment. It's a real rare occurrence, though. Maybe it's just a rumor. I've never actually seen it happen."

The rain stopped and the sun came out hotter than ever.

"We may as well eat lunch here," said Popov. "They have great food in this camp."

We flew over to the POL and refueled. Then we parked at the visiting tie-downs and walked to the mess hall to get lunch. Dau Teang had been a French plantation. There were still civilian buildings there. The buildings' exteriors were brownish orange and had rounded corners and stucco-like walls. Inside, there were high ceilings and arched doorways. Popov was right about the food—it was good.

Between bites, Popov asked if I'd noticed the name of the area to the east northeast of Dau Teang.

"No. I didn't pay much attention."

"Would you believe it's the Michelin rubber plantation?"

"No kidding? Do they still work the trees?"

"Someone does. I don't know if it's Michelin or what, but they do work the trees. We had to cut back the trees from each side of the road through the plantation because our guys kept getting ambushed. I think we paid someone for every tree we cut down."

Because 1-1's ship had taken a hit, we flew back to Cu Chi and were done for the day. I used the unexpected free time to get a much needed haircut. I was told I could get a haircut at either a GI or a Vietnamese-run shop. The Vietnamese shop was supposed to be better and less expensive. I crossed the road into the armored troop's compound. The "shop" turned out to be one old, beat-up barber chair sitting outside a hootch. I was the only one there. The chair sat as low to the ground as it could get so that the short Vietnamese papa-san could reach my head. From what I could tell, the barber did a decent job. We communicated in pidgin English. For the finishing touches the barber produced a straight razor. Of course, my paranoia worked overtime; there really wasn't any way to tell the good guys from the bad guys. The straight razor made me nervous. The barber pulled back my collar and shaved not only around my ears and the nape of my neck, which I was accustomed to, but he shaved way down my back. This was followed by a liberal dose of witch hazel, which burned like hell.

I got the rest of my haircuts from GIs.

★ CHAPTER 13 ★

A Target, Too?

I was assigned to be Conners's copilot on the number-one gun team. It was 1700 hours (five P.M.) and it had been a busy flying day. My body was coated with a layer of grime.

"Hey, Mike, would you stand in for me on number one while I get a shower?" I asked.

Mike was busy studying technical manuals, and without looking up he answered offhandedly, "Sure, no problem, but try not to be too long." Most times I tried to not take a shower when I was on scramble standby. Fatalistically, I figured I should fly all the times it was my turn and none of the times when it wasn't. It would have been a downer for someone else to get killed while flying in my place. Even worse, I didn't relish the thought of getting shot for someone else.

I stripped down, wrapped a towel around me, and walked past the one row of hootches between my residence and the shower hut. There were a couple of fifty-five gallon drums on top of the shower shack. The drums were periodically filled from water trucks. To get a hot shower I would have to climb up on the roof, light a gasoline immersion heater, and wait for twenty minutes. Not many guys, including me, thought it was worth the trouble. My showers were nearly all cold.

After my shower, I sat at my homemade desk and wrote my daily letter to my wife. My letters tended to be rather long, sometimes running on to twenty pages. I made sure I wrote my wife every day. In the back of my mind I figured that she would forget me if I didn't stay in contact. By the time I was done writing, it was dark. I strapped a .45 onto my hip and headed for the mailbox at the operations shack.

Conners looked at me quizzically. "Where you going all loaded for bear?"

"Just to mail this letter."

"Do you think the pistol's really necessary?"

"It makes me feel better to have it on. I remember my first five nights in-country too well not to be armed at night. We seem to win in the day, but I think Charlie owns the night."

"You're right about that, I guess," Conners said.

Mess was served and we returned to the hootch to get some sleep. Normally, the number-one gun team scrambled to provide close air support for someone every night. Getting to bed early got me at least *some* sleep. Before lying down I took the .45 out of its holster, loaded a round into the chamber, uncocked the hammer, and put the pistol under my pillow, as had become my habit. I took off my shirt and lay down on top of the covers, letting a fan blow directly on me. In a few minutes I was asleep.

"Ahooooga!" rasped the Klaxon horn. I jumped out of bed, threw on my shirt, and quickly laced up my boots. I grabbed both my weapons and ran out of the hootch in time to meet Conners, who was also on his way. We ran together until Conners peeled off into the operations shack to pick up the mission location and radio contact information while I continued into the Corral. I unhooked the main rotor blade from its tie-down point on the revetment, stowed my weapons, donned my chicken plate, and climbed in. Conners reached the ship, climbed in, and began the start sequence while he buckled into his seat. Our wingman was starting up at the same time.

"Four-three, this is 4-5. Are you up?" Conners called.

"Four-three's up."

"Roger, come up tower."

Four-three clicked the microphone twice to acknowledge. While communications were being established, both Cobras hovered into the middle of the Corral. As he pushed the cyclic forward to start the takeoff, Conners called the tower, "Cu Chi tower, this is Centaur 4-5, scramble takeoff east."

"Four-five, Cu Chi tower, roger. Four-five's clear for takeoff."

It was a good thing we were clear, because we were going anyway. By the time the tower cleared us, we were halfway to the perimeter of the field. The whole scramble sequence was designed to be accomplished inside three minutes from the time the Klaxon sounded. Most times we made it. Our adrenaline surged in response to the Klaxon—not unlike Pavlov's dogs.

When we arrived at the enemy contact site, we learned that another fire team had already been there and that it had taken some antiaircraft fire—.51-caliber machine-gun fire, to be exact. In flight school we'd been taught to evade antiaircraft fire by turning perpendicular to it and then descending rapidly, even to the point of entering autorotation. I was glad the antiaircraft fire had not been heard from since it was first used. I wasn't anxious to use my training. Conners set up our runs so that we wouldn't be silhouetted by the moon, and the two Cobras pelted the target area with rockets. The flash from each pair of rockets temporarily blinded me, as well as Conners. We flew through clustered specks of burning solid rocket fuel that twinkled like fireflies. In the daytime they were invisible parts of the smoke trails, but at night they made quite a display. Our rockets expended, we asked the troops if they needed another fire team and headed for home. Our ship was in the lead with the wingman flying 200 feet higher and to our rear. The wingman could provide us with covering fire at any time as he zigzagged back and forth across the flight path. That increased the chances of our being able to roll in to cover him if he was shot at.

Ever so calmly, the ground troops called to us, "Four-five, you're rear ship's taking fire from behind."

Conners's reaction was different from flight school training. A lot different! "Son of a bitch!" he shouted loudly enough to be heard without his activating the intercom. Conners rolled the ship violently to the left, past the vertical plane, pulled back on the cyclic, and increased collective pitch to tuck the nose down and around. We inscribed an oblique plane through an imaginary cylinder of air and were headed back to our rear very rapidly. The turret sight, which I hadn't yet stowed, crashed into my legs. Conners rolled the ship upright and continued the dive. I grabbed at the turret sight and finally was able to move it into a ready position. A large bright white muzzle flash stood out against the apparent sea of black. It was smack-dab in front of us.

"Nail that fucker!" Conners directed me.

I sighted and squeezed the minigun triggers. My aim was a little low and I walked the tracers up to the muzzle flash, which immediately stopped. I let off the triggers. In the brief instant I relaxed, the intensely bright muzzle flash started again. I hosed down the area while Conners continued the dive. Our speed was building and the ship began to vibrate, but I kept the tracers flowing. Immediately before Conners broke off the dive the muzzle flashes once again stopped. I stole a quick glance at the altimeter. We were down to 500 feet. As we broke directly over the target, I continued to strafe it until the turret reached its travel limits. Conners climbed to higher altitude, and we circled the site like buzzards, waiting. After five minutes with no more action, Conners called to the grunts.

"Thanks for the warning. We're returning to base now."

"Anytime, Centaurs. Thanks for all your help. Hope we don't need you for a while. Out."

It gave me a sense of satisfaction to stow my sight knowing that I'd been able to do what was necessary when it was necessary. Conners let me fly back to the base. The air seemed smooth as silk and the Cobra flew like it was part of me.

★ CHAPTER 14 ★

Going Ballistic

Flying close to the Cambodian border was always a high-risk proposition. The Big Rubber was a huge rubber plantation reasonably close to Cambodia that was used by the enemy to set up ambushes and infiltration routes from the Ho Chi Minh trail. Recurring VR of the Big Rubber was a necessary defensive and offensive tactic.

The LOH pilot on one of these missions was reasonably new and I'd never worked with him before. We'd covered his descent down to the deck and he was working the LOH back and forth vigorously, but still kept up his speed. I liked his style. The LOH crossed from my right to my left. Without any warning, the little ship tucked its nose down and slammed into the ground. Pieces flew off and the remains rolled a couple of hundred yards. Somehow, there was no fire. Before the crash, the LOH hadn't slowed down or made any kind of preparatory maneuvers. There were no calls for help from the pilot. One moment the LOH was flying nicely and the next moment it was a pile of junk.

We circled the downed LOH. None of the crew was in sight. "Mayday, mayday, mayday," called the aircraft commander. "This is Centaur 4-7 on guard. Any slick pilot in the vicinity of the Big Rubber come in."

"Centaur 4-7, this is Bandit 2-4."

"Roger, Bandit. Come up two ten point three."

"Centaur, this is Bandit. How can we help?"

"I've got a crashed LOH. No indication of enemy activity."

"Roger, Centaur. We're five minutes away. We'll be coming in from the north."

The Huey arrived as promised, circled the area at altitude once, and made a steep approach to a clearing close by the downed LOH. We flew along with the slick during his approach, but stayed higher and to his right to provide cover if he needed it. After the slick touched down, the two door gunners got out and trudged through the brush to the LOH. They made two trips, carrying one of the three LOH crewmen back to the Huey on each trip. On the third trip, only one crewman went back to the LOH.

"Damn! I don't believe it!" I said to the pilot. "Look at that! One of the LOH crew members is relatively unhurt. He's walking back with that door gunner helping him."

"It is kind of unbelievable, isn't it? I don't think I'd have believed anyone could survive that crash unless I'd seen it with my own eyes."

"Centaur 4-7, this is Bandit. We've got your guys and are proceeding to Cu Chi medevac."

"Bandit 2-4, roger. We're a little short on fuel. We'll fuel up at Tay Ninh and return to base shortly. Thanks for your help."

Checking in at Base Operations, we learned that the LOH pilot was dead and that there would be a safety meeting that night. Even in a war zone, aviation safety was nothing to ignore. I hoped to learn something useful about the crash that might help save my own neck. The meeting turned out to be a big disappointment.

I entered the briefing room at the appointed time and found half the troop was already there. I took a chair. The CO began to speak and the murmur of idle conversation died down.

"I'm not sure how many of you know it, but Lieutenant

Black here is our safety officer. He has something he wants to share with you tonight which arises from the crash that occurred this afternoon."

Lieutenant Black stepped forward and paused for effect. His hands were clasped behind his back.

"As many of you know, two months ago we were given ballistic flight helmets to use. I've been trying to get you guys to use them ever since, but you don't seem to want to cooperate."

This sounded to me like sour grapes from Lieutenant Black. Some of the guys had tried out the new helmets. They were supposed to help deflect shrapnel, or if you were real lucky, even a bullet. But there were problems with the helmets. First, they were round, not oval like a person's head, and the pressure from the round shape on the front and rear of the head was severe. It was impossible to get one to fit. Everyone who tried the new helmets got excruciating headaches. Second, the helmets were too heavy to wear while vibrating and maneuvering, sometimes violently, through the air.

"Well, look at this!" said Black as he pulled a flight helmet out from behind his back. "This is the helmet Swenson was wearing today. Look hard at it. Then decide if you can afford not to wear a ballistic helmet."

The helmet Black held up had a bullet hole smack-dab in the middle of its visor with a larger bullet exit hole in the rear. The inside had been cleaned up, but it was still evident why we called our flight helmets "brain buckets."

I looked at the guy on my right, raised my eyebrows, and said, "I was covering Swenson today. Now I know why there wasn't any indication of trouble from the LOH. The pilot died instantly. But I don't get Black's point. The bullet entered through the visor, not the helmet. All a ballistic helmet might have done was stop the bullet from exiting. Guess Black would prefer it ricocheted around on the inside before stopping."

"Maybe so. Black is kind of weird," my colleague replied.

The CO stood up and motioned for Black to sit down. "That'll be all for tonight," he said. "You're dismissed."

The meeting broke up and we filed out the door. There was distinct muttering as we walked back to the hootches in clumps of five or six. There never was any demand for the ballistic helmets, and I never heard of any other pilot getting it right between the eyes. No doubt about it. Everyone felt the way I did. Swenson's number had come up. Nothing would have helped him.

★ **CHAPTER 15** ★

Merry-go-round

The ground unit we were to support contacted us as we neared its position. "Centaur 4-9, this is Fox 2-8. We're heading out on azimuth zero three five. Need you to VR in front of us. S-2 [intelligence] thinks we'll flush out Charlie."

I was the front-seater for Tom Brewer. Tom was the thinnest guy in the outfit. When I flew a ship after Tom, I'd have to loosen the seat belt to get it around me. Tom was the only pilot for whom I had to do that. For everyone else, I threw on the belt and tightened it. Tom was a natural pilot. He had reactions like a cat and could make the Cobra do whatever he liked. It was good flying with him. Tom's skill gave me a sense of confidence.

"One-seven, this is 4-9. You got the grunts in sight?" Tom asked our assigned hunter.

Rick James replied in his normally short manner. "Yep."

"Okay, 1-7. Let's do it."

"One-seven's on the way down."

"Fox 2-8, this is Centaur 4-9. The LOH is on its way. Make sure your guys know he's going to be in front of you so they don't fire in his direction."

"Four-nine, will do."

The LOH got to ground level behind the troop column and then flew over their heads to set up his basic direction of search. He started his bob-and-weave routine as he passed the point men. The LOH crisscrossed the line of march and was putting some distance between himself and the troops.

"Four-nine, I've got some spider holes here," Rick said.

I wrote down the location on the canopy with a grease pencil and advised the ground troops: "Two-eight, this is 4-9. There's a tunnel complex fifteen degrees left of your current heading and a couple of klicks out." I looked back and scanned the forest to relocate the LOH. Rick had begun to concentrate his flight over the area where the tunnel entrances had been spotted. Suddenly a small black puff of smoke was floating above where a hole had been reported.

"One-seven, we roger your black smoke," Tom said.

This was a way, as cover for the LOH, to make sure what we were seeing was being purposefully caused by the LOH crew and not something about which to be alarmed. LOH pilots didn't always tell us everything they were doing when they got busy.

Rick's two clicks of the microphone was reassuring. Our unit's normal LOH crew complement was nonstandard. LOHs were supposed to run reconnaissance with only a pilot and an observer. There was a standard arrangement for a forward firing minigun, but our guys didn't use it. The forward-only firing of the standard arrangement was ineffective for defense. Our guys normally carried the pilot, a copilot with an M-16 rifle, and an observer with an M-60 machine gun. Besides the guns, the LOHs carried a variety of grenades: white phosphorous smoke grenades, standard smoke grenades, tear gas grenades, concussion grenades, and fragmentation grenades. Sometimes I wondered how the LOHs got off the ground.

Rick was having his crew drop grenades into the spider holes. They were trying to kill anyone close to the entrances or to flush them out. Rick must have seen some signs of recent activity or he wouldn't have bothered. The big problem with dropping grenades was that the LOH slowed down over the targets to achieve the accuracy needed for the hand-dropped munitions. The LOH was circling left, coming around for a second "bombing" run. We were orbiting left in a much larger circle. The LOH came in close to our orbit and I was looking almost straight down at it. As Rick passed the line of my left shoulder, bright orange flames erupted from the engine compartment and wrapped themselves forward into the area behind the cockpit. The whole ship was ablaze in an instant. The LOH rolled out of its left turn, its nose came up momentarily, as if it was slowing down, and then it crashed into the ground, rolling over and over and over for what seemed like an eternity. It finally stopped, but continued to burn.

I'd not heard or seen anything that indicated the LOH was taking fire and the crash was already a fact. Mentally, I calculated that responding with the minigun wouldn't do anyone any good, so I held my fire.

Tom rolled the Cobra left and down into a rocket-attack dive. We were aimed where the LOH had first "exploded," and I waited for rockets to launch, but none were forthcoming. Tom must have had the same idea I did.

As Tom pulled out of the dive, we got a good look at the destroyed LOH. Tom called back to Troop Operations, "Centaur Ops, this is 4-9. One-seven's crashed in flames. Expect no survivors. Will advise."

"I think we ought to take a closer look," I said.

"Yeah, I'll make another pass."

We made a left circle, and Tom entered another dive at the LOH. This time he didn't pull out until we were down to 300 feet. As the LOH passed to my left rear, I saw one guy standing up with another crew member lying at his feet.

"Hey, Tom. There's two guys down there! Did you see them?"

"Sure did. I don't believe it, but they're down there all right. . . . Fox 2-8, this is 4-9. Did you see the LOH crash?"

"Four-nine, this is 2-8. We didn't see the crash, but we can see smoke to our eleven o'clock. We ought to be able to push through this brush and get to him in half an hour or so."

"Two-eight, this is 4-9. Understand . . . Centaur Control, this is 4-9. Be advised, there are at least two survivors from the crash. I'm going to land and pick them up."

"Four-nine, this is Control. Troop is scrambled. They'll be there quick."

"Four-nine, roger. Out."

For some reason Tom's instinct told him that the survivors couldn't wait for either the grunt column or our own troopers. Tom's decision to pick up the survivors was extraordinary: there was nowhere to put extra people on a Cobra. We'd heard rumors about a Cobra rescue up north, but nothing official had come down to us. No one in our own troop had ever tried it.

Tom began his landing approach to an area immediately downwind of the burning LOH. From altitude, the area didn't look too inhospitable. As we got closer, it became clear that the area surrounding the LOH was covered with dense underbrush and small trees. Tom ignored the ground cover and set the ship down thirty yards from the LOH. That was as close as we could get.

"I'm getting out to help them," I said.

"Okay," Tom said. "When you get them over here, open up the ammo bay doors and have them lie down on them. We'll fly them out that way."

I reached up with my right hand and pulled the microphone cord to my helmet from its jack, opened the canopy hatch, and climbed down into the boonies. Most of the brush was grayish brown and two to three feet tall. I turned away from the Cobra and saw the two survivors trying to reach us. They weren't doing very well. One was pulling the other through the brush. I pushed through the brush toward them and the burning LOH, and was breathing hard with the effort. The weight of my chicken plate didn't help the situation. As I reached the shaken GIs, the LOH's grenades and ammunition started exploding. I could feel the heat from the fire on my face and the concussion of the explosions through my body. I thought my chicken plate would protect my torso. It didn't occur to me to think about my extremities.

"Let's get the hell out of here!" I screamed at the standing survivor over the roar of the Cobra and the exploding LOH. I took the incapacitated guy under his right arm and the standing GI took the other. We heaved through the brush and bushes over to the Cobra.

"Wait a second right here," I told them. The ammo bay doors were one and a half feet wide and four feet long. They were hinged at their bases and opened sideways. A strand of one-eighth-inch-diameter stainless steel cable at each end of the doors was all that stopped them from opening past the horizontal plane. I pushed in the two spring-loaded catches on the left ammo bay door and lowered it to the horizontal position. I ran around the front of the ship, repeated the process on the right side, then sprinted back to the downed crew.

"We have to load him onto the ammo bay door," I shouted above the Cobra noise to the healthier survivor. With some effort we lifted the injured man onto the left door. He yelped a couple of times. Something was hurting him.

"Go around and get on the right door," I said to the standing survivor as I motioned for him to circle around the front of the ship.

He waved to say he understood, then limped around to the right side and got on. I climbed back in, closed the hatch, strapped in, connected my helmet, and said to Tom, "Let's go."

Tom pulled in 100 percent of the available power and we barely lifted off the ground. The ship was extremely nose-heavy. It immediately started to drift forward and to turn slowly to the right. Tom added more left pedal. That took more power, and we started to settle a little, so he pulled in more collective pitch. The ship didn't have the power to spare. It started spinning to the right. The main rotor rpm dropped. The master caution annunciator in the center of the instrument console flashed and the aural warning unleashed siren-like whoops. Tom fought for control, but the ship wasn't cooperating. We had lateral motion and were spinning simultaneously. I thought a crash was unavoidable. I counted three complete spins before Tom gave up and bottomed the collective pitch. We sank down, hit the ground hard, and swayed side to side. Luckily, the ship didn't topple over.

"We're too heavy," said Tom. "Get out and off-load the guys. I'll lighten the armament load and come back for you."

I climbed out, taking care not to step on the injured man. It was hard to reach the canopy hatch with the ammo bay door open, and I didn't close it. As I tried to get around to our other passenger, I noticed the brush in this area was a lot more dense than where we'd been before.

"Get off and move to the side," I shouted, and motioned. The right-side passenger jumped down and moved into the brush beside the Cobra. I could barely see him in the heavy foliage even though he was only a few feet away. I moved back and hefted the wounded soldier off the ammo bay door, then dragged him ten feet to the left and lay on top of him to shield him from flying debris as the Cobra took off. As the Cobra climbed up to 100 feet and began firing rockets all around us, my thoughts turned to first aid for the injured man. I steeled myself for the blood and guts I knew would be the result of the tremendous crash I'd witnessed. I raised the man's helmet visor and saw that it was Rick.

"Where do you hurt, Rick?" I asked.

"My ankle's broken and the back of my neck hurts," he said.

I didn't think I could do anything for the broken ankle in the time we had, so I peeled back Rick's shirt collar and looked at his neck. There was a burn ring around the back of the neck. The skin was pink and raw, with some blisters and scorch marks.

"Is that all?" I asked.

"Is that all?" Rick yelled. "It damn well hurts!"

I didn't take the time to explain that I had been expecting to find blood shooting from torn arteries or foaming from a sucking chest wound. Instead, I started to size up our predicament. We were lying out in light brush. I was the only one armed, and I only had my .45 with its few rounds of ammo. I suddenly felt very alone. I remembered how I'd been such a poor shot with the pistol that I'd had to cheat on my qualifying scores to be eligible for a combat assignment. Keeping in mind the NVA's reputation for mistreating Cobra pilots, if I ended up in a firefight with the bad guys, I resolved to save the last bullet to kill myself.

"What happened to you guys, Rick?"

"I saw something off to the right front just before all hell broke loose. It looked all the world like a grenade suspended in some kind of parachute."

"You were knocked down by Charlie?"

"Yeah."

"Oh, shit."

I took out my .45 and cocked it. Boy, did I wish I was a better pistol shot!

About the time our being alone started to get real tense, Tom returned with the Cobra. I holstered my pistol and we reloaded the passengers. With the lightened ship, the takeoff was almost normal. We headed for the medevac pad. On the way back we got up to 100 knots one time and I had to keep reminding Tom to hold his speed down because we had out-board passengers.

"How are they doing?" Tom asked.

I peered over the edge of the cockpit, looking out and down on each side. Rick and the other guy had their hands wrapped tightly around the ammo bay door front cable and were clinging for dear life. The wind was buffeting them and their flight suits flapped wildly.

"They're still there," I said. "But they're holding on real tight."

About then I felt an unusual, very high frequency vibration.

"Do you feel that vibration?" I asked Tom.

"Yes, but it's not serious. Don't sweat it."

Tom called the tower, "Cu Chi tower. This is Centaur 4-9, five miles north for landing at dustoff."

"Four-nine, this is Cu Chi tower. Roger. Call right base for landing."

"Uh . . . tower, this is 4-9. Notify medevac we have two injured on board."

"Wilco, 4-9."

We entered the traffic pattern and located the white medevac pad with the great big red cross in the middle. Right after we touched down, several hospital people rushed out to us and unloaded the two crash victims. As I watched Rick go in on a stretcher, I still felt the nagging vibration.

"Tom, why don't we shut down here and take a look at the ship?"

"Nah, that's not necessary," Tom said. "We're fine."

Tom made the required radio contacts and told me to fly around to the POL. The ship handled okay, but the vibration was still bugging me. We refueled but decided not to rearm just then. We wanted to get back to see how the guys were doing. I flew the ship around the pattern, landed in the Corral, and parked between our assigned revetments. Tom shut down the engine and electrical systems. I retrieved the green five-by-seven-inch loose-leaf logbook from its spot between the right-side top of the instrument dashboard and the canopy. I filled in the flight hours data and stored the book back in its place. When the main rotor slowed I climbed out and waited for it to stop. I looked up to hook on the rotor tie-down bar and was surprised to see the bottom of the main rotor severely scarred. It had obviously been used as a giant rotary mower blade! The underside had punctures into the honeycomb structure from just behind the leading edge running the span of the blades all the way back to the trailing edge. Some of the punctures were up to two inches wide and one inch deep. Puncture lines were evident from the rotor tips to within four feet of the main rotor mast. It was amazing the main rotor hadn't flown apart, but that damage couldn't account for the high-frequency vibrations I'd felt. High-frequency vibrations were most commonly associated with the engine or the tail rotor. I walked to the rear of the ship. Sure enough, both ends of the tail rotor were bent sideways and rearward like pretzels. Puncture striations added to the unnatural sight. The ship was obviously not fly-able. I walked to the front of the ship, stepped up onto the foot rest, retrieved the logbook, and entered a big red X in the block for aircraft status.

Tom said that for him the worst part of the experience was firing rockets with the front hatch open. The smoke and hot sparks from the left-side rockets had come inside, temporarily blinding him and stinging his exposed face.

We went to see Rick in the hospital the next morning. His right leg was in a cast up to the middle of his thigh. "How you doing, Rick?" asked Tom.

"Pretty well, considering, I guess."

"That was quite an experience yesterday. We didn't think anyone could have survived that crash," I said.

Rick's eyes grew large as he spit out his own reflection, "Hell, the crash was the easy part. I thought the ride back was going to kill me!"

At least Rick got to go home. The troopers found the remains of the third crewman, who had been sitting in the rear seat of the LOH. The body was located 200 yards from the crash site, and both its legs were missing. Rick swore something Charlie did had knocked them out of the sky, but the way I figured it, one of the grenades the observer was dropping got away from him and exploded inside or close to the LOH. Either way, it was a mission all the survivors would remember.

B.J. Scammell had the room next to mine. He was also a warrant officer Cobra pilot. B.J. was "more mature" than the rest of us kids and had a slight beer belly complemented by a friendly round face. B.J. was from South Carolina and talked with a characteristic slow drawl. Having spent my childhood in North Carolina, talking with B.J. made me feel like I was at home. B.J.'s plan for after his tour was to get assigned to the 82nd Airborne at Fort Bragg and to retire from the service. When I came back from my visit to Rick, B.J. knocked on my door.

"Spalding, are you in there?"

"Yeah, come on in, B.J."

B.J. opened the door and entered the room, leaving the door open behind him. "So, how's Rick doing?"

"Seems okay to me. He's been over here long enough that they're going to ship him home. He got the million-dollar wound."

"Reckon so. Did you hear about Mamma-san and the AK yet?"

Mamma-san was a Vietnamese maid for our hootch. She lived in Cu Chi village, immediately to the south of our camp. Each hootch had a maid whose jobs included sweeping out the dust, washing clothes, shining boots, and the like. Some hootches had a baby-san maid. Baby-sans were younger women. Ours was definitely a mamma-san. She stood only four feet tall, was of very slender build, and chewed betel nut, which had given her teeth a shiny black coating. She was personable enough, though, and she did her work with enthusiasm. I guessed that Mamma-san had seen several sets of pilots come and go from what she probably considered "her" hootch.

"No," I said. "I haven't heard anything about it."

"Samuels was given a captured AK by the grunts for a mission on which he'd helped them out. He was trying to figure out how to field-strip it so he could clean it when the mamma-san happened by and saw the trouble he was having. After some sign language and pidgin English, Samuels understood that she wanted him to let her have a try. The way Samuels is telling it, it only took Mamma-san about thirty seconds to strip down the rifle, a couple of minutes to completely clean it, and another minute to reassemble it. Samuels swears she could have done it in the dark!"

"Guess Mamma-san has talents we're not aware of," I said.

"Yeah, I never doubted that," said B.J. "It wouldn't bother me a bit if it had been an M-16. Any of the guys could have taught her about cleaning them. But where in hell did she learn about AKs? Kind of makes me nervous. Know what I mean?"

I sure did.

★ CHAPTER 16 ★

Strange Beasts

Frank Meyers was wingman on a night close air support mission over the Boi Loi woods. I was his copilot/gunner. Meyers was a happy-go-lucky guy with more enthusiasm than most any other three people. Boi Loi was a hotbed of enemy activity. The area was covered with dense jungle, and the North Vietnamese Army (NVA) used it to full advantage. One of our ground squadrons had spotted a column of enemy moving out of the wood line and had called us in to assist in the attack. There was a single small hut, the remains of a village, that the ground-pounders had designated as our target. It was a very dark night and the hut was just a slightly lighter speck against the dark ground. We'd made two passes and neither the lead ship nor Frank had been able to hit the hut. As the lead ship called "Breaking right" out of his third run, Frank rolled our ship right and into a thirty-degree nose-down dive. The first pair of rockets looked slightly long. Frank corrected and fired the next pair. Still long. Frank was holding too much power. He corrected, pushing the nose farther down, and fired the third pair of rockets. The sparks and brightness of the rockets began to dissipate, and then there was a large bright orange fireball on the ground. Through the floorboard I felt several jolts in quick succession. They were accompanied by deep thuds. Frank was yelling something and I tried to see what was going on by looking in my tiny rearview mirror. In the glow of the red low-intensity cockpit lights I could barely see Frank's head moving up and down rapidly in an exaggerated "yes" motion. Frank hadn't keyed the intercom, but I could hear him yelling, "I got hit! I got hit!" The g's piled on when Frank broke off the attack.

My heart rushed as the adrenaline pumped into my bloodstream. "Frank, calm down!" I said. I asked the most important questions by spitting them out in rapid-fire succession. "Do you want me to fly? Where are you hit? How bad is it?"

Frank stopped jumping around and asked, "What do you mean, where am I hit?"

"You shouted you were hit."

"No I didn't. What I yelled was, 'I got *it*.' I'm okay. We didn't even take any fire."

"If you're not hit, and we didn't take any fire, what were all those bumps and thuds?"

"That was just me stamping my feet on the floor. You know, it's really exciting to get a secondary explosion from a target. That's the first time it's happened to me."

If Frank hadn't been the aircraft commander, I would have told him I didn't appreciate his taking several years off my life with his exuberance, but remembering my place, I kept my mouth shut.

Later in his tour Frank's luck ran out. He landed at the Tay Ninh VIP pad to get briefed for a mission. Frank's front-seater was filling in the logbook, and Frank climbed out of his ship just in time to get hit by a piece of shrapnel from an exploding enemy rocket. The front-seater wasn't even scratched, and there was no damage to the Cobra, but the shrapnel sliced off the back of Frank's head. The front-seater said that Frank died instantly. I was assigned to pack up Frank's things to be sent back to the real world. It was unpleasant duty; I kept thinking about how Frank's family was going to feel when they received what I packed.

A new captain came into the outfit and was going through in-country orientation. He got assigned to set out some permanent boundary lines for our dirt-surface volleyball court, which was located immediately behind the shower shack. The captain was laying out the rear baseline when a water truck backed over his legs and crushed them. The captain's total time in the unit was three days.

One of our slick pilots was seriously injured on a troop medevac mission. Actually, it isn't fair to call it a mission. When the scramble horn sounded, the pilot bolted from his hootch and ran toward Operations. To get there faster, he decided to cut between two other hootches. The pilot was plunging full speed ahead through the darkness while simultaneously putting on his shirt when a thin steel cable strung between the barracks as a clothesline caught him in the mouth, penetrating far enough to sever his jaws at the hinge point. A strange wound to be found in a frontline Army hospital, to be sure, but it was, nevertheless, an incapacitating one.

There were supposed to be two types of LRRP teams with which we worked, long-range patrols (LRP) and long-range reconnaissance patrols (LRRP), but from the way they operated, it was never clear to me what the real difference was. In either case, my involvement with them seemed to prove a common theory—LRRPs were nuts!

LRRP missions were conceived to accomplish two main goals: gather intelligence on enemy troop strength or movement and, when advantageous, ambush the enemy in its own backyard. The Centaurs' role was to insert five- or ten-man LRRP teams into the boonies, to respond with close air support if needed, and to extract the teams when their missions had come to an end.

At the first briefing I attended for a LRRP insertion, we were given a large-scale (1 to 25,000) photoreconnaissance map of the landing zone (LZ). An F-101 Voodoo had snapped pictures of the area in question and map grid coordinates had been superimposed on the developed photos. (When we were flying VR, the Voodoo missions posed a midair collision threat to us. All of a sudden, they'd come screaming by at high speed and at our altitude. At night, when the ships dropped flares to light the ground for their cameras, it looked as if the aircraft were shitting little balls of flashbulbs.) The LRRP team leader looked at the map provided for this particular mission, studied it for a minute, pointed to a large bush, and said, "Put us in right there."

Sometimes, from the air we had trouble finding whole landing zones; these people wanted us to put them next to a particular bush! The LRRP team, the slick pilots, and our fire-team pilots walked to the Corral for the start of the mission. The LRRPs were carrying very full field packs, and they had to lean forward to maintain their balance under the load. On each LRRP, there seemed to be at least one of every kind of infantry weapon: electrically fired claymore mines; trip flares; grenades; pistols; light antitank weapons (LAWS); and various types of rifles. Many of the LRRPs had CAR-15s, like mine. LRRP patrols carried so much weaponry that we could only haul five of their men in a single Huey. Normally the Huey was rated for up to ten troops.

One of the LRRPs was carrying two rifles. One was an M-14 with a sniper scope. The other was, to my amazement, a relatively diminutive Remington Nylon-66 .22-caliber rifle. When I was thirteen a friend had owned one. We used to hunt rabbits together and I was jealous of his rifle; it was a lot better than my own. But the bullets fired by the Remington were not very powerful.

"What in the world do you use that Remington for?" I asked the LRRP.

A sly grin crept over the LRRP's thoroughly camouflaged green, black, brown, and tan face. He reached into his right-front pants pocket and pulled out a silencer. "I use this for real close-in work," he said. "You know, like when the gooks are within two or three meters of us and they don't know we're there. I can put a round right into one of their heads and the others still can't tell where it came from."

Our four-ship formation took off and headed up into the Boi Loi, where we were supposed to drop off the team. I was flying as copilot/gunner for the Cobra fire team leader, Mike Crist. The Cobras soon outran the slicks on the way to the LZ, but that was part of the plan. Mike kept the fire team above 3,000 feet. He found the landmark we'd selected as the initial point (IP) for the LRRP insertion approach and flew past the LZ to familiarize himself with the area. He then turned in a wide circle and proceeded back to the IP by a different route. The idea behind this tactic was to give Charlie as little idea about what was going on as possible.

The slicks arrived at the IP at the designated time, 0900, and we made contact.

"Two-seven, this is 4-6. How do you hear?"

"Two-seven's up and reads you five by five."

On the FM ground communication channel, Mike made sure the LRRPs could talk with us. "LRRP 7-5, this is 4-6."

"Got you loud and clear, 4-6," said the LRRP team radio operator.

"Two-seven, this is 4-6. Take up heading zero seven five and descend to low level," said Mike. "The LZ is five miles."

Two clicks of 2-7's microphone acknowledged his "Roger." The two slicks turned to the proper heading and began a steep descent. The second slick dropped back into trail formation from his original left-echelon spot. Mike would now provide navigation for the slicks and would actually talk them into the LZ.

"Continue zero seven five. LZ is two miles. . . . Come left to zero seven zero. LZ is one mile. . . . LZ is five hundred meters. Start your deceleration. . . . Come right to zero seven three."

The slicks' noses began to rear up as they braked for the LZ, which they could not see but we could. As we got closer and closer to the LZ, Mike's chatter continued with increasing frequency.

"Head zero seven zero. . . . LZ is two hundred meters. . . . LZ is one hundred meters. . . . LZ is fifty meters. Twenty-five meters."

Breaking the tension, a call came from the slicks: "Two-seven's got the LZ."

We flew past the LZ while the slicks very rapidly touched down next to the chosen bush and immediately began to take off. Their time in the LZ was twenty or thirty seconds. They held their heading for a while after their departure.

Mike turned to the right, back toward base, and checked in with the LRRPs. "LRRP 7-5, this is 4-6."

A barely audible whispered voice came back on the radio. "LRRP 7-5's in. See you in three days."

The LRRP radiomen wore headphones so the crackle of the radio wouldn't give away their position and they whispered when they wanted to talk to us. Later in my tour I found it hard not to whisper back, and sometimes did. The LRRPs thought it was funny.

The planned three-days-later LRRP extraction was moved up to 1400 hours that very afternoon, when the scramble horn blared. The LRRP team had been searched out and attacked. For all the tactics we used to try to make the teams' location an unknown to Charlie, I never thought much of the basic secrecy idea. How could we possibly be stealthy when the distinctive whopping of the Hueys' main rotor blade could be heard for miles?

We scrambled to the LRRP team location.

"LRRP 7-5, this is 4-6," called Mike. There was no answer. "Seven-five, this is 4-6." There was still no answer. "Seven-five, this is 4-6. Please acknowledge."

A very out of breath LRRP panted back, "Four-six, this is 7-5." The LRRPs weren't whispering this time. "We're on the move. Heavy forces have been encountered. We're two hundred meters away from the initial drop point on azimuth two three five. We . . . we're taking mortar fire!"

"Roger, 7-5. We have your location. Where do you want our stuff?"

"Put some fifty meters from us on azimuth zero five five!"

Mike rolled the Cobra into its attack run and fired several pairs of rockets. As we broke to the right I could feel the thuds from our wingman's rockets underneath us.

"Four-six, this is Centaur 2-7. We're at the IP with a flight of three."

Mike was rolling in for another attack but still let the slicks know what was going on. "Roger, 2-7. Bad guys are in contact. Stand by . . . 7-5, how're you doing now?" Mike asked.

"Seven-five's still taking sporadic rifle fire, but the mortars have stopped."

"Can you make it into the bomb craters due south of your location?"

"We'll try. We got one wounded so far."

"Understand. Let me know when you're there."

Mike headed for the IP.

"I've got the slicks at one o'clock low and two miles," I announced over the intercom to Mike.

"Two-seven, this is 4-6," Mike said. "We've got you in sight. Start your approach."

Two of the slicks started down and took up the rough heading to get to the old LZ. Mike started talking them into the new makeshift LZ.

"Seven-five's in the craters," called the LRRPs.

"Roger, 7-5. We're on the way. . . . Two-seven, you're one thousand meters from the LZ."

"Receiving fire! We're taking fire!" the slick pilot yelled. Mike rolled in and put some rockets to the right side of the two-ship formation while our wingman worked over the left side. Big green tracers were heading for the slicks. This wasn't the way LRRP extractions were supposed to develop. Taking fire a kilometer away from the LZ was not something that happened.

"Two-seven's hit. We got a wounded door gunner and fluctuating turbine rpm."

The slick began to turn to the right to head for home. Now the extraction mission was coming apart. There was the distinct possibility that we might not get the LRRPs out in time to stop them from being overrun by the enemy.

"Okay, 2-7. Let us know if you need further help. Uh . . . Trail, talk to me," said Mike.

"This is 2-9."

"Two-nine, continue present heading. You're five hundred meters from the LZ. . . . Four-three, head back and pick up the backup slick. Escort him into the LZ after

2-9's clear. . . . Two-nine, you're two hundred meters from the LZ."

"Receiving fire! Receiving fire!" 2-9 shouted.

I opened up with the minigun, hosing down the area to the left of the slick where I saw some muzzle flashes; 2-9 continued his approach.

"Seven-five, we'll be there in a minute. Pop smoke . . . Two-nine, you're one hundred meters from the LZ. There'll be two bomb craters to your left. Pick up the squad in the far crater."

An intense pinpoint of red burst forth on the ground and gradually billowed into a swirling haze wafting on the wind around the bomb craters.

Mike called to the LRRPs. "Seven-five, we have red smoke."

"That's a roger, 4-6," said the LRRP. "We're taking more small arms fire now!"

The slick pilot pulled up his nose like a bronco and decelerated into the LZ. "Two-nine's got the smoke. Understand the LZ's hot. . . . Receiving fire!"

Mike threw the Cobra into another rocket attack dive and fired many rocket pairs. The explosions formed a half moon around the LZ. When we broke out of the run, Mike turned left and I pummeled the area with the automatic grenade launcher. Dust flew up from enemy bullets striking the ground in front of the slick. Mike tightened up his break turn and rolled in for another run. Toward the bottom of the run we ran out of rockets.

"Two-nine's coming out," the slick called.

The lone Huey moved slowly forward, his door guns blazing away at the tree lines. The ship staggered and barely cleared the trees, but finally his speed built up and he was on the way home.

"Two-nine's clear. We've got six on board. There's three healthy and one wounded left."

"Four-three, this is 4-6. Two-nine's clear. Where are you?" asked Mike.

"We're a klick out."

"Two-four's taking fire!" the backup slick screamed.

We saw 4-3 make his run, rocket explosions bursting in the woodlines on the slick's left side. He pulled out, circled tightly to the right, and made another run.

"Two-four's got red smoke."

"Two-four, this is 4-6. Red smoke is correct. Good guys are in the first bomb crater you'll come to."

Our wingman formed up on us and checked in. "Four-three's back up on your wing, 4-6."

The single Huey decelerated into the landing zone while raking the trees with its M-60 machine guns. Muzzle flashes winked in the trees and tracers headed for the slick. Dust was getting knocked up into the air from small arms fire all around the LRRPs' bomb crater.

"Four-three, take the right side," Mike commanded.

We were out of rockets, and Mike held the ship steady at altitude so I could use the turret weapons. I pushed the grenade launcher buttons. There were two distinct *poomps* and then nothing. I switched to the minigun, but there was no response.

"Mike, I'm out of ammo or jammed," I said. "Looks to me like they're still taking fire from the northern tree line. Maybe a low pass would help?"

Mike didn't hesitate. He moved the cyclic rapidly left and forward. The weaponless Cobra followed Mike's control inputs and we were soon diving at the tree line on the left side of the slick, but in the opposite direction. Mike held the dive until the last instant possible and then pulled out hard. We zoomed over the tree line at 180 knots. Tracers from our own slick bounced underneath us. Green enemy tracers whizzed by from our rear and crossed from left to right, but we took no hits.

"Two-four's clear," called the slick.

That call was one of the best things we'd heard in what seemed like an eternity.

*   *   *

Back at the base camp, 2-9 told the story from his perspective. When coming out of an LZ, the slick copilot was supposed to monitor the engine instruments for any sign of trouble. The copilot with 2-9 that day didn't have a lot of experience. When they had begun their takeoff with six LRRPs on board and were receiving intense fire from the ground, the new guy unholstered his pistol, slid back his door window, stuck his left arm out with the gun, put his head down in the crook of his right arm to hide his face, and squeezed off all the rounds in the gun. It was the guy's first firefight. We decided he had done okay even though he neither watched the instruments nor provided effective counterfire. He did try. A little hazing with a reminder to watch the instruments was his only "discipline."

In the war zone on both sides, animals had a somewhat confusing status: some were off-limits and some were fair game. There were lots of dogs in the base camp. All the dogs would run around and play intensely for an hour immediately after the sun rose. Then as the heat built up to extreme levels through the day they'd find a cool place in the shade and sleep until evening, when they'd play a little while again. I was told that to keep down the risk of disease, every so often someone would be assigned to round up a bunch of the dogs, take them outside the perimeter, and shoot them. But there was one dog no one would ever have thought to destroy.

Slick was a pure-white shorthaired dog that looked like a cross between a beagle and a bulldog. His legs seemed too short for his body. Slick had an endearing habit. Like firehouse dogs who responded to the fire bell, Slick sometimes responded to the Klaxon horn. He'd run to the Corral with the troopers and jump on board a Huey that was cranking up. Slick had flown on many missions and was, of course, considered to be good luck for the unit. Slick seemed to have his pick of all the bitches on the base, and a few months into my tour there were cute puppy-Slicks popping up. Slick was friendly with everyone, and many times his wagged-tail greeting after a mission was enough to cheer us up.

Like everywhere else in the world, Vietnam had buzzards. Some of these birds would grow to have what seemed to be six- or seven-foot wingspans. Sometimes midair collisions between us and them would seem assured. The flight rule was to try to go over the birds, because they tended to tuck in their wings and dive for the ground when frightened. There was a standing joke about "buzzard dogfighting."

On one otherwise uneventful day I got to try out some dogfighting with a local buzzard. We were west of the Big Rubber and on our way to refuel at Tay Ninh when we spotted a gigantic bird right in our path. He was floating lazily on the air currents, not even bothering to flap his wings.

"Think you're a good-enough shot to get that buzzard?" asked the pilot-in-command.

"Should be easy with the minigun."

"Well, go ahead and try, then."

I unhooked the turret sight from its rest and raised it to my eye level, sighting the buzzard in the recticle. I tried following the bird's movements for fifteen seconds to get a feel for it. Then I fired a short burst. Tracers sped out from the minigun at their furious pace toward the unwary bird. Nothing happened. I'd missed completely. And as far as the bird was concerned, I wasn't even in the sky. I resighted and held back the triggers, trying to hit the bird by following it as I would have with any target. The ten-second burst was completely ineffective. The bird continued to soar in its big sweeping arcs, waiting for whatever it saw on the ground to be ready to eat. I pulled the triggers and held them in the firing position. I moved the sight left and right, up and down, and in infinite combinations to try to home in on the big bird.

It was impossible to move the sight with the same speed and precision as the buzzard's seemingly gentle maneuvering. Tracers were spewing all over the sky. Then I ran out of ammunition.

"Reckon he wins," said the back-seater.

"Reckon so," I said. "The real pisser is, he doesn't have to expend any more energy, while I, on the other hand, get the privilege of reloading the minigun."

In the middle of the night, one LRRP unit called us for an extraction after popping an ambush on what they were sure was an enemy patrol. By the time we arrived on-site they'd discovered they'd used their deadly claymore mines to kill one great big wild boar.

We ate pork for three days.

Samuels bounded into our hootch one evening clasping a three-inch-long, one-inch-diameter glass vial in his hand. He held the vial out between his thumb and forefinger for me to see the contents and said proudly, "Look what the LRRPs gave me for the mission I ran with them last week."

I looked carefully but couldn't make out the contents of the vial. To me, the contents looked only like two pieces of shrunken, blackened meat.

"I give up, Samuels. What is it?"

Samuels looked genuinely disappointed, and his voice came down an octave as he calmed down.

"You really can't tell?"

"That's right."

"It's the ears off of one of the gooks we got for them, that's what. LRRPs said they were my very own trophy for a job well done."

Some people thought the LRRPs were animals. Given our circumstances, this was, of course, a form of the ultimate compliment! Besides, the LRRPs sometimes encouraged the view.

★ CHAPTER 17 ★

Agent Orange

Howard Stevens came out of his hootch, which was opposite my own, at the same time I started to go to eat dinner. What Howard lacked in stature, he made up for with quickness. This was a trait most welcome in LOH pilots. Howard and I approached each other on the boardwalks that led from our hootch doors, and our combat boots clunked in step with each other. Howard had a dark complexion and usually had a five-o'clock shadow even early in the morning. But that night, Howard was clean-shaven.

"Haven't seen much of you lately," I said.

"Guess we've been on opposite schedules. I've been flying my butt off."

As we turned and walked together toward the mess hall, the stench of burning human shit and jet fuel assailed our nostrils. The outhouse was upwind of the mess hall, and it seemed that whenever it was time to eat, the Vietnamese on burn detail decided to do his job. When I first arrived in-country, the smell nauseated me; now I was used to it.

"So, how're you doing?"

"Today I'm great. Last night, I wasn't so sure," said Howard. "I sacked out all day today. Must've needed it."

"What was the trouble last night?"

"You heard the dustoff signal, right? Well, when our slick got to the pickup point, the LZ was too small for him to get into. The grunts were in pretty heavy contact, and they had one wounded who couldn't wait. The slick called for a LOH to try to make the pickup. I volunteered. I grabbed my observer and we ran out to our ship, cranked, and were en route for five minutes when the twenty-minute fuel-low warning light came on. Someone had flown my ship and not refueled it. I figured if everything went smooth I could make the pickup and get back, so I kept going. We took some fire on the way in, but once inside the defensive perimeter, the grunts gave us great covering fire. There was no room to set the ship down, and we managed to get the wounded grunt on board by lifting him into the ship. On the way back it was like someone had speeded up time. Twenty minutes was flying by in no time. The ass-pucker factor got real high. Even my observer asked me if we were going to make it. Finally, as I was easing the ship's weight on the skids at the medevac pad, the engine died from fuel starvation. It was too damn close for comfort, I'll tell you."

"So how come you forgot the prime directive—'don't volunteer'?"

"Something had to be done. It was my turn. That's the last time I take fuel for granted, though. Say, did you hear about Phil King's disaster this morning?"

"You mean how he got his slick shot up while flying low-level along Highway One on his way to Tay Ninh?"

"Yeah, but that's not the reason I call it a disaster. The gook that shot him was lucky enough to hit the main fuse-lage spar. The ship has to be sent back to the States to get fixed. That made the CO so mad he assigned Phil to the scout platoon. Said if Phil likes low-level so much he could get his bellyful in the scouts. Phil's a damn fine slick pilot. It seems a waste to have to train him in LOHs."

"I guess it isn't well known, but Phil told me he was qualified in the LOH already. Being a second-tour guy, and with only six months left in the Army, he requested slicks when he got to our unit. You're right about his slick talents, though. He was an IP at Rucker. Sometimes I've wondered if Phil has ice water for blood. I've flown cover for him on some LRRP extractions and medevac runs. His 'receiving fire' call is the calmest I've ever heard."

The evening flight briefing indicated I'd get a new experience the next day. I was going to fly cover for some Air Force C-130 Agent Orange spray aircraft over the Boi Loi. Everyone assured me this was one of the most boring assignments around.

We took off in the morning and headed for the Boi Loi. Arriving at the assigned rendezvous point five minutes ahead of time, we lazily orbited the general area and searched the sky for our escort objects.

"Centaur 4-1, this is Spray-8. We're two miles west of the rendezvous point and lima lima."

I searched the ground west of our position and quickly located the low-level flight of five four-engine C-130s headed for us. Light black smoke trails came from their engine exhausts and they were flying in a V formation.

"I've got 'em," I told the rear-seater.

"Spray-8, 4-1's got you in sight."

As the flight of C-130s got to us we fell in to their immediate rear but stayed at altitude. Even with the specially outfitted transports fifteen hundred feet below us they seemed large. The flight of five wasn't flying a tight formation. The spray equipment, which I could barely see, hung down and aft of the rear edge of each wing. When Spray-8 reached the edge of the Boi Loi, they turned on the sprayers. A fine mist trailed behind each airplane as it sped along at treetop height.

"Uh ... Spray-8's leftmost ship took a little fire back there," said the lead C-130 pilot using a bored-with-it-all voice. Before I could react, the intercom clicked on and the rear-seater said, "Hold your fire, Spalding. Mark down the location."

I didn't like not shooting back worth a damn, but I pulled my grease pencil from the built-in pocket on my upper-left flight suit sleeve and wrote down the grid coordinates on the canopy. The answer to my unasked question was forthcoming from the back-seater.

"Unless one of these fat boys gets shot down, and they never have to my knowledge, we don't waste the ammo now. It's more important to keep up with the flight, which we barely can. We note any place they take fire and come search it thoroughly after the spray takes effect in a couple of weeks."

Two weeks later the path the spray ships had covered was completely devoid of living vegetation. Even from altitude we could see all the way to the ground. The LOH's view was even better. He found a bunker complex very close to where Spray-8 had taken fire. We inserted our aero-rifle platoon to search the area. They didn't find any enemy, but they did find an intriguing tunnel entrance. A couple of specialist tunnel rats were flown in from another unit. After thirty minutes in the tunnels, the rats came out. They'd found a reinforced concrete bunker, forty feet underground, full of weapons and two surprise items—new Briggs and Stratton generators, still in their crates with Canadian shipping marks!

For some time we had all contributed to a fund that was being used to renovate an empty building and turn it into a Centaur officers' club. We all put in construction time when we could, too. The work went slowly since time off was a luxury not often received. Finally, the day came when the club opened. The outside looked like all the other buildings, but when I opened the front door to visit for the first time, the blast of cold air startled me. It was over a hundred degrees outside, but inside it was a pleasant eighty. The interior was a big square open area with some reasonably soft chairs and a couple of cocktail tables. The rear of the room had a semicircular bar. We couldn't buy drinks, but each person could keep his own booze, with his name on it, behind the bar. A refrigerator behind the bar was stocked with people's beer. I turned around and faced the door through which I had entered. There was a mantelpiece in the left front corner of the room. One engraved brass plaque was affixed to the mantel. It bore the name of the only Centaur pilot who had been killed up to that time. I never knew the fellow, as he was killed a year before I showed up, but I was told that Frank Meyers was operations officer when the NVA mortared the Corral. He had walked out and stood in the door of the operations building to watch the fireworks. A stray round landed close by and that was all she wrote.

When I left the outfit there were seven brass plaques. Except for Frank Meyers, they all died while flying.

* **CHAPTER 18** *

First-Light Mission

One of the commonsense tactics ingrained in our heads during Army flight training was "Don't fly the same route at the same time every day." In theory, this advice was mostly for slick pilots, who sometimes flew what boiled down to a schedule for resupply or troop transfer. We called those "ash and trash" missions. But the advice seemed to me to be sound for all missions. Nevertheless, our unit received orders to fly a first-light VR mission over the area between the Top Hat and the Mushroom every day. This area had been the subject of many VRs and troop insertions. Typically, the NVA who tried to control that part of the river would not engage in firefights with ground troops. They'd merely fall back into their extensive mazes of tunnels and bunkers and wait until our troops left. Artillery and air strikes had little effect. From the air, the whole area could be seen to be pockmarked from all the shell and bomb craters. In spite of the first-light missions' clear violation of sound tactical doctrine, no explanation was provided as to why the missions were necessary. Nevertheless, orders were orders. Howard Stevens was the missions' LOH pilot.

The first day out, Howard saw some gooks right after he started into his bob-and-weave. The Cobra brought Howard to altitude and called in an artillery strike. The second day, Howard had been looking over the area for ten minutes when he got shot at. The third day, Howard took fire and got shot through both arms. Severely wounded, Howard still somehow managed to fly his bullet-riddled chopper back to base. When Howard wrote us from the Tokyo hospital, his writing was barely legible. Howard wrote that no one there believed he was a LOH pilot. Everyone in Howard's ward was sure LOH pilots got shot in the legs, not the arms, and most especially not in both arms. The fourth day, Gerry Green and I took our turn as the killer half of the first-light VR hunter/killer team.

Gerry was an enigma for a Cobra pilot. He was a devout Mormon. I had the impression that the Mormon religion preached nonviolence, and I once asked Gerry how he could be an attack helicopter pilot—or, for that matter, serve in the Army at all. Gerry said something about having to obey both God's and man's laws. I thought his answer left many unresolved conflicts. Gerry had been in-country for only two months longer than I. During the entire time we served together, I never saw Gerry drink a Coke or heard him swear. There was more to this than self-discipline. Gerry had an aura about him. He was extremely self-assured and serene.

Phil King was newly assigned to be the first-light mission hunter pilot. Phil was a heavy guy with a dark complexion and a short haircut, no one's portrait of a LOH pilot. How he squeezed into the small ship was a mystery. Once in, he seemed to completely fill the cockpit. I was finishing the pre-flight of our Cobra while Phil walked past the revetments on his way to his own ship. He stopped to chat.

"You ready, Spalding?"

I closed the nose compartment door, snapped the latch shut, and turned around to face Phil before I responded. He stood there, chicken plate draped over his right shoulder and M-16 in his left hand, waiting for my reply. I looked him in the eyes and an eerie feeling came over me. For a split second I was certain Phil was going to die. The fleeting feeling was unnerving, but as any "scientific" person would, I naturally dismissed it.

"Sure I'm ready," I said. "You be real careful."

"Always am, always am," Phil said as he walked away in the direction of his LOH. We took off into the dawn calm, heading for the assigned VR area. The sun shone in and warmed the cockpit. Because the sun was low on the horizon, and very bright, I had to consciously make myself look to the east for conflicting air traffic. The river water glistened beneath us and there were no clouds.

"One-two, this is 4-7," said Gerry. "Anytime you're ready."

"One-two's ready. We're on our way down."

I unhooked the turret weapon sight from its mount, letting the sight bob up and down lazily between my legs. Phil got down to the deck and began to circle around in the area. I took the turret sight in hand and loosely tracked the LOH. Phil's moves were not nearly as erratic as most of the LOHs' I'd covered, and he seemed to be going slow. I keyed the radio transmitter.

"One-two, keep your speed up," I cautioned.

I heard two radio clicks and saw the nose of the LOH drop a little to pick up speed but the LOH's movements remained disquietingly smooth. The VR continued, with Phil reporting the usual bunker complexes and recent traffic.

"Four-seven, 1-2's coming around for another look. Gunner said he saw something in a tree line."

I activated the turret and tracked behind Phil's ship as it made a wide sweeping left turn back over the area he had just covered. A kind of pig squeal came over the radio. It was barely distinguishable to me as "Receiving fire." I pulled the minigun triggers. The gun fired a one-second burst and jammed. I watched as the LOH rolled level and the nose came up to decelerate. I pressed the grenade launcher buttons. One round fired and the launcher jammed. Gerry made no move to provide covering fire.

"Roll in! Roll in! He's taking fire!" I cried. Gerry slowly rolled the nose left and down. He took a long time before firing the first pair of rockets. As we pulled out at 1,000 feet I heard an unfamiliar sound—*phhhit, phhhit, phhhit.*

"We're taking fire," I told Gerry.

"I don't think so," he replied.

I was looking down at the LOH. It was wobbling into what looked like a clearing, its nose high in the air. It seemed to land a little hard. There was a puff of an explosion inside the LOH and instantly a big orange fireball exploded from its tail, engulfing the whole ship. We circled left back to the point from where we'd initiated our rocket run.

"Phil, get out of there," Gerry called.

There was no answer. The LOH burned fiercely for what seemed like a million years. I wondered what was taking the crew so long to get out, and I was mentally urging the LOH crew with a kind of silent prayer—Get out, get out, get out! We entered another rocket run. I could see the billowing purple smoke of the smoke grenade the LOH observer had dropped when they took fire. Gerry hesitated. It seemed to me he didn't know what to do.

"Shoot the smoke. Shoot the smoke," I told Gerry. The Cobra rockets launched out and exploded all around the rising smoke. I craned my neck around to the left rear and looked down at the furiously burning LOH. Phil tumbled out the left door. He was on fire. His whole body was scorched black, and whiffs of smoke rose from it. He rolled over and over on the ground. Then he sat up, motionless.

"Gerry, I see Phil."

"Where? I don't see him."

"Never mind. Get some help in here fast."

Gerry flipped the radio switch to guard frequency and called for help. "Mayday, mayday, mayday. This is Centaur 4-7 on guard. Any slick in the vicinity of the Top Hat, please come in."

"Four-seven, this is Centaur 2-5. Be there in two minutes."

"Two-five, roger. You'll see smoke from a downed LOH. Recommend you make your approach from the west. Bad guys east."

"Four-seven, will do. . . . Got the smoke. Two-five's one mile out."

I looked to the west and spotted the slick. He was already starting his approach. "Tell him Phil's ten meters south of the LOH," I said.

"Two-five, be advised. Downed pilot is ten meters south of the LOH."

"Four-seven, roger."

The single slick slowed down as it neared the still-burning wreckage. The slick completed the approach without taking fire and landed. As soon as the skids touched down, the two door gunners got out to look for survivors. One man looked like he was heading right for Phil, but he turned around before he got there.

"Four-seven, this is 2-5. We don't see anyone down here."

I keyed the microphone. "Phil's down there all right. I saw him get out. He's still sitting up ten meters from the LOH and at your two o'clock. He's all burned up. Go look again."

This time the crewmen found Phil, picked him up, and loaded him into the ship.

"Four-seven, this guy is hurt real bad. We don't see anyone else. I'm coming out the way I came in."

The slick lifted to a high hover and made a tail rotor pedal turn to pivot around and face the direction from which it had entered the LZ. The slick's nose dipped slightly as it started its takeoff. A new voice crackled over the radio.

"Four-seven, this is 4-6. We're overhead with the aerorifles. How's your fuel?"

"We're bingo in ten minutes," said Gerry.

"Roger, understand," said 4-6. "We've got the LOH in sight. You can return to base."

"Four-six, this is 4-7, roger. Be advised. Bad guys are east of the downed LOH."

"Four-seven, thanks. See you later."

Gerry shut down the ship at the rearm point. I climbed out and looked for damage. I worked my way aft from the nose, bending over occasionally and looking at the Cobra's underside. I reached the halfway point of the tail boom. Three bullet holes loomed into view. It was a good thing we had been fast at the bottom of our attack run. At 100 knots, instead of 170, the holes would have been in the cockpit. Whoever hit us was a good shot—and not scared of Cobras, to boot.

The first thing I did when I got back to the Corral was walk into Operations and call the hospital to see how Phil was doing. A female voice answered the phone at the hospital. Having spent many months in the men-only war business, the sound of a woman's voice seemed very out of place. "Hi, I'm Warrant Officer Spalding," I told the nurse. "One of my buddies came in to your unit a little while ago. He was burned. His name is Phil King. Can I come over and see him?"

"Phil's doing okay, considering, but he's in no shape for visitors. Not only is he burned badly, but he was shot three times in the legs and butt. He's in intensive care now, and fighting hard. The prognosis is as good as can be expected. It helps that you guys got him here fast. Why don't you call back tomorrow? Maybe you can see him then."

"Thanks, I'll do that."

The aero-rifles returned an hour and a half later. They'd spent a long time looking for the other two LOH crew members. One of the crew members was found right away, but the searchers couldn't locate the second guy. After forty minutes, they looked in what was left of the LOH cockpit, for the third time, and realized they'd been looking at the copilot's corpse all along. It was burned so completely there wasn't much of the body left—to the ground troopers, it had looked like twisted and melted LOH debris.

Centaur 2-5 was one of my hootchmates. Our conversation turned to that day's rescue, and I made some comments about not allowing LOHs to carry white phosphorous grenades on my missions. I didn't want the secondary explosions in a crash to make other people, including me, risk their lives so that the LOH guys could think they were part of killer/killer teams.

"Yeah, that was a bad deal today," said the slick driver. "Once we found Phil and got him into our ship, the mission wasn't over by a long shot. Phil was burned so badly that his skin came off in the swirling wind blowing through the cabin. Coming out of the LZ, a piece of skin flew up and covered part of my visor, making it hard for me to see. Some of the skin stuck to the floor and the crew had to wash it out using scrub brushes."

After the next day's last VR mission, I called the hospital to see about visiting Phil. The nurse hesitated for the briefest moment. "I'm sorry, Mr. Spalding, he died during the night from pulmonary complications."

I was stunned. I hung up the phone without saying goodbye. I had been ready to visit my friend and now he was dead. Phil only had a couple of months left in the Army and he hadn't made it. He had a wife and a small child. His death mission seemed to have had almost no point to it. The waste was too much to bear. I walked into the officers' club, went to the refrigerator, removed someone else's six-pack of beer, and set it on a table as I sat down with two other pilots. I didn't even like beer. I intended to get drunk, and I did. The next day, I barely remembered having started to cry. I didn't remember the guys taking me to my room at all. I did remember waking some time later and realizing I was going to vomit. I couldn't walk, but I managed to crawl on all fours to get out of the hootch. I heaved up a huge volume of beer onto the dusty ground, and my head involuntarily fell into the puddle. I couldn't move. My dazed mind worked in a fog. I thought about how revolting it was to be wallowing in my own puke, and to not be able to do anything about it. Mercifully, two of my compatriots, unidentifiable in my stupor, lifted me by the arms and put me back in bed.

Phil wasn't the only guy doing a second tour in-country whose first-tour luck didn't hold. A lot of them seemed to get shot up. One man thought the situation over and refused to fly. He became the rearmament pit officer. This was a manual-labor, hot, dirty, and potentially dangerous job. He still wouldn't fly. Shortly after Phil's death, Gerry Green became the maintenance test pilot. The troop CO somehow got the area between the Top Hat and the Mushroom designated as "no low-level operations." The operations map was modified to show the area striped in red diagonal warning lines. We named it LOH Alley.

I continued my normal duties. The next VR I was on, my adrenaline pumped the whole time the LOH was low-level. I was keyed up, and I kept the turret slewed most of the flight even though there was really no need. My trigger fingers were a hair away from raining volumes of lead onto the peaceful countryside. It was not a safe state of affairs for anyone. I went to the Cobra platoon leader and explained.

"Mike, I need to talk to you in private."

"Okay, let's go into my room."

Mike busied himself with organizing some personal effects while I explained my concerns.

"I'm too tense," I said. "I'm afraid I'm going to get somebody killed for nothing. I need a couple of weeks' rest."

"There's no way I can do that, Spalding. You'll just have to work through it somehow."

"How about taking me off VR? I don't think I've got a problem with attack missions."

"Let me look into it. I'm not promising anything, but I'll try."

"Thanks a lot, Mike."

I never received any official notice, but for two weeks I was on either the number-one or the number-two gun team. That was all it took. After the brief respite from VR, I was back to normal.

Although I had drunk myself stupid over Phil's death, normally I only rarely drank alcohol. In fact, before the Army, being only twenty, having worked toward being a pilot since I was a teenager, and not having had much social life, I had only drunk booze a few times in my life. In comparison to many of the older pilots, I was a real teetotaler. This was especially true if I was compared against the infamous hootch-5 inhabitants. Hootch-5 housed the rowdies in our outfit. They'd never bothered to build any rooms, except for one, so the hootch remained an open bay with no privacy for anyone. There was a locker in the middle of the hootch-5 floor where food was kept. The guys weren't too neat about food storage, though. One time we decided to spray for bugs and made the mistake of spraying inside the locker. I don't think we killed any bugs—they seemed to be immune—but a million inch-long cockroaches crawled out from the locker's nooks and crannies. They formed a solid cover on the concrete floor. The boiling mass headed for the sides of the hootch, where it was darker. Deciding discretion was the better part of valor, the hootch-5 human residents dedicated the locker to the roaches. Bugs needed a home too, they figured. Charlie Riggs was a hootch-5 tenant.

Chuck was a pretty good pilot. He had done a tour in Germany before coming to Vietnam and he had plenty of flight experience. Chuck had thinning hair and was fun to be around, even when he was drinking, which was anytime he didn't have to be on call to fly. Chuck and I were to fly up to Tay Ninh early one morning to augment fire support for another unit's operations. Chuck got drunk with his buddies the night before.

I got up before dawn, walked to Operations, found out what ship we were assigned, and preflighted it by flashlight. There was a thick fog. As I was finishing up the preflight, it had grown a little lighter, but the fog was delaying dawn. I walked back to Operations.

"You guys seen Riggs?" I asked.

"Nope. You're with him today, aren't you?"

"Yeah. I figured he'd be up by now. We're supposed to be on our way to Tay Ninh. At least, assuming the weather lets us go, that is."

I bought two Cokes and drank my normal breakfast while I waited for Chuck to come into Operations. Halfway through the second Coke I began to wonder what was keeping Chuck so long.

"I'm going down to hootch-5 to see if Chuck's up yet," I told the ops officer. "If he shows up here, tell him I'll be back in five minutes."

When I entered Chuck's hootch, it became clear that my assigned pilot-in-command was still in bed. Actually, "in" bed wasn't quite the right description. Chuck was stripped down to his underwear with his upper body draped crosswise over his bunk and his arms hanging limply over the far side. His legs were on the floor.

"Hey, Chuck. Wake up," I said quietly, so as to not wake up the other sleeping residents. There was no response. Not even a grunt. I reached down and shook Chuck by his shoulder and pleaded.

"Come on, Chuck. Get up, will you? If you don't get up you're going to be in a shit load of trouble."

Chuck moaned a little and turned his head toward me. One eye opened into a small slit and squinted.

"Go away," he grumbled.

I could smell the strong stench of booze from Chuck's mouth even with that small utterance. He was obviously still drunk. He wasn't going to wake up easily. I went into my hootch and found Conners making coffee.

"I need you to give me a hand with Chuck. I think he's still drunk, and we're supposed to be on our way to Tay Ninh right now."

"What do you want me to do?" Conners asked.

"Come with me. I've got a plan to at least get him on his feet."

Conners and I walked across the drainage ditch, into hootch-5, and over to Chuck's slumping figure.

"You've got to be kidding me," said Conners. "You're going to fly with that!"

"Just help me roll him onto his back, will you?" Conners and I lifted Chuck's feet onto the bunk and then rolled him over so that his mostly naked body was on its back. I went over to a cupboard, retrieved some rubbing alcohol, walked back to Chuck, and poured the alcohol all over his chest and belly.

Chuck bolted upright. "Holy shit!" he screamed. "What are you doing to me? That stuff's really cold."

The rest of the sleeping pilots stirred in their bunks, and someone told us to shut up, but at least Chuck was awake. He wasn't sober, but he was awake.

"Get dressed and get up to 825," I said. "We're late already."

I walked back to the Cobra and swapped Chuck's and my gear between the rear and front seats. As I finished the gear transfer, Chuck walked up unsteadily.

"I'm in no shape to fly," he said. "How're we going to do this?"

"I'm going to fly back-seat. That's how."

"You can't do that. You're not in-country qualified for the back yet."

"I don't give a crap about qualifications. I'm not riding in the front with a drunk pilot-in-command in the back. We do it my way or not at all. It's your choice."

"Okay, okay. Let's go."

I helped Chuck pour himself into the front seat, walked around to the right side, and climbed into the rear seat. I hadn't been in the rear seat of a Cobra for four months. It felt only vaguely familiar, so I took my time doing everything and double-checking. The fog had lifted some. There was a 100-foot ceiling. I cranked the ship and called the tower using Chuck's call sign.

"Cu Chi tower, this is Centaur 4-8. What's Tay Ninh weather?"

"Four-eight, wait one . . . uh, Tay Ninh reports a fifty-foot ceiling. Visibility, three quarters of a mile."

The weather was dicey, but as long as there was some room between the ceiling and the trees, I figured I could make it without flying on instruments. I'd never flown the Cobra on instruments, and I hadn't flown on instruments at all for almost a year.

"Roger, 4-8's ready for takeoff."

"Four-eight's cleared for takeoff," called the tower. With no other flight traffic in the area, the controller took liberty with radio procedure. "Ya'll come back now, ya hear?"

I started the takeoff and clicked the microphone twice. When I cleared the base camp perimeter, I descended to just above the ground and accelerated to 130 knots. I kept the ship low, hopping over rice paddy dikes and hedgerows. Pretty soon I picked up Highway One and began following it toward Tay Ninh. I zigzagged back and forth across the road. Chuck didn't say anything for fifteen minutes. He sounded almost normal when he finally spoke.

"Hey, Spalding. You're doing okay and I'm not feeling

too bad now. Why don't you arm the turret weapons, just in case."

That seemed to be a reasonable precaution. I located the armament circuit breakers and pushed them in. "Guns are hot," I told Chuck.

Passing the little market town of Trang Bang, I worked my way westward to pick up the Vam Co Dong River. I figured there was less chance of an established chopper ambush over the river than along the road. As a tree line I hopped over fell behind us, we were suddenly twenty feet high over the smooth water of the river. Without warning, Chuck opened up with the minigun. Tracers spewed out, striking the water close in front of us. The bullets glanced off the water and flew up past our fuselage. I scrambled to find the turret circuit breaker and pulled it. I pushed the intercom button and spoke. My frustration came through in my voice. "What the hell are you doing? Are you trying to kill us all by yourself, or what?"

"You know what?" said Chuck.

"What?"

"I'm really glad I'm drunk enough to enjoy this."

"Wish I was," I replied.

We flew on to Tay Ninh in silence. When Chuck sobered up, I made him reload the minigun.

★ CHAPTER 19 ★

Better to Be Bored

My hootchmates and I were sitting around the table frying bacon to make BLTs when Popov walked in through the door. Years of hitting his head had conditioned Popov to be careful when going under things. Although he didn't have to, he bent slightly when he walked across the threshold. Straightening up, he looked right at me. "You've got tomorrow off, don't you, Spalding?" Naturally suspicious of such questions, I replied slowly, "That's what the duty board shows for now. Why do you ask?"

"We're kicking off a little project to differentiate the Cobra platoon from other units in the area and I'm looking for volunteers to help."

There was that word, *volunteer*. I was still skeptical but decided not to withdraw from the yet-to-be-defined task at that moment. "What is it you've got in mind?"

"We're going to paint teeth on the Cobras. You know, like the Flying Tigers had on their P-40s in World War II. If each guy with a day off does two ships, we can get them all done in a week. What do you think?"

I looked at the other guys sitting around the table. They seemed to have perked up at the idea, and some of them nodded their heads yes. Conners's face was puzzled.

"I don't get it," said Conners. "We wanted to do that when the Cobras first came into the unit, but we got orders that unofficial decoration was not allowed. What gives?"

"Hell, I don't know why the change of heart," said Popov. "Maybe it's the 4th Cavalry's new CO. All I know is, our own old man has sanctioned the effort."

The others seemed to be willing to do their parts, so I said I'd cooperate.

I met Popov in the maintenance hangar at 0800 the next day. Popov showed me the stencil to use, where the paint and brushes were, and how to position the stencil on each side of the Cobra. There was to be a black upper gumline starting under the nose above the turret. It was to run up each side and then down past the back lower corner of the ammo bay. It was shaped like the top half of a wing. The lower gumline was only slightly arched and ran forward along the lower edge of the fuselage. At the front of the ship it curved inward behind the lower rear edge of the turret. The gaping mouth was to be painted fire-engine red, with a row of bright white triangular teeth jutting from both the lower and upper gumline. Painting was hot work in the tropical sun, and as the Cobra's sides heated up, the paint seemed to dry instantly. I could stand only two hours of it at a time. The end result of the work was quite pleasing in a brutish sort of way. To me, the mouth looked more like a shark's than a tiger's, but that really made no difference overall. The Cobra seemed to be looking for something to gobble up. Only a few weeks later we saw that the Diamond Heads had painted teeth on their ships, too. The Diamond Heads' painted mouths were different from ours and, also unlike ours, were not all the same design. (Later in my tour, we were told that word had spread through the enemy ranks to not draw attention to themselves when helicopters with teeth were seen in the area.)

Popov inspected my painting handiwork when he came in from his day's last mission. He walked directly from the Corral to my room. Popov's heavy footsteps got closer and closer until they finally stopped outside my door.

"I'm awake. Who's there?" I said.

"It's me," said Popov.

"Come on in."

Popov opened the door, entered the room, and sat down on my steel card-table chair.

"The tiger mouth looks good, doesn't it?" he said.

"I thought so. It looks real mean."

"We'll be flying that ship together tomorrow on a sniff mission. I came to brief you about it."

"A sniff mission? What in the world is that?"

"They rig up a Huey with some special equipment that does chemical analysis of the air. Supposedly, the machine can distinguish extremely faint aromas created by man. You know, things like ammonia from urine, cigarette smoke, things like that. We fly along at altitude with the slick to give him cover if he needs it and to note the machine's findings. It's mostly like being on an extraboring VR except that the machine spits out a lot of information. But all this isn't the reason I wanted to brief you. I wanted to let you know about Fort Polk East."

"I give up. Is this someplace we're going to get fuel that's not shown on the map, or what?"

"No way! We won't be landing there. At least I hope we don't land there. Fort Polk East is a very large encampment of the NVA that sits on the other side of the Cambodian border, but just barely. It's heavily defended. We're going to be flying close to it tomorrow, and I wanted you to know what it was you were looking at, just in case."

We rendezvoused with the sniff slick at 0900 the next day. The designated sniff area was between the Vam Co Dong River and the Cambodian border in an area that could be considered the northwestern tip of the Mekong Delta. In contrast to the heavy woods north of Tay Ninh, this area's terrain was characterized by wide-open swamp that looked much like the river plains around Savannah, Georgia, where I had trained.

The lone Huey descended to the deck and flew a straight line toward the Cambodian border. The pilot didn't use any evasive maneuvers, he just flew straight. Every so often, we'd receive a call from the slick indicating the equipment had sensed something. The call was merely a color—green, yellow, or red. I marked "g," "y," or "r," as appropriate, at the map grid coordinates where the call was made. When the low ship got to the limits of its westward search, Popov would tell it, "Sniff 2-1, time to turn."

The slick would take an initial heading forty-five degrees away from the side of its flight path on which the return leg was to be flown. Then it made a smooth turn back to head in the opposite direction. The return leg was fifty meters south of the westward leg. The Huey repeated these search patterns until the entire area had been covered.

The closest we came to Fort Polk East was five miles, but even from there I could see what looked like substantial structures. They could have been barracks, but it was hard to tell. Whatever they were, they were definitely there and, for us, untouchable. It was more than a little frustrating to know of prime targets that the rules of engagement forbade us from attacking.

Our CO, a major, was, of course, a rated pilot. He happened also to be Cobra rated. Like all commanding officers of aviation battalions, the major was busy keeping the outfit running and didn't normally pull flight duty. In comparison to the line pilots, it could have been argued that he almost never flew. This meant that, for all the prior flight time the major had, his current capabilities weren't honed to the fine combat edge of the rest of the unit's population. Nevertheless, there were times when the major had himself put on the gun team mission roster. The major flew as fire-team leader, and I was selected to fly as his copilot on several occasions.

In the predawn hours of one dark night the major and I scrambled out to assist Fire Support Base Diamond, which was under attack. Diamond was close to the Cambodian border and was a staging area for a small contingent of Special Forces troops as well as an artillery fire support base. Because of its strategic location, the NVA had decided to try to overrun it.

As we approached the location, we could see tracers streaming out from Diamond as well as some small muzzle flashes outside its perimeter. The major was talking to Diamond's defenders. To my lower right front I saw the unmistakable large bright-white muzzle flash of an enemy .51-caliber machine gun. I sighted on the flash and let loose with the minigun. The major figured out what was going on and rolled the ship's nose right and down to point it directly at the muzzle flash. I kept pouring on the minigun fire, but as the ship rolled left to a level attitude, it rocked back and forth violently. The rocking made it hard to hit the target, but I kept trying. I'd never felt such a vibration before. I tensed, waiting for something to break, but soon the ship steadied. Shortly after that, as I continued to hose down the target area, the muzzle flash from the antiaircraft machine gun stopped. Without firing any rockets, the major pulled up and to the right as our wingman gave us cover with his rockets. We ran the rest of the mission as needed by Diamond's troops, and there was no further antiaircraft fire. Then we headed back to base.

"What was all that vibration on our first run?" I asked the major.

"I think the rounds from that fifty-one came real close," he said. "Of course, there's no way to tell since they weren't using any tracers."

"Yeah, that was weird, huh? How could they expect to hit us without using tracers? I'd think it would be next to impossible."

"Me, too," said the major. He paused, contemplating the issue. "You know, maybe they think it's harder for us to locate them if they don't use tracers."

"If that's so, they're dead wrong. All not seeing any tracers does as far as I'm concerned is make it less scary."

I didn't really think machine-gun bullets coming close to our ship would have made it rock so violently, but the major was the boss. Besides, maybe he was right.

When we got through rearming, Diamond was still under attack and the number-two gun team was about to leave to return to base. We headed back to Diamond. By then, Diamond's defenders had called in a Spooky gunship, which was also dropping aerial flares. The flares were five feet long and six inches in diameter. They were housed in a shiny metal canister that fell away after the flare's parachute opened. The flares burned brilliantly and made the ground show up about the way it looked at dusk. Shadows danced on the ground as the flares swung lazily under their parachutes. The Spooky orbited a thousand feet over us and dropped a flare each time one started to go out. The flares were a big help in picking up targets at night, and, of course, the ground troops liked being able to see probably even more than we did. There were some drawbacks to working with flares, though. If we happened to be close to a flare when it ignited, our night vision would be destroyed for a long time. But the worst scenario about flare work was the one in which the flare canister dropped on top of us. The damage that could be caused was considerable, and the idea plagued me whenever I worked under a Spooky. It was particularly disturbing to think of a flare canister's coming right through the canopy. By the time we had expended our armament and repelled the attack on the fire support base, we'd managed to dodge a very large number of flares.

Truck convoys made repeated trips to Tay Ninh on Highway One. These convoys consisted of long lines of Army trucks, equally spaced and moving at a reasonably slow pace. Normally, the convoys proceeded uneventfully, but not always. Ambushes sometimes occurred. Land mines were another hazard with which the convoys had to contend. The three-quarter cavalry was charged with convoy escort to minimize the problems. Tanks and APCs would be placed at the front and rear of the convoy, as well as being interspersed throughout it. If there was significant intelligence that a convoy was going to be ambushed, the Centaurs would be dispatched to fly escort as well. Of course, even if we weren't flying escort, we'd get called to provide close air support for our tank squadrons if they engaged the VC. That's what happened one day when I was again flying with the major.

We scrambled out of Cu Chi and headed west on Highway One. The weather was fine with ceiling and visibility unlimited. It felt good to get to altitude, where the air was a little cooler. A convoy had been ambushed out of some hedgerows to the north side of the highway. When we got on station, the convoy had actually moved up the road and left a contingent of the escort squadron to finish the counterattack.

The major contacted the ground troops. "Fox 3-7, this is Centaur 6 on station," he said.

"Six, this is 3-7. We're one hundred meters north of the road and fifty meters south of the stream that runs north and south."

"Uh . . . roger. Pop smoke for identification."

On the ground, the red spot of a smoke grenade billowed up and spread out. I could see three APCs and a tank pointing to the south. They were about to go through a hedgerow and had stopped for the time being.

"Six has red smoke."

"That's a roger on red," said Fox 3-7. "How about working over the area between us and the road? We know the bad guys are in there somewhere."

"Will do," said the major. "Keep your heads down. Four-two, this is Centaur 6. Use a racetrack pattern, parallel the road, right turns."

"Four-two's got you covered," answered our wingman.

Our two Cobras pounded the area with rockets for two attack runs. I noticed that there was a tree line about fifty meters north of the road that hadn't been touched.

"Major, you see that heavy foliage area closest to our troops?"

"You mean the tree line we just hit?"

"No, not that one. The one even closer to the troops and a little more to the west."

"Oh, yeah. What about it?"

"Nothing's gone in there yet. No tank rounds, artillery, or rockets. Let's lay a few rockets in there and see what happens."

The major rolled in on the target I'd pointed out and let fly with three pairs of rockets. We were pulling up hard and were halfway through our breakout turn when the wingman finished his rocket run. As our ship banked back to level, but continued its climb, I watched the target area. A uniformed man sprang from the bushes running for all he was worth toward the stream.

"I've got a gook!" I said as, without hesitation, I tried to take aim with the turret sight. The turret reached its limits before it could be brought to bear.

"Break right, break right," I told the major.

The ship rolled right. I sighted on the running man and pulled the minigun triggers. Tracers spewed out. Simultaneously the man started to zigzag in an unpredictable manner. Bullets seemed to be hitting all around him. I couldn't believe he wasn't being hit in the hail of bullets headed his way, but he didn't go down. I moved the sight around, trying to track his movements, but was always a little behind. By now, the ship was in a steep dive headed in the general direction of the running man. The major started firing rockets and that intermittently interrupted my firing, making it that much harder for me to track the speed demon below us. The man headed straight for the stream. We were down to 700 feet. The major punched off rocket pairs one right after the other, walking them up to the man from behind. Dirt and water exploded into the air, but the man kept running. He reached the edge of a hedgerow and dived for the stream as our last pair of rockets hit right where he entered the bushes. The major pulled up hard and to the left. I struggled to keep the sight from hitting my legs under the g's. As we gained altitude and got back into our regular race-track pattern, the ground troops acknowledged our efforts.

"Nice moves, Centaurs," said 3-7.

After dinner, I ran into one of the hootch-5 residents on the way back to my room.

"You coming over tonight for the movies?" he asked.

"No. You know I never go to the troop movies. All those

guys sitting together in the bleachers seems to me to make too good a target for the VC for him not to take a shot at it with mortars some night. When it happens, I'm going to be safe in my room."

"I didn't mean those movies. Haven't you heard about the blue movies one of the fellows bought?"

"What are you talking about? What the hell are blue movies?"

"You know, sex movies. They show people screwing and things like that. We're showing them in our hootch tonight. You gonna come? I'll save you a seat."

"Guess I'll be there. What time are you going to start?"

"We're supposed to start at nineteen hundred hours. See you then."

Besides a scene involving a long-necked wine bottle, the main thing that struck me about the films was the fact that all the women had large tufts of hair under their arms. There was no doubt they weren't Americans, but there was also no doubt they were women! There was no sound with the movies, and the brutish audience made jokes about almost everything in the films.

Joking did wonders for our morale.

★ **CHAPTER 20** ★

The Shadow of Death

I was walking between Operations and the flight line on my way to preflight my ship when the scramble horn squawked its call to action. The run to my assigned ship was easier than it might otherwise have been as I didn't have my equipment with me. I'd left my helmet and chicken plate in another ship the previous day. I unhooked the rotor tie-down and stowed the hook in the nose compartment. I looked around and saw that my assigned ship from the day before was in a different revetment. Someone else must have flown it the previous night. I ran the thirty yards to the seven-foot cube of an overseas shipping container in which we stored other people's gear when we took over a ship they were previously assigned. I opened the heavy hinged front of the container and entered. Having come in from the bright morning light, I found the dim light made it almost impossible to see. After some time groping around, I located my gear among lots of other people's. I quickly grabbed my helmet and chicken plate, exited the dimness of the shipping container into the bright light, and ran back to my newly assigned ship, squinting until my eyes adjusted to the light. Charlie Riggs was already cranking the ship. I donned the chicken plate hurriedly, putting it on like a life preserver. I put on my helmet and climbed into the front seat. I closed the hatch, and as I rotated the hatch handle forward to secure it, Charlie picked up to a hover. Charlie called for scramble clearance, and we were off to the west. I plugged my helmet cord into the ship's radio cord and, as we cleared the base camp perimeter, I made my first communication with Charlie.

"Where are we headed, Chuck?"

"We're on our way to Nui Ba Dinh by Tay Ninh," said Chuck.

I called Cu Chi arty for firing information in their sector. We were clear on the way up Highway One and I let Chuck know. My head started to itch. I moved my helmet around to get some relief, but it didn't seem to work. Then my scalp started to sting like it was on fire in places. I banged my helmet with my hands, and that seemed to make things worse.

"What's going on up there?" asked Chuck. "Are you okay?"

I couldn't stand the stinging anymore. I took off my helmet. Over the unmuffled jet engine and wind noise I could still hear Chuck asking what was going on. I reached both hands up to my head and scratched violently. That helped some. I looked inside my helmet. There were hundreds of red ants crawling around in it. They must have thought the glue used to fasten the Styrofoam cushions in place was some kind of delicacy. I turned my helmet right side up and banged on it hard.

"What the hell is going on?" cried Chuck over the noise.

Chuck must have thought I'd lost my mind or something. "I've got ants in my helmet," I yelled back. Chuck, of course, still had his helmet on and didn't understand what I'd said.

"What?"

"I said, I have ants in my helmet."

"I can't understand you."

I ignored Chuck for a couple of minutes while I alternately banged on my helmet and rubbed my head hard. When I put my helmet back on and connected up to the ship Chuck still didn't understand what had been going on.

"What's the problem, Spalding? You gone nuts or what?"

"I had ants in my helmet," I said.

"Ants?"

"Yeah. Ants."

"You okay to fly?"

"Sure. No problem. Unless, of course, they were some kind of godforsaken poisonous gook ants on the VC's side."

"I always disliked people leaving my stuff in those shipping containers. I'm afraid of running into a snake in there. I never thought about ants."

"Guess we better pass the word around when we get back."

"That's for sure."

Chuck turned on the low-frequency radio and tuned it in to Armed Forces radio. We listened to "Rocket Man" and "The Year 2525" on the way to the mission.

*   *   *

The mountain of Nui Ba Dinh, otherwise known as the Black Virgin Mountain, was a geologic oddity. The mountain was solid granite and rose from the ground to an altitude in excess of 3,000 feet. There were no other mountains around it. It stood like a lonely sentinel guarding the way between Dau Teang and Tay Ninh. We had a radio relay and electronic listening post on top. There was an operating gravel quarry at the bottom. Everything in the middle was "owned" by the NVA. I found out one of the people I flew with, Ron Jacobs, had a college degree in geology. On the way back from a mission in the vicinity of Tay Ninh, I looked to the north to admire the spectacle of the mountain and was reminded of Ron's degree.

"I heard you've got a degree in geology. Is that right?" I asked Ron.

"Yes, I do. I haven't had much use for it lately."

"Well, maybe you can answer a question for me. How in the world can such a large mountain exist when there's no mountain range? I learned about mountain building in high school geology, but Nui Ba Dinh doesn't seem to match what I know."

"That's because it wasn't made by mountain-building processes."

"Now I'm really confused."

"Nui Ba Dinh is the remains of a gigantic fissure in the earth's crust into which molten lava oozed. As the crust and the lava cooled, it solidified into granite. Then the softer material all around the granite was washed away by the rains and wind. That material is what formed the Mekong Delta. The process is still going on today."

"You mean three thousand feet of dirt and softer rock over this whole region washed away!"

"Yep. It took eons, but that's the way it happened."

Ron and I landed back at the base and were walking into

Operations. Ron looked across the road to the area used by our sister ground troops and muttered, "Uh-oh."

"What's wrong?" I asked.

"Nothing really. It's only that one of the ground troops is in from the field for a rest."

"So, what's the big deal about that?"

"Being as these guys are in the field a lot, they're not all that civilized. A lot of times their horseplay can get out of hand. Even though they love us when the pressure's on in the field, when they come into the base they sometimes think we've got it too easy. They occasionally harass us with pranks."

"What kind of pranks?"

"Well, for one thing, they like to gas us with tear gas grenades. Depending on their mood, they might even use the kind that has vomitory agent in it."

"Oh, great. We get gassed by our own guys."

"Not always. Sometimes nothing at all happens."

I took Ron's warning to heart and made sure my gas mask was close by my bunk when I went to sleep. Sure enough, an hour or so after I went to bed I woke up to the unmistakable eye stinging and throat closing caused by tear gas. Someone in the hootch yelled, "Gas," but I was already donning my mask. It wasn't very comfortable, but it beat the hell out of breathing the gas. I lay back down and went to sleep with my mask on.

Ron was an interesting person in one key respect. He could, and would, eat almost anything. One evening I watched as he made his dinner. He mixed a can of Beenie Weenies, peanut butter, and eggs together and heated them on his single-element burner. Ron ate every bite right out of the pot while we chatted. When he finished, he looked at me, his expression serious.

"Don't ever eat that mixture," he said. "That really tastes like crap warmed over."

I don't know what made Ron think I'd have ever tried it.

* * *

Ron and I flew as the major's wingman right after the rainy season had started. The troop's pilots joked that there were two seasons in Vietnam—hot and dry, and hot and wet. On the way back to base there were scattered heavy rain squalls all over the area. The squalls were relatively isolated, and we could see the dark gray streaks of rain falling between the bases of the clouds and the ground. Circumnavigating the squalls would present no problem. For some reason, the major decided he was going to fly through one of the larger squalls. Not being current on instruments, I would have elected to go around the storm, but Ron was flying and he followed the major dutifully.

"Hey, Ron. Why don't we just go around this one?"

"No need," said Ron. "We'll be in it for just a bit and then pop out the other side. The major made it."

We flew into the edge of the storm, and I scanned the flight instruments. It grew darker in the cloud, and I snuck a peek at Ron in my rearview mirror. Ron was looking all around the canopy, watching the rain streaks and the clouds as they sped by. Assuming he had ever learned it in the first place, Ron had obviously forgotten everything the Army had taught him about flying on instruments. Looking outside was definitely not the way to do it. I thought this would be kind of a test to see if what I'd learned as a flight instructor was really true. I scanned the instruments with expectation. The nose of the Cobra gradually but deliberately pitched up. This was, perhaps, the beginning of a classic "graveyard spiral." My suspicions were confirmed in short order. The ship rolled into a sixty-degree right bank and headed for the ground. I waited awhile, giving Ron time to pull out. Maybe he was just turning back out of the storm. The ship's speed built up very fast, and we were losing a lot of altitude. As we passed through 1,000 feet and 170 knots I knew I had to take some action.

"If you can't do this, I can," I told Ron calmly.

I was extremely relieved to hear Ron's immediate reply: "You've got the aircraft."

At least I didn't have to fight for control with Ron, who was quite a bit larger than I and who had the four-to-one mechanical advantage on the controls. I rolled out of the bank and pulled the nose up to level. The ship vibrated in the pullout, but we were soon straight and level, although we were down to only 500 feet. We still couldn't see the ground or the horizon. It was raining hard. I kept the ship level and waited to fly out of the squall. After a couple of minutes, Ron clicked on the intercom. "You're heading for Cambodia," he said. "I've got the aircraft."

I let go of the ship's controls. I hadn't been thinking about my heading. Now I focused on the radio magnetic indicator. It showed we were heading due west. Ron started a left turn but made it too steep for an instrument turn. I looked in the mirror and saw Ron still trying to fly by looking outside. In no time, we were nose down and picking up speed. There was very little time before we would collide with the ground close below us.

"Ron, you're going to kill us. I've got the aircraft," I said. Again, Ron relinquished the controls. I took up a heading of 125 degrees and continued to fly. Ron tuned the radio to Cu Chi tower frequency. "Cu Chi tower, this is Centaur 4-1," called Ron. There was only silence.

"Cu Chi tower, this is Centaur 4-1."

Still no answer.

"Cu Chi tower, this is—"

A loud feedback squeal radiated into my earphones.

"Damn thing's gotten wet from a leak," said Ron. "Descend down to two hundred feet. Maybe we can see the ground."

I cautiously descended to 200 feet indicated altitude. In the driving rain, we could barely make out the ground below us. Forward visibility was still virtually nonexistent.

"I think I can fly now," said Ron.

"Okay, you have the aircraft."

The ship's nose pointed down and the speed built up as Ron once again headed for the ground.

"No good," he said. "You take it."

"I've got it. I'm on the instruments. You watch out the front. We should be coming up on the base, and I don't want to hit a radio tower or something."

Almost immediately Ron cried out, "Break left! We just overflew the perimeter." I turned to the left, which put us on a downwind leg for the main runway at Cu Chi. Of course, I couldn't actually see the runway. I was guessing as to our position. When I reached a point that should have been where to turn on the base leg, I turned ninety degrees to the right. The rain continued to pound on the canopy, but Ron said, "I can kind of see the runway."

I sneaked a quick glance to the right and barely made out the runway centerline stripes. We were almost in position to turn onto our final approach. When I moved my gaze back forward to the instruments, a white light, at our altitude and off to our left front, caught my left eye's peripheral vision. It was a landing light! A large transport airplane was on final approach. I threw the ship into a steep-banked left turn to avoid the imminent midair collision. When we turned through a complete circle, I made my right turn onto final approach. I hoped the tower could see us and would keep any other craft on approach from landing on us. As I brought the ship down to the runway and slowed it from forward flight, I discovered I couldn't see well enough in the rain to hover. The ship wobbled in the air, and I thought I was going to lose it right there.

"I can't see. Can you?" I asked Ron.

"I think I can. I've got the aircraft," he said. The canopy's shape let Ron see well enough to hover. It wasn't a smooth precise hover, but we weren't going to crash. Ron slowly and carefully hovered down the runway and then left into the Corral, eventually setting the ship down in its revetment.

Ron shut down the engine. The two of us sat there without saying a word while the rain poured down around us. The gyros wound down with their characteristic decreasing-pitch whine. Except for the rain pelting the canopy, it was very still. I finally broke the silence.

"Cheated death again, didn't we?"

"Yep. But let's not do it again," said Ron.

"Okay, you've got a deal as far as I'm concerned."

I flew with Ron off and on over the next three months. Each time we flew, Ron would want me to help him with his instrument work. We'd look for cloud decks and fly in them to and from our missions. I also made Ron shoot some GCAs (ground-control approaches) into Cu Chi. For some reason, Ron was unable to master the talents needed to be a good instrument pilot.

On one VR mission, Ron and I arrived over the assigned area and found it covered with an almost solid cloud layer. The ground troops we were to support reported the ceiling as 800 feet. Clearly, they weren't trained weather observers.

"Want to see my new instrument flying technique?" Ron asked me. Not anticipating what was to come, I answered sarcastically, "You've been practicing without me, huh? Well, go ahead and show me your stuff."

In my mirror, I saw Ron looking around at the clouds below us. Then he rolled the ship into a steep left turn and pointed it at what looked like a less-thick part of the clouds. Ron was going to dive steeply through the clouds!

"Ron, don't do this," I pleaded.

"Don't worry about it," he said. "I've been doing this a lot lately. I don't have to be on instruments for very long this way."

I tensed and rode through the insane maneuver. The ship entered the clouds at 1,700 feet. It screamed toward the unseen ground below and burst out of the clouds at about 600 feet. Ron pulled three g's and used the excess speed to get back to altitude. He put the main rotor in the clouds but kept the canopy just below their bases. Trying to do the VR was futile. Standing orders were that we weren't supposed to do VR missions unless there was at least a 1,000-foot ceiling. We gave the mission our best shot but couldn't keep the low ship, which had flown up to the area low level, in sight. It didn't help matters that, at 600 feet, we felt like sitting ducks and spent a good deal of time looking for bad guys ourselves. Ron finally aborted the mission.

A vision of .51-caliber machine-gun tracers streaking directly toward my head made me wince—

I awoke from the nightmare with a start and immediately realized the scramble horn was blaring. I was flying with Ron as the major's wingman again. We headed toward Tay Ninh. As we got nearer to the contact area we could see a lot of tracers and flares from a Spooky operating over Fire Support Base Crook. The NVA were making a major offensive in the Tay Ninh area and they were attacking Crook en masse. Our own mission was farther south. The NVA were attacking an Army of the Republic of Vietnam (ARVN) airborne unit located between the straightedge woods and the Vam Co Dong River. The good guys were taking some heavy casualties. It was two o'clock in the morning. There was only a half-moon. The major had the ARVN mark their position as we approached and found out that they wanted our fire to be 100 meters to the west of their position. The major led us in from the east at 3,000 feet. He had turned for the base leg of a right-hand race-track pattern, and I was watching his ship through the right front part of the canopy. Without warning, a burst of green-blue .51 tracers launched from the darkness below toward the major's ship. They looked real close. The major's position lights winked out as he rolled in on the position that shot at him. He launched a pair of rockets, which were answered from the ground with more tracers. He fired a few more rocket pairs and started his pullout. Ron rolled our ship hard right and down in a steep dive to fire at the antiaircraft position, which was still shooting at the major as he made his attack breakout. By this point in my tour, the troop had decided not to use miniguns against antiaircraft positions at night. The two-foot-long flame from the barrels of the minigun made a great target for the enemy gunners to aim at. Two pairs of rockets leapt out toward the enemy position as Ron pushed the firing button. To our great surprise, *numerous* heavy machine guns opened up on us. It was as if they had planned to get the wingman! Ron kept firing rockets. At the bottom of the run Ron pulled up and to the right while he turned off our own position lights.

"Four-one, this is 6," called the major.

"Go ahead 6."

"We're at five thousand feet at your eight o'clock."

I stretched my head around to our left rear and looked up. I could make out the faint glow of the major's red rotating beacon against the main rotor, but only barely. "I've got him," I told Ron.

"Six, 4-1's got you in sight."

"I'm going to make another pass," said the major. "Let me know when you can cover."

The major maneuvered for his next run while Ron turned left and then right to get into his optimum position. The major made his attack. He didn't ripple-fire all his rockets, but he punched one whole hell of a lot of them off one pair right after another. The major took fire, and Ron immediately rolled in again. Up came the tracers. Somehow we weren't hit again.

"Four-one, this is 6. I'm out of rockets. Time to return to base."

"Six, we're not out yet. We'll be ready after one more pass."

Betraying serious concern, the major asked, "Are you sure?" Obviously, the idea of a single-ship attack in the face of such a large number of antiaircraft positions wasn't something the major thought to be too wise.

As Ron climbed the ship to an attack altitude he answered, "Six, 4-1's sure."

"Tonto say 'Speak for yourself, Lone Ranger,'" I quipped to Ron.

Ron's first pair of rockets caused the NVA to open up on us with a vengeance. I started counting positions firing at us. I got up to twelve! The green and blue tracers started out small and slow. But as they got nearer, their apparent size and speed increased until they were the size of basketballs and whizzed by at a million miles per hour! The tracers were swarming all around us. I involuntarily ducked as a burst went between the canopy and the main rotor. The major said, "Get out of there, Ron!"

Everything went into slow motion. There was no fear involved in any of this. It was like watching a movie rather than being in the middle of real life. I wondered what it was going to feel like to get shot. I considered whether or not I could move my chicken plate to an angle that would turn the inevitable bullet strike into a glancing blow so that I might survive. Then my mind leapt to consider exactly where I was going to land our ship after Ron was killed. Answer—to our right front, on the other side of the river, so the bad guys wouldn't get to us too fast. Ron fired the last pair of rockets and broke out to the north. Somehow we were still in one piece.

Back at the base, Ron shut down the ship to rearm. I opened the hatch and got out slowly. I was exhausted. I took the flashlight and inspected for damage. Our main rotor had a half-inch-diameter hole in its underside. On top, the rotor had a much larger section of skin peeled back from the bullet's exit. Now, while in the relative safety of the base camp, the completed mission became scary. I shook all over, like I was shivering. It wasn't cold.

That afternoon I got up and walked to the Corral to retrieve my flight gear. On the way back, I stopped and read the bulletin board. There was a large notice posted.

ALL PILOTS
MEETING TONIGHT—1900 HOURS
SUBJECT: NEW MALARIA STRAIN

The briefing room was packed when I got to the meeting. The major introduced a doctor from headquarters. The doc explained that they had discovered a new strain of malaria in our sector of the country. The half-inch-diameter orange "horse" pills we took once a week were ineffective against this particular strain. We were supposed to take a little white pill once a day from then on, until we left for home. We were given a pill bottle with a two-month supply in it and told to start our dosage the next day.

"Any questions?" asked the doc.

Someone halfway to the front of the room spoke up. "I've got a question."

"Go ahead."

"How many other units are getting the same pills?"

The doc walked over to the operations map and pointed to it. "All units west of the Mekong River over to the Cambodian border and north to Tay Ninh City are affected. Any other questions?"

There were no more questions, and we were dismissed. I had been extremely conscientious about taking the horse pill. If I made it back to the real world, I certainly didn't want to take home malaria. Everyone in-country took the horse pill. But this was different. There was some discussion among us concerning the necessity of taking the new pills. Most of us had been in-country for some time already.

Maybe we were already infected. If not, why not? I considered the likelihood that there was some new strain of malaria limited to the area we'd been briefed about, and decided it was unlikely. I didn't take any of the pills. Several years after I'd returned to the States I heard about a medical experiment the Army had run on its troops in Vietnam. The scenario seemed to fit the "new strain of malaria" routine I'd been exposed to. Apparently some of the human guinea pigs had died or become extremely ill. Curiously, I didn't get angry. Finding out about this incident seemed merely like getting one more confirmation of the "Vietnam experience" the country suffered through. All I wanted to do was forget about it.

My last mission with Ron was uneventful but for one occurrence. We were on our way back to Cu Chi from Tay Ninh, flying at 4,000 feet along the right side of Highway One. Listening to the radio and watching for conflicting air traffic, I was enjoying the ride when a pair of rockets launched and sped out of sight. "Oops," said Ron.

"What happened?"

"My thumb slipped. Hope the rockets don't hit anything friendly."

"If they do, I'm sure we'll hear about it later."

No one noticed. At least, we never heard anything about two stray rockets impacting along Highway One.

★ CHAPTER 21 ★

Aberrations

Our Cobra fire team climbed out of Cu Chi on the way to Tay Ninh. Two of our sister armored cavalry troops were in heavy contact with the enemy on the southern outskirts of the city. Since the 1968 Tet offensive, no enemy force had penetrated that far into any city within South Vietnam. Arriving overhead, I surveyed the situation. The squadron commander was orbiting the area in a LOH and giving tactical direction to the troops below. The area of contact was along a main city road running east–west. Both sides of the road were lined with one-story, tin-roofed shops and residences. Mature trees were set in rows between the houses and shops to serve as windbreaks and natural fences. Apparently, one enemy force had dug in within two or three of the buildings and was holding out. Other enemy elements ringed the area. One of our ground troops was north of the road and one was south of the road. They were trying to squeeze the enemy between them. Both sides of the contact area were sealed off by armored forces farther down the road.

The fighting went on for hours. Our fire team made numerous attacks in the surrounding area to support the grunts, but striking the town itself was not authorized. The enemy had managed to kill off a couple of our tanks and numerous APCs. In fact, while we listened, we deduced that every officer on the ground, except for one, had been killed. These particular bad guys really knew what they were doing.

"Fox 3-7, this is 6," called the colonel from the LOH. "There's no response from 3-6. We need to have him sweep east fifty meters and then swing to the north. See if you can raise him."

The northern troop platoon leader, 3-7, tried calling several times with no result.

"Six, 3-7. I'm going to dismount and go over to see what's going on with 3-6."

My back-seater clicked on our internal intercom. "That's a big mistake. I don't think he'll make it."

Five minutes passed while we orbited, waiting to see what happened. Finally, an unfamiliar voice came over the radio. It sounded on the edge of panic.

"Uh . . . anybody this frequency, we need some help. The lieutenant from the other troop bought it trying to cross the road. Guess I'm in charge. What should I do?"

"Damn, damn, damn," said my back-seater. "I knew that guy pretty well. He was a good man."

The colonel answered the panicky grunt. "Who is this?"

"Sergeant Burdick."

"Sit tight, Sergeant." There was a minute's pause in communication and action. At that moment two armored cavalry troops were under on-the-spot command of a not-too-sure-of-himself sergeant. The opportunity for defeat loomed, and the colonel was obviously thinking over what ought to be done.

"Four-two, this is 1-7. The old man wants me to land him down there. Can you guys give cover?"

"Where's he want you to land?"

"Right in the middle of the southern troop."

"One-seven, we really won't do you much good. The troops are too close to where they're taking fire from to put in any ordnance."

"Okay, 4-2. I'll tell him. . . . Four-two, this is 1-7. We're going to do it anyway. See you later, I hope."

I watched as the LOH headed for the ground in a steep spiraling autorotation descent. The pilot pulled out at the last possible moment, and the colonel jumped out and ran over to the command APC. He took over direct command of both troops and began to get them organized.

"Six, this is 4-2."

"Go ahead, 4-2."

"I've got an idea how to wrap this up. Why don't we load up with white phosphorous rockets and burn the place down around their heads?"

"That might work. I'll try to get permission," said the colonel.

We orbited and waited for word.

"What the hell is taking so long?" I asked my back-seater.

"Anytime populated areas get involved this kind of stuff goes all the way back to Washington for decisions. The communication takes a while."

"Oh, great," I said. "The colonel's men are in the middle of an intense firefight, and he has to wait for someone in Washington to make a decision. That's just terrific."

Suddenly, my right foot was propelled violently upward. My leg hit the turret sight. The leg and foot crashed back down. I tried to push the floor intercom button to tell the back-seater we'd taken fire, but I couldn't. I gently grasped the cyclic, so as to not interfere with the other man's flying, and clicked on the handle's intercom switch.

"We just took a hit!"

"Where from?" asked my back-seater.

"I can't tell. It was only one round. I didn't see any tracers or muzzle flashes. I felt the round hit under my foot."

"You okay?"

"Think so, but my floor switch is inop. If I'm using the sight I won't be able to talk to you."

We made another set of attack runs for the grunts and went back to Tay Ninh to rearm. As the ship's rotor turned more slowly, the back-seater got out, walked around to the front, and climbed up on my entry step to peer into the front cockpit. He leaned in, blocking my upper torso.

"See," I said, trying to point to the floor. "Look at the foot armor right around the intercom switch. See how it's bent upward?"

"Yeah. Good thing the armor was there, huh?"

"No doubt."

External inspection showed that the bullet had entered the left lower side of the ammo bay and stopped when it hit my foot armor. How the bullet didn't contact any of the ammo bay contents was anybody's guess. We loaded up with standard high-explosive rockets. As we were putting in the last couple of them, a jeep approached at high speed and screeched to a stop. "You guys the Centaurs?" asked the driver.

"That's right."

"Word just came through. Load up with willy petes." We unloaded all the rockets we had just then finished loading and reloaded with white phosphorous rockets. There weren't many willy petes already assembled. We had to demate the standard warheads from their rocket motors and put on the willy petes. Considering that a battle was going on and lives were at stake, this took a very long time. We worked hard, and the sweat poured off our bodies, but it was somewhat comforting that the cause of our extra labor was our own idea. We climbed into the ship while we were still out of breath, and scrambled back to the contact area.

Our next attack run was directly in the town. The willy petes hit in the houses and shops, blowing pieces into the air. The brilliant white puffs of the exploding rockets were deceptively gentle looking. Fires started in lots of places. In another hour the engagement was over. The enemy had inflicted great damage and significant casualties. He had been tenacious as hell, and he had died rather than surrender.

My control of the Cobra was purely subconscious when I made the approach into the Corral. My ass had gone numb many hours before, and it seemed as if my brain was in its own holding pattern. I strained to make myself think about what I was doing. I'd flown eleven hours in a fifteen-hour period. This was a flight time rate roughly five times that of the official "allowed" average daily flight time over any thirty-day period. The platoon leader thought enough was enough, and uncharacteristically, he switched the assignments between the number-one and -two gun teams. I went right to sleep after dinner. Even though I was now on the number-two, backup, gun team, there was still a lot of action going on, and I got scrambled out at around two A.M. After the last mission that night, I sacked out until five P.M. the next day.

We got word two days later that the enemy inside Tay Ninh City had been women! They had apparently been led by a male Caucasian. Rumor had it that the women had been NVA widows and their leader was a Russian. There was no official confirmation of either theory.

Captain Eric Brahm had thick black hair and was, for a Cobra pilot, almost fat. Brahm had significantly less time in-country as a pilot than I did, but he seemed to fly routine okay. Brahm had done a prior Nam tour as a ground-pounder before becoming a pilot. I don't know if that had anything to do with it, but Brahm seemed tensed up all the time he flew. Brahm and I drew each other for a convoy escort/VR mission. These combination missions happened sometimes. When the chance of ambush was judged low, higher command would send a hunter/killer team to VR in front of the convoy, instead of using a regular two Cobra fire team.

As we flew back and forth across the road in front of the convoy the LOH came across a group of villagers in the fields doing their farming. The LOH circled the villagers.

"Look at how strange those villagers are acting," said Brahm. "They don't seem to want that one guy to be close to them." Brahm called to the LOH, "One-seven, this is 4-1.

See if you can get that individual to the east of the main group to show his ID."

The LOH hovered around the lone man and herded him away from the others. In these situations, the LOH observer would take out his wallet and open it, showing the subject they wanted to see an ID. Sometimes the communication worked and sometimes it didn't. This time it didn't seem to work. Or, at least the man under surveillance made it appear he didn't understand. Brahm then directed the LOH, "One-seven, come up to altitude." We waited for the LOH to get to 1,500 feet. Then Brahm descended to 1,000 feet and began to orbit around the man he was interested in. The villagers stopped farming and headed for home. The lone man was too far away to catch up.

"I think that guy's VC," Brahm announced to me.

"What makes you think so?" I asked.

"Look at the way the villagers were treating him. They sure acted funny. Besides, he didn't show the LOH any ID."

Even though the villagers had behaved funny, I thought to myself, that might mean the guy was VC or it might not. There didn't seem to me to be any way to tell.

Brahm called the base tactical operations center, "Base TOC, this is Centaur 4-1. We've got a suspicious individual, military-age, male at grid coordinates 254293. He's been trying to group up with some civilians that don't want anything to do with him. Request permission to fire."

I couldn't believe what I'd heard. As I had expected, the TOC denied permission to fire. Brahm got very irritated and began to argue with the TOC about getting permission. The TOC wasn't budging. Then Brahm became inspired.

"Base, this is 4-1. The guy just picked up an AK. Request permission to fire."

"Four-one, this is base TOC. You say he's got an AK?"

"That's affirm," Brahm lied.

"Permission to fire granted," said the TOC.

I keyed the intercom and said, "That guy doesn't have a weapon."

Brahm spoke in a tone that was authoritative and crisp. "Don't worry about it. Just sit there and keep quiet," he ordered.

Quickly, my mind ran through what was happening. Brahm was pilot-in-command, air mission commander, and a captain to boot. To try and stop what was about to happen, even if I could, would be what, mutiny? Brahm had a four-to-one leverage advantage on the flight controls and the physical position advantage of being above and directly behind me. Besides, the man below very well could be VC. As long as Brahm didn't tell me to do the killing, I'd do as ordered.

Brahm rolled the ship right and down into a steep dive at the VC. A pair of rockets sped out and exploded behind the man. He didn't move. Brahm steepened the dive to almost vertical and fired several more rockets. None of them hit home. The man stood frozen in the field, looking up at us, not moving. I watched the altimeter rapidly unwind at an increasing rate. We reached attack breakoff warning altitude.

"Five hundred feet," I announced.

Brahm didn't pull out. He fired another two pairs of rockets. They missed. By this time, I was close enough to see the man's face. It was still cocked upward into the sky from which death rained down. He seemed to be looking straight at me and to have an expression of resignation. I cross-checked the airspeed. We were screaming toward the ground. To get Brahm's attention, I yelled, "One hundred seventy knots!"

I reached to pull back on the cyclic, but Brahm started to break out of the dive at that very moment. The ship shuddered as it struggled under the high speed and the g's. We zipped over the man and mushed down toward the rice paddy. Right when I was sure we were going to hit the ground, the ship steadied. I looked to the right and saw we were below the level of the rice paddy dikes. One of the dikes loomed large in my windshield.

"Watch the damn dike!" I yelled.

Brahm pulled in more collective pitch. The rotor rpm drooped down into the lower part of the green arc but held there. We cleared the dike by inches. Brahm climbed to 1,000 feet in a left turn. He lined up for another run and rolled in. His aim was better this time. The first pair of rockets struck five meters in front of the man and he collapsed. Several more rockets landed right next to him. This time, Brahm terminated the dive when I announced 500 feet. He climbed back to 1,500 feet and circled. The man lay motionless in the field.

Brahm rendezvoused with the LOH and we headed back to the base.

"You've got the aircraft," Brahm said.

I took over the controls without comment and made a slight turn to the left to get on a heading I thought would take us directly back to the base. After a few minutes, I heard Brahm key the intercom.

Apologetically, Brahm said, "Sorry about almost driving us into the ground."

I didn't feel able to reply. I concentrated on my flying and Brahm didn't say anything else to me.

Back in the States, a year or so after this episode, I ran into one of the guys who flew as my copilot. Naturally, we swapped information about what happened to whom.

I asked, "Do you know where Captain Brahm got reassigned?"

"Sure do. He got 'reassigned' to the great beyond. Brahm killed himself in a LOH. His own overaggressiveness got the best of him. He was doing some VR by the Boi Loi. He hovered over a tunnel opening to have his guys drop grenades. A gook stuck out his AK and blasted the LOH. The LOH exploded and killed all three crewmen."

It was unfortunate two other men were taken with him, but as for Brahm, things felt evened-out to me.

We got a new CO for the unit. One of the first things he did was hold a meeting in the officers' club. He announced that from what he could see, the commissioned officers had been getting preference in being assigned as aircraft commander in the Cobra platoon. The new CO thought the warrant officer Cobra pilots would do at least as good, and maybe even better, a job. Right then and there, he reassigned several Cobra qualified captains and first lieutenants into the scout and slick platoons. I was quickly designated to become an aircraft commander.

Tom Brewer had gone to Cobra Instructor Pilot school at Vung Tau and was our unit's official IP. I met Tom in the Corral for my back-seat check ride. Tom had me take off and head south of the camp. This was an area we almost never operated in as it was designated pacified. I did all the maneuvers Tom asked me to.

"Let me have the aircraft for a while," Tom said. "I want to demonstrate a low-level, one-hundred-eighty-degree autorotation. You don't have to do these, but you ought to see it once at least."

What Tom was talking about wasn't part of any normal training curriculum I knew about. I wasn't sure it could be done. Tom dropped the ship to the deck and accelerated to get as much forward speed as he could. He flew down the center of a dirt road.

"Okay, Spalding. Anytime you want, cut the throttle on me."

I reached down with my left hand and rapidly rotated the throttle to the flight idle stop. Tom immediately bottomed the collective and pulled the nose up while simultaneously banking hard right. The speed bled off fast. At fifty feet, Tom threw the ship into a steep left bank and pulled the nose around underneath us. I thought the main rotor was going to strike the ground on the left side, but Tom leveled the ship and sucked in a ton of collective to cushion us onto the road. We hadn't bled off all our forward speed, and the ship skidded and swayed on its skids as it ground to a halt on the hard-packed dirt.

"Pretty slick, don't you think?" said Tom.

"Terrific, if you can do one and get away with it," I said. "How long did you have to practice before you mastered it?"

"They had us do one every day at Vung Tau. I'm still not as good as the guys down there. I don't get to practice enough."

We flew to the Top Hat area to shoot some rockets. I was in the middle of my second pass at a designated target when a transmission oil pressure warning light flashed on. Stateside procedure would have had us make an immediate precautionary landing. If the transmission oil quit lubricating, the multitude of gears between the jet engine and the main rotor driveshaft could seize up, stopping the rotor.

"I've got a transmission oil pressure light," I said.

"What do you do?" Tom asked me.

I was already turning to head for the base. "Stateside, I land. Here, I try to make it back to base. There's no way I'm landing out here in LOH Alley when I don't even have a wingman for cover and rescue coordination."

"I agree," said Tom. "Keep an eye on the oil temperature gauge. If it gets into the red, we'll land."

The oil temperature rose slowly, steadily increasing the ass-pucker factor as we went. By the time we got to the base camp perimeter it was real close to the redline. We declared an emergency and shot a straight-in approach to the runway rather than to the Corral. I shut down in front of the maintenance hangar. The next day, Maintenance told me they had replaced the transmission oil pump. My check ride had been cut a little short, but Tom signed me off anyway.

★ CHAPTER 22 ★

Beginning Again

The Army engineers did a good job with some things. They used their gargantuan Rome plows, which, as far as I could tell, were tanks converted to bulldozers, to plow out entire sections of the Boi Loi woods. I provided cover for the crews of these huge machines a few times. On one such occasion my hunter/killer team had completed a VR in front and to both sides of a Rome plow expedition. We'd found nothing, and after twenty minutes I told the LOH to come up to loitering altitude. I set up a large orbit over the plows. Three of the huge machines were proceeding, line abreast, through the deep woods. From my vantage point, they seemed to move without hindrance, knocking over trees and everything else in their path. The smoke belching from their diesel exhaust stacks was testimony to the false impression of easy effort. Without warning, the telltale dense black smoke of a fairly large explosion erupted to the immediate front of the leftmost plow. It stopped in its tracks.

"Mustang 6, this is Centaur 4-4," I said, using my very own newly assigned call sign. "You got a problem?"

"Centaur, wait," replied the ground troops. A few moments later they called back. "Four-four, be advised, we hit a large booby trap. Looks like it was made from part of a hundred-and-five millimeter artillery round. It dented our dozer blade some, but we're okay. We're proceeding with the operation."

The column of behemoths started forward on their

purposeful rampage through the forest. The Rome plows were amazing machines. Not even artillery shell booby traps could stop them.

In contrast to jungle clearing, the engineers did some things less well. During the dry season the Corral was extremely dusty. It was possible to lose control of a chopper when landing in dust because, if enough dust was kicked into the air, the pilot would lose sight of the horizon as well as his ground reference. Our solution was to make the landing approach so that it could easily be continued all the way to the ground without having to come to a hover. The engineers' solution was to cover the ground with tar. Admittedly, the tar did reduce the dust. It also stuck to our boots. Repeated trips to the Corral eventually pulled the heels off my boots! Fighting the tar seemed futile. I went heelless until the tar soaked into the ground. Meanwhile, the sides of our ships got tar all over them where we climbed in. Our shark teeth looked like they had cavities. In the cockpit, tar covered parts of the floorboards and tail rotor pedals. It was a real mess.

"How do you like this tar?" I asked my copilot as I cranked my assigned ship for a VR mission.

"What's to like?"

Jokingly, I replied, "Well, for one thing, I bet I can fly with only one foot. That way, if either leg is seriously wounded we can still get home under complete control."

"No way. It's not that bad, Dan."

"Bet ya a buck."

"You're on."

With both feet, I pushed hard on the tail rotor pedals. The tar that had built up on the pedals, and that which my own feet had brought along, merged with a squishing sound. With considerable effort, I twisted my right foot back and forth, unstuck it from the rotor pedal, and placed it flat on the floor. I picked up the ship to a low hover, adding left pedal. Once into the center of the Corral, I tested my theory. It worked. There was so much tar that I could "add" right pedal by pulling back on the left pedal with my stuck foot.

"You lose," I said. "Pay up. I only need my left foot on the pedals."

"Okay, okay. You proved your point. Now, put both feet back on the rudders, will you? You're making me nervous."

Tay Ninh had the unenviable nickname "Rocket City" because of the heavy enemy barrages it sometimes endured. But its proximity to the Cambodian border made for some different missions.

Yellowjacket alerts, for example, were particularly frustrating. The listening post at the top of Nui Ba Dinh, and other facilities, would triangulate radio transmissions that weren't known to be coming from good guys. We'd scramble out over the jungle to the locations where the bad guy radio transmissions were theoretically located. The trouble was, the system was full of bugs. Most times what we'd find was an element of ARVN. They knew where they were—it was their country, after all—but the U.S. Army hadn't been informed. When a LOH overflew a bunch of armed, uniformed men while looking for bad guys, things could go wrong in a big hurry. Normally, when they heard us coming, the ARVN would pop a smoke grenade to show us where they were. Most times that stopped unfortunate "misunderstandings."

There was a fat, balding, good-natured major who worked in Army Intelligence at Tay Ninh. One very early morning the major shook me out of a sound sleep.

"Get up, Spalding," he said. "We need to go fly."

"Okay, okay," I said as I sat up on the edge of the bunk, barely awake. "Let me wake my copilot."

"There's no need for that. I'm your copilot for this trip."

"Isn't that a little irregular? You aren't a pilot."

"That's not important. We're only going to fly around the base camp perimeter."

I walked out, preflighted the ship, loaded the major, and took off.

"Where to?" I asked.

"Fly around the base camp. Start at the bunker line and work your way out in concentric circles until I tell you to stop."

I reached the bunker line and started to climb as I banked the ship left to circle the base.

"No. No," said the major. "Don't climb. Keep us at fifty feet and don't go too fast."

"Even without bad guys, that's not too safe, Major, but you're the boss. If we get killed, it'll be your fault."

"That's okay by me."

I flew the circles the major requested. After only fifteen minutes the major said he was done and we could land. As we walked away from the ship, my curiosity got the better of me.

"So, Major, what the hell were we doing up there? It didn't seem to me that you needed a Cobra for that."

"I was looking for signs that we'd been probed last night. Little buggers like to test our perimeter alertness from time to time. I like to fly in the Cobra for this part of my job because it's smoother than the other choppers."

"Oh. Well, did you see any signs of trouble?"

"Not today. But, of course, there's always tomorrow. Remember my motto, Spalding, and you'll be fine."

"What motto is that, Major?"

The major grinned. His large cheeks moved upward, narrowing his eyes. "Napalm sticks to kids. Remember it."

Gallows humor was everywhere the Army was.

The next time I worked with the major it was on a different kind of mission. The strategists in Washington had decided they had to try to do more to stop the flow of enemy troops and materials into South Vietnam from Cambodia. They preferred gadgetry over infantry, so a plan had been

developed to "seal off the border." I met the major in the Tay
Ninh TOC for our briefing.

"Hey, Spalding, what d'ya know?"

Remembering the last time I worked with the major, I
gave him an answer with which he'd be comfortable: "All I
know is—napalm sticks to kids."

"Glad to hear it, glad to hear it. Let's go outside and I'll
show you what we're up to."

We walked out to the parking pad, where a slick was
being loaded with some unfamiliar camouflaged objects. As
I neared the slick, I saw that the objects were four-inch-
diameter cylinders having one pointed end. The other end of
the cylinders had what looked like green plastic branches.

"What we have here," said the major, patting one of the
objects, "is a self-contained seismometer. You're going to fly
cover for the slick while he dumps these out along the border
in the Elephant Ear. When the bad guys come through the
area, these babies vibrate and send us a signal. Then we dump
lots of artillery on 'em. Great plan, don't you think?"

"Whatever you say, Major. But if the VC see the tops of
these things they aren't going to be fooled by that fake bush
stuff. They'll walk around it, or destroy the device."

"By the time they see the device it's too late, and so
much the better if they touch them. They're booby-trapped.
If they're disturbed, they blow the ass off the bad guy doing
the disturbing."

I walked around to the right side of the slick to talk to its
pilot. He was constructing a homemade bombsight by
making an X on his lower chin bubble with black plastic
electrical tape.

"Show me where you're going to drop these things," I
said. The pilot reached down beside the seat, produced a
map, and pointed to several small black spots that ran a distance of five kilometers. They were going right on the
border.

"You familiar with that area?" I asked.

"Sure am."

"You know they have some radar-controlled thirty-seven-millimeter flak up there?"

"Yep. That's why I asked for you guys. They thought I was going to fly there all by my lonesome, but I'm not that dumb."

I went back around to talk with the major.

"Major, you know that's a hot area up there. They even have some radar antiaircraft guns, don't they?"

"Yeah. It's my guys that found out about 'em. So what?"

"I'm not a fire team. All I've got is the one Cobra and a LOH. The LOH is useless on this mission. Another Cobra would be a big tactical advantage. How about if I try to scrounge up a fire team for you?"

"Nope. Can't wait. You guys leave in five minutes."

Unlike Air Force planes, the Cobras, as well as the Hueys, had no sophisticated threat-warning equipment. The only way we might be able to tell if a radar was locking on to us was that it might create a buzz or a beep in our FM radio. That wasn't a comforting thought as we flew to the drop area. Finally, the slick descended to 100 feet above the top of the jungle. I stayed at altitude. Every time the slick dumped one of the spook devices, he'd say, "Mark number so and so." My copilot put a point on the map where the device was, and numbered it. I didn't fly straight and level. I danced the Cobra in an imitation of a LOH bob-and-weave, only I varied the altitude plus or minus 1,000 feet. I didn't want to present a convenient target for anyone who might be thinking of engaging me.

A faint sound came through my headset.

"Two-eight, was that you?" I asked.

"Was what me?"

"That beep."

Another one sounded, a little louder and longer—*beeep*.

"I didn't say anything," said 2-8.

I jammed the cyclic hard left and forward. As I dove for

the cover of the jungle I rolled back and forth rapidly. The noise sounded in my headphones intermittently on the way down and stopped abruptly as we passed through 1,000 feet.

"Two-eight, this is 4-4. We're low-level with you. I'll zig-zag behind. Recommend you get closer to the trees right now."

The Huey nosed over. He was soon level with me, barely clearing the trees. When we got back to base we turned in our marked map so the artillery boys could preaim at the appropriate targets. That night, based on reports from the sensors, the arty pounded the area. The next day we got to do a VR to see what had happened. There was no sign of anything, except for the artillery shell craters. This happened a lot. Most of us pilots figured the arty was killing off a lot of the wild animal population, but there was absolutely no way to tell if this idea worked.

Chuck Riggs and I went to the Tay Ninh officers' club to relax after a day of VR. I was Chuck's copilot. We were assigned to be the rapid reaction team for the base if it was attacked. I never quite understood this assignment. Tay Ninh was home to the Blue Max Cobra outfit of the First Air Cavalry, but somehow the brass felt it was necessary to drag Centaurs up to Tay Ninh to provide additional support. Eighty percent of the time we didn't get used. The Tay Ninh rapid reaction assignment did have some benefits. The officers' club was pretty nice, and there was also a steam bath on the base. Steam baths offered a place to cook out the grime of long flying days, and I learned to enjoy them. A massage was included with the price of the steam bath. The massages were given by Vietnamese baby-sans.

The first time I took a steam bath it was eye-opening. I went into the locker room, disrobed, and wrapped a towel around my waist. When I opened the door to the steam room, I couldn't believe anyone could stand to be in it. Steam boiled out of the door. I hesitated. Two or three guys shouted simultaneously, "Close the door! You're letting the steam out."

I entered the damp, misty, stifling atmosphere, holding my breath, and closed the door behind me. Finally, I had to take a breath. The heat and steam cooked into my nostrils and throat. I felt as if I couldn't breathe. I took shallow, quick breaths. After five minutes or so, I got used to the environment and relaxed while the grime and tension of the day melted away. After the bath, I took a luxurious hot-water shower. When I came out of the shower room, I was herded into a massage room by a mamma-san. A girl came in and motioned me to lie facedown on the massage table. With her small hands, she kneaded my shoulders, neck, arms, back, and legs. The massage felt great, but I was very uncomfortable with the overall situation. I'd heard the girls worked for tips, and I suspected they would accommodate those people who desired a sexual massage in addition to the therapeutic one included in the price of the steam bath. The girl pulled on me and motioned for me to turn over onto my back. I stood up, keeping my towel around me, and headed for the door. The baby-san protested, telling me in pidgin English that she wasn't through. I left anyway. I visited the steam bath whenever I had the opportunity, but, except for the first time, I always declined the massage. For this seemingly wanton waste of money, all the baby-sans named me "Number-One Dinky-Dow GI." "Number one" meant the best, as opposed to "ten," which was bad, and "dinky-dow" meant crazy. They meant I was most crazy. Maybe they were right.

It was 2015 hours. Chuck and I were sitting at a cocktail table while I drank the one Chivas Regal I allowed myself. Drinks were a quarter no matter what they were. Some Tay Ninh pilot had introduced me to Chivas without telling me it was scotch. It wasn't until I ordered a Chivas back in the States that I learned I was a scotch drinker but had a beer budget. Chuck was sipping a beer. The O-club door opened and a LRRP captain came in. He walked directly to the bar and turned around to speak to the small crowd.

"Listen up, you guys. We got a problem. A LRRP team was inserted beside the river up close to the border yesterday. The last radio contact we had with them was at ten-thirty hours today. From the way the radio was transmitting at that time, we think it's crapped out. We want a slick to fly up there now and lower a radio to the team. The slick will need gun cover, too. I'm asking for volunteers."

Chuck looked at me with a "what do you think" expression.

"Look, Chuck, if you think we can do it, I'm game," I said.

Chuck spoke up over the low murmur the captain's announcement had begun. "We'll fly cover."

No one else spoke up for a minute, but finally the pilot of the general's command-and-control ship volunteered. We walked over to the TOC for a briefing. Weather had begun to move into the area, and the sky showed no moon or stars. There was a solid overcast, and the wind was blowing at ten knots. The LRRP team was about as far north along the Vam Co Dong River as you could get without being in Cambodia. The jungle grew tall in that area.

"Up there, with the higher elevation, we'll only have about a hundred feet of clearance between the trees and the overcast," I said.

The slick pilot wasn't so worried about the weather. Of course, his canopy wasn't tinted blue. He was going to have to come to a hover over an area where friendly troops were supposed to be. If they weren't there, maybe unfriendly troops would be.

"Can you give me cover with so little room?" asked the slick pilot.

Chuck qualified his answer. "We'll be able to use the turret weapons, but our rockets won't be effective because we most likely won't be able to get a firing angle."

It began to dawn on all of us why this mission had been volunteer. With only 100 feet between the trees and the clouds, the chances of crashing were good. The area we were going into was hot with enemy activity. It wasn't going to be easy even if everything went well. We didn't dwell on what would happen if it went badly. We walked the fifty yards to the VIP pad from the TOC. There was a light drizzle, and the ceiling was maybe 300 feet. We cranked the ship and made contact with the slick.

"Hornet 2-1, this is Centaur 4-8. You ready?"

"That's a roger, 4-8."

"Two-one, come up tower freq. . . . Tay Ninh tower, this is Centaur 4-8, flight of three, ready for takeoff from the VIP pad."

There was no other air traffic. The tower was surprised to hear from anyone. "Where are you guys going on this dark and stormy night?" the operator asked.

Chuck was in no mood for chitchat. "Is 4-8 clear or not?"

"Jesus! What a grouch. . . . Four-eight's clear."

As the slick took off to the east and climbed to the grand height of 100 feet, all I could see was his flashing red, green, and white position lights. The idea of what we were doing played in my subconscious. Fright started to solidify deep inside me. This was different from going up against someone shooting at you with antiaircraft fire. That happened instantaneously. This we got to think about.

When the slick was halfway to the perimeter of the base, Chuck made our takeoff and followed him. The perimeter of the base was ringed with bright streetlights that were aimed outward to illuminate the perimeter defenses and the cleared ground out to 100 meters from the bunker line. On a dark night, at 3,000 feet, I could see Tay Ninh, Cu Chi, and Dau Teang from the Boi Loi woods. From a distance, the bases looked like diamond bracelets resting in the unbroken dark purple velvet of the night. We passed the perimeter lights.

"I don't have the slick," I told Chuck.

"Me either. It's like he disappeared."

"Hornet 2-1, this is Centaur 4-8. We've lost you."

"Four-eight, 2-1's due north of the base, half a klick."

"Okay. We'll come over and find you."

Chuck made a left turn. Outside the base, we had no visual reference. It was like being inside an inkwell. Normally, in this situation we'd fly on instruments, but we had to look outside to find the slick and avoid the ground.

"I'm getting vertigo," said Chuck. "Can you fly?"

"I've got the aircraft," I said. "You look for the slick and I'll fly." I flew for five minutes. We couldn't see the slick in spite of multiple position reports from both him and us. "Now I'm getting vertigo. Can you take it?"

Chuck took the controls. "I've got it. Man, this is murder. We'll have to trade off to keep from plowing into the terra firma."

We never did see the solitary Huey. Finally, after twenty minutes of switching control, fighting off vertigo, and almost hitting the ground a couple of times, we all agreed to abort the mission. I was flying and landed in the POL to refuel. While I was pumping JP-4 into the hungry Cobra, the wind started blowing like there was a hurricane. Chuck leaned out and yelled above all the noise, "Shut that stuff off and get back in!"

I ran around and hoisted myself into the front seat. Before I got the hatch closed, a torrential rain started. The tower called us in an excited pitch: "Four-eight, you're on your own. We're abandoning the tower. I think it's going to blow over. We had a fifty-mile-per-hour gust!"

Chuck stayed on the controls while we just sat there waiting for the wind to abate. A big gust hit us. The ship swayed and scooted across the pad while twisting us into the wind. After the initial big gusts of the weather front moved through our area, the wind remained very strong and rain streaming down the canopy looked like folds of heavy drapery. Chuck clicked on the intercom. "I don't think we ought to fly in this, do you?" he asked.

"No way. I've tried that before. But I tell you what we

might be able to do. I know there's a truck road a little to our front. If we can get to it, maybe we could hover up to the VIP pad."

"Sounds good to me. We'll give it a try. The way the lights reflect off the rain on the canopy, I can't see very well from here. How about you?"

"I'm not too bad. As long as I stay close to the ground, I think I can hover."

"Okay, then. You've got it."

I tentatively lifted to a two-inch hover. The wind knocked the ship around, and I had to fight hard with the tail-rotor pedals to keep from being spun around unwillingly. When I reached the road and pivoted right toward the VIP pad, the wind was more off the nose and it became easier to control the ship. I inched us forward slowly.

"Watch that sign on your left," warned Chuck while he angled the landing light to shine on a large piece of plywood mounted between two four-by-fours. As I nudged the rotor over the sign, I could barely make out what it said.

SPEED LIMIT 20 Mph
CAUTION: LOW FLYING HELICOPTERS

"Boy! They aren't kidding with that sign, are they?" I said.

Chuck didn't answer, but I could hear him laughing hard.

When we got to the VIP pad, the slick was already there and shut down. We waited for the rain to slack off, and then shut down ourselves before walking into the TOC to see what was going on. The slick pilot was standing by the situation wall map.

"So where'd you guys go?" Chuck asked.

"We were there. We could see you fine, like we said."

"I don't get it. Something doesn't make sense. If you could see us we should've able to see you."

"I wonder if it had to do with us putting our position lights on the flash dim setting?"

"Shit. That's what was wrong. What'd you do that for? Don't you know we have a hard time seeing because of our blue-tinted canopy?"

"Nope. I never thought about it until now, but if we try again I'll leave the lights on bright till we're closer to the drop area. I'm still going dim when I have to come to a hover, though. I'm not going to be a big bright target. You guys will have to do the best you can."

"Okay, if that's the way you want it. Let's not have a midair, though."

The LRRP captain was talking on a radio. He finished and came over to us. "You guys can quit arguing over who did what. The team called in about five minutes ago. They got the radio working and they're okay. You can go back and enjoy what's left of the evening if you want."

"Captain, do you know where we're sleeping tonight?" I asked. We didn't have permanent quarters, and different areas were available on different trips.

"I'll show you. Give me a minute to finish up here."

The captain led us out to the VIP pad and into a barracks to its immediate west side. In the barracks was nothing. Well, not exactly nothing. There were four standard cots. That was it.

"Does anyone live here?" Chuck asked.

"Yes. At the far left corner you'll find a hole in the floor that leads to an underground area. Everyone assigned to this hootch lives down there. It's a lot safer down there when the rockets start flying. I'm sorry, but there's no room underground and this is the only area we could scrounge up tonight."

The mosquitoes were biting like mad. "I'll be back in a minute, guys," I said as I headed out of the hootch. I went to the ship and retrieved my flight helmet and gloves. When I returned I went to the last remaining cot and sat down on it. I tightened the Velcro fasteners of my flight suit sleeve and pant leg openings around my wrists and boot tops. Then I put on my flight gloves and helmet. I lay down on my back and pulled down the flight helmet visor. Fully clothed, and with the "hatches battened down," it was hot as hell. Sweat dribbled down my sides, tickling me. But at least the bugs were getting only a small piece of me. That is, except for those big and mean enough to bite through the flight suit.

★ CHAPTER 23 ★

Rocket City

I was walking to Operations from the Corral when I noticed two American men in civilian clothes entering our officers' club. Because there were numerous civilian representatives from American companies on the base, I wouldn't have thought twice about them except that one of the men was wearing a sport coat and the other one was wearing a suit. For someone grown used to the olive-drab-everything style, the incongruity of suits and coats stuck out like a sore thumb.

I filled out my required after-action forms. The form contained spaces to identify myself, the Cobra I was in, where we fired any of our weapons, and how much ordnance was expended. It seemed to me to be a tedious and useless task, but I guessed there must have been some purpose to all the detail demanded even in the middle of a war. The ops officer seemed busy with a mountain of paperwork. I figured he could use a break, and I wanted some information.

"What's with the two civilians I saw going into the O-club?" I asked.

"Those are special accident investigators sent out by

Washington to do interviews about what happened to Popov last week."

"Damn, that happened fast. Somebody must be real interested."

"Guess so. Nobody here thought that much about it, except Popov, of course. Anyway, I guess we'll find out from Popov soon enough about why all the hubbub."

"Yeah, see you later. Don't work too hard."

I checked my mail slot and went to the hootch to grab a Coke or two to pass the hour I had to myself before I was to depart for Tay Ninh rapid reaction duty. I was reading a magazine when Popov came in and flopped his lanky frame onto our blue-vinyl-covered couch.

"You got a Coke I can bum?" he asked in a worn-out tone. "Those guys grilled me for over an hour. I had to tell the story over and over with them asking different questions every time. I think if they knew how, they would have hypnotized me to see if they could squeeze out any more information."

I leaned forward half out of my chair to reach our small communal refrigerator, pulled out a Coke, and tossed it gently to Popov, who caught it with one hand.

"So what's the big deal? Why are these guys paying you so much attention?"

"Seems I'm the only one to have survived an incident like I had last week. Everyone else has died."

Popov had been on a maintenance test flight. One of the maneuvers he had to do was designed to check for transmission mount and stabilization system function. The Cobra was flown to 2,000 feet, slowed down below translational lift speed, and the cyclic was stirred around in a left and then right circle. The artificially induced vibration was supposed to stop within a certain number of seconds. On Popov's second try, the vibration didn't abate but got a hell of a lot worse. He had thought the ship was going to come apart right then.

"I took the investigators out to the ship and showed them how the main rotor mast was dented inward one inch on both sides immediately below the main rotor. One of them whistled when he saw the damage. The other one said, 'That's the worst case of mast bumping I've ever seen, except, of course, for those cases where the main rotor broke off the mast.' They kept asking me what I did to get out of the mast bumping. Truth is, I wish I knew all the details of what I did, but all I really remember is bottoming the collective and entering autorotation. Oh well, maybe that will help someone else sometime."

"Maybe we ought to eliminate the maneuver that caused the problem from the maintenance checkout routine."

"These guys didn't think so. They emphasized making sure we keep some positive g on the ship while we do the cyclic stir, and that's all they had to say."

"Listen, Oscar, I'd like to stay and talk some more, but I've got to be on my way to Tay Ninh for the evening. Any messages I can give the guys up there?"

"Yeah, tell 'em to keep their heads down."

As Popov spoke I was already up and moving through the hallway. I turned my head and raised my voice to be heard. "I think they already know about that," I said. From one of the other rooms in the hootch someone chimed in: "No shit!"

"See you tomorrow night, guys," I said.

Since my last night of sweat and mosquitoes, I'd found two "secret" sleeping places at Tay Ninh. One was in the LRRP's bunker. They built a damn fine bunker. It was roofed with railroad ties, three layers of them, with sandbags between each layer. The bunker looked like it could take a direct hit from a 122mm rocket without those inside being injured. Besides the protection, sleeping with the LRRPs gave me some new perspectives on their operations.

"I hear you guys call us in real close to your own positions sometimes," I said.

"Sometimes," grunted the LRRP closest to me.

"What's the closest you've ever been to our rockets?"

"We called in some within twenty meters of our position a couple of months ago."

"I don't want to destroy your confidence in us, but you ought to know, sometimes we aren't all that accurate with our rockets. For one thing, the ship has to be in perfect trim. Once fired, the rockets are like arrows. They turn into the slip stream, as well as drifting with the wind. Sometimes, the rocket motors bake in the sun for a long time or they get dropped without us knowing it. They can develop fissures that make them burn unevenly and they go wild when we shoot them. That doesn't happen often. Maybe once in a thousand firings, but the bottom line is, the damn things don't always go where we point them."

"Look," said the LRRP, "I don't give a crap about any of that. When I'm down there and Charlie is after my ass, you just put the fuckin' rockets where I tell you to. That's the way it has to work."

The LRRP went back to cleaning his M-14 sniper rifle. I guessed that if I were doing his job, I wouldn't want to know the details of what might go wrong either.

The other sleeping place I found was in the TOC. The TOC was well fortified since it was the command-and-control center for the entire first brigade area of operation. There was a gigantic table in the middle of the situation map room. I'd stretch out on the table and sack out. There was only one problem with this. My sleep would be disturbed anytime something happened anywhere in the area. One night, I was half sleeping when the door to the room opened. In my twilight consciousness I was vaguely aware of the heavy treading of several pairs of combat boots on the concrete floor. I was tired and didn't move. Maybe the intruders would work around me if they thought I was sound asleep.

"Who the hell is that?" asked a voice.

"That's Warrant Officer Spalding from the Centaurs," said a second voice. "He sleeps here."

"What for?" said the first voice.

"I'm not real sure about that. I've never really asked him."

"Well, wake him up and get him out of here. I need to use the table. Besides, he doesn't need to hear everything that's going on."

Someone came over and nudged me on the shoulder. "Come on, Spalding, up and at 'em. The general says you can't sleep here."

I sat up and looked around the room. Through my sleepy haze I saw that there was indeed a general standing by the table. He was going to unroll a map on the table to plan some mission or other. I got up and walked out thinking how unfortunate it was that one of my good sleeping places was no longer useful to me. I walked through the pitch-black night toward the LRRP bunker. Normally, my way would have been lit by the red reflections from anticollision lights atop the numerous antennas surrounding the TOC, but since the evening a hundred rounds of enemy heavy mortar fire had been directed onto that area of the base by sighting on the lights, they were kept off. The downside of the arrangement was that our anticollision arrangements became "Be careful," but in my opinion that beat the hell out of getting the shit blown out of the whole area and maybe me. When I reached the LRRP bunker there was no sign of life except for a few snores that echoed up through the narrow opening. I made as much noise as I could on the way in so the guys didn't think I was sneaking up on them, groped in the dark until I found an empty cot, lay down, and sacked out for another few hours of fitful rest.

The next day, I flew VR missions all around the straight-edge woods up close to the Cambodian border. The LOH found many indications of recent enemy activity, but beyond that the mission was routine. We headed back to Tay Ninh for refueling. My front-seater was doing the refueling honors.

"Centaur 4-4, this is LRRP 6."

"Go ahead 6," I replied.

"LRRP team 3-9's in heavy contact. You're the nearest asset. What's your status?"

"LRRP 6, wait one." I leaned out and yelled to the front-seater, "Get in right now! LRRPs need help. . . . Six, 4-4's ready to go. Got a location?"

"Roger, contact is at grid 347621. Radio frequency is one zero one point four."

The contact area was southeast of the city about ten miles. "Centaur 1-8, this is 4-4. We got a LRRP support mission. You stay here. See you back at the VIP pad later." I picked up the ship to a low hover, made a left pedal turn into the wind, and started my takeoff.

"Tay Ninh tower, Centaur 4-4, scramble takeoff from the POL."

"Four-four's clear. Frequency change approved."

Immediately, I flipped the radio selector switch to the FM radio and contacted the ground forces who needed our help; "LRRP 3-9, this is Centaur 4-4."

"Four-four, this is 3-9. We're behind a rice paddy dike and taking heavy fire from the north. What's your ETA?"

"Be there in seven minutes."

The sky over Tay Ninh had scattered clouds at 1,300 feet. Looking out to where we were going, I could see the clouds became more dense and were at a lower altitude. I wouldn't be able to make high-altitude runs when I got there, so to save time I stayed low-level on my way to the target area. About the time I was supposed to be at the target, all hell broke loose. There were large explosions on the ground all around us. Concussions rocked the ship. The LRRPs had called in an artillery strike! I rolled the Cobra hard right and went back out of the area the way I'd come in.

"LRRP 3-9, call off the arty if you want 4-4's help."

"Four-four, wilco. Sorry about that."

I began a climb up to the base of the clouds. I stopped at

1,000 feet. "Listen," I told the front-seater, "we don't have a wingman so we're going to be exposed on our breaks. I'll roll the ship hard out of our runs. You hose down the area under us with the minigun or grenade launcher to give us some cover. If we're breaking over the LRRPs, don't forget to stop firing or the shell casings may hit them. Got it?"

"Got it."

I turned the ship around and headed back to the target area. The artillery was stopped. I saw the LRRPs crouched down behind a rice paddy dike. Bullets were hitting the top of the dike.

"LRRP 3-9, how far out do you think the bad guys are?"

"Try fifty to one hundred meters."

I overflew the target heading east. The area was covered with dense brush. Even from my relatively low altitude, no enemy could be seen in it. I thought I saw a small muzzle flash. When I'd flown past the target area a requisite distance, I rolled the ship hard left and tucked the nose down underneath us. I rolled right, leveling our bank, and the sight pipper was right where I wanted it. I let the first pair of rockets go. They hit where I wanted them to. I was able to get off three or four more pair before I got down to 500 feet. I broke hard right in a forty-five-degree banked climb. The front-seater hosed down the area with the minigun, which, thankfully, worked perfectly. At our bank angle the gunner was looking straight down while he fired. I saw what I thought was a couple of small tracers speed by us.

"Four-four, 3-9. You're taking fire from your right."

"Yeah, I noticed. Thanks for spotting. I'll see what I can do about it on this next pass."

I made the next run lined up farther to the north, and, not to be predictable to the enemy gunners, I broke hard left, over the LRRPs. The front-seater stopped firing like he was supposed to.

"Four-four, 3-9 saw no counterfire that time."

The next pass I kept firing and didn't break out of the run

until we got too close to our own rocket explosions. "Shoot out to the right," I told the front-seater.

I held the dive until the last possible moment and then broke straight ahead, purposefully just clearing the trees and bushes that whizzed past while the gunner continuously worked the area over with the minigun. I made a climbing right chandelle and rolled in from the opposite direction. I fired the last of my rockets and broke straight out to the east.

The front-seater clicked on the intercom: "I think I'm about out of minigun ammo."

"LRRP 3-9, this is 4-4. What's your status now?"

"Incoming fire has stopped. An extraction team is on the way. Should be here in five."

"Okay. We're out of ammo except for grenades. You need us to hang around?"

"Don't think so. Great job. Thanks."

"Glad to help. Four-four's returning to base. Out."

After the intensity of the past twenty minutes, the Cobra seemed strangely quiet on the trip back. The front-seater flew with competence and I relaxed. In the POL it was my turn to get the fuel.

When we weren't scrambling, normal procedure had the copilot stand outside the aircraft as a fire guard. This was mostly a holdover from procedures with piston-engine aircraft, but the safety precaution was still followed rigorously. Hard-learned safety lessons in aviation aren't dropped easily. Typically, the copilot stood on the right side of the ship beside the pilot-in-command's hatch. As we did for the Huey, when we started up a Cobra we monitored the engine temperature, rpm, and time to know if we were having a hot start.

Joe Chavez had flown with me quite a lot. We were scheduled together for a routine VR. Joe stood outside my hatch as expected. I decided to have a little fun. I squeezed the engine starter trigger and the jet engine began to come to life with the usual clicking of the ignitors and increasing whine. Joe was watching me instead of the ship. As the rotor came up to speed, I leaned forward a little and stared intently at the temperature gauge. I suddenly widened my eyes, opened my mouth, and drew my head back in fake surprise. Joe jumped up and down, looking back at the ship for the fire that must be there.

He yelled over the noise, "What's wrong? What's wrong?"

I relaxed my expression and posture, turned to Joe, and smiled, letting him know it was a joke.

Joe's agitation eased. He shouted over the engine noise, "Damn your hide! You sure had me going with that one. I think you took a year off my life."

Joe and I were flying together when a new weapon was invented by our slick pilots. We were flying as wingman on a close air support mission for two of our sister troops who had been trying to penetrate a woodline for a couple of hours. Every time they'd start to advance, the gooks would pop up out of one hole or another and hit one or two of the tanks or APCs with rocket-propelled grenades. Then the grunts would call us in to work over the area. We didn't seem to be doing much good for the troops. Collisions with the trees made our rockets go off high over the ground, and because Chuck was dug in, he wasn't being affected much. Even bombs from a B-57 Canberra didn't stop these NVA from shooting back. We'd gone through half of our rockets when our fire team got a call from a slick.

"Four-two, this is Centaur 2-8. We're inbound with a flame bath." Dean Priest was the slick pilot. Dean had been a race car driver before he enlisted in the Army. He was one of those guys who never held much for spit and polish but who seemed to always get the job done.

"Two-eight, 4-2. You're inbound with a what?"

"A flame bath. You'll see. For right now, how about breaking off and orbiting south of the contact area?"

"Wilco. Four-four, this is 4-2. Follow us to hold south."

"Four-four, roger that."

While we orbited at 3,000 feet I saw the slick fly by under-neath. He looked to be at only 1,000 feet. The Huey was carrying a cargo net sling load of three fifty-five-gallon drums on their sides. The drums formed a small pyramid with two on the bottom and one on top. We heard the slick working with the ground troops.

"Fox 3-8, this is Centaur 2-8. We're inbound with a pres-ent for all the little Chucks who are hiding in their holes. Pop smoke."

The grunts popped a smoke grenade to ensure positive identification of their position. We never told the ground troops what color to use. If the enemy was listening in he'd pop a same-color smoke grenade and things could get very confusing and maybe deadly for the wrong side.

"Two-eight rogers purple smoke."

"That's affirm, 2-8," said the ground troop.

"So, where would you boys like me to put this stuff?" said Dean.

"Two-eight, 3-8. Hit some holes that are fifty-five meters to our northwest just inside the woodline. One of the biggest trees in the area stands right beside them."

"Roger, understand. I'll be making one dry run. Say wind direction."

"Wind is from zero three five degrees, about ten."

Dean maneuvered his ship to the southwest of the target area and then made a beeline for the tallest tree he could see. When he'd overflown the target, he swung back around and headed for it again.

"Three-eight, 2-8's inbound, hot."

As the slick closed on the target, it slowed until it looked like it was going to come to a hover. The sling load was released. It dropped the 1,000 feet to the ground and hit dead center on the target. When the barrels hit, there was a huge explosion and fire that burned intensely but briefly. I didn't think this was what they'd had in mind when we went through our sling load training in the States. Everyone wanted to be a bomber. First the LOHs, and now the slicks.

"Four-two, 2-8's heading back to base. Hope that helps."

"Couldn't hurt. See you later," said 4-2.

At dinner, I sat down beside Dean and asked, "What exactly was that 'flame bath' stuff you used today?"

"Oh, nothing special, really. It's merely three drums of JP-4 jet fuel and some trip flares tied onto the drums and cargo net to ignite the fuel when it bursts out."

"Kind of homemade napalm, huh?"

"Guess you can think of it that way, but we can get in a lot closer than the jet jocks. The grunts can use us when they can't use the jets because of close proximity to bad guys. Also, because the JP-4 isn't jellied, it runs down into tunnel holes better than napalm. Since we started doing this, we keep getting special requests from the troops in contact. It must work for them."

"One thing, Dean. You almost come to a hover and you're only at a thousand feet or so. If you do this long enough, some gook is going to nail you or your load. Have you thought that through?"

"I thought about it some, but the way I figure it, if I can help the grunts, it's worth the chance."

We were finished with our meals and went our separate ways for the evening, but it wasn't the last time I'd work with Dean.

Once again, I pulled Tay Ninh duty. We went up early to enjoy a steam bath. On the way up, the lead ship gave me a challenge.

"Four-four, this is 4-3. Think you can wax my tail in a dogfight?"

Dogfighting wasn't something even remotely mentioned in any of our training, but it would be interesting, I thought. "Worth a try," I said. "Two bucks says you can't shake me."

"You're on."

The lead ship immediately started some violent maneuvers to get away. It rolled left in a fake turn and then back hard right. I easily stayed with him. He dove and pulled up into a steep pedal turn, but again, it was pretty easy to stay with him. In fact, I found that no matter what the lead ship did, it was always possible for my turret gunner to keep him in our sights.

"Okay, you win," said 4-3. "Give me a chance to win my money back. Let me on your tail and see if you can shake me."

"Roger that."

We set up and 4-3 said, "Go."

I rolled the ship hard left past vertical and pulled the nose around in a half-assed split-S. When I came screaming out the bottom, I checked my six o'clock; 4-3 was right there. I pulled the nose up and let the airspeed bleed off. At twenty knots, I fake-rolled right and then kicked in all the right pedal I had. I'd hoped this would get my gunner a line on 4-3, but he blithely slid to the left and I couldn't get around fast enough. I pointed the nose straight down. I shot a glance over my right shoulder; 4-3 was still there, but he was lagging back and starting a break from the dive.

"Three hundred feet!" yelled my front-seater.

Oh, shit! We had both lost track of altitude. I hauled back on the cyclic and pulled in collective. The Cobra seemed to react in slow motion. It mushed and didn't stop its downward plunge until it was below the trees on each side of the field we had luckily descended into. The field and trees raced rearward as I gently lifted the nose farther to initiate a climb before we got to the end of the field. When things settled down, and I allowed myself to breathe, I called 4-3.

"Four-three, this is 4-4. That's enough for today, don't you think?"

"Whatever you say, sport. Cut it kind of close down there, didn't you?"

"Just a tad."

After all the real threats to my well-being that were beyond my control, I thought it would be a rather foolish thing to buy the farm while horsing around. I made it a point not to play dogfight anymore. It wasn't worth two bucks even if I could have won.

We met in the officers' club later. The place was unusually crowded. Everyone was talking and having a really good time.

"What's going on?" I asked the closest guy.

"You didn't hear? Ho Chi Minh died today."

This news perked me right up. It was like I hadn't flown at all that day.

"Well, that certainly calls for a celebration. Maybe with Uncle Ho gone, this whole mess will stop in short order."

I walked to the bar and ordered a drink. The bartender, a Vietnamese girl, noticed my grin. "Why everyone so happy?" she asked.

"Ho Chi Minh died."

"Oh. So what?"

I thought she must not understand. "You know. Ho Chi Minh, the ruler of the communists."

"Oh, yes. I know," she said matter-of-factly. "But why you happy?"

I dropped the conversation. Maybe the girl knew something about the situation in her country that I didn't. Or maybe she just didn't care who ran the place. This girl came from one of the purportedly most anti-communist parts of Vietnam. If she didn't care, what the hell were we doing there? It was better not to dwell on it. I still had missions to fly.

Back at Cu Chi, when I arrived the next night, the operations officer made a point of telling me to congratulate B.J. Scammell, but he wouldn't tell me why. I walked into my room and stowed my gear. I went out into the hall and knocked on B.J.'s doorjamb. B.J. didn't have a real door. He said it was too hot for doors. A red piece of cloth hung in the doorway to give him some privacy.

"Come on in," said B.J.

I brushed back the door cloth and took two steps into B.J.'s room. "I hear I'm supposed to give you some congratulations."

"Yep. That's a fact."

"Right." I paused, waiting for B.J. to tell me why he was owed congratulations. There was a pregnant pause. A little exasperated, I said, "Well, are you going to tell me why?"

"Not until you congratulate me."

"For crying out loud! Okay . . . Congratulations."

"I reckon that was sincere enough for government work. Today I became the Centaur who's actually seen the most enemy troops."

"What are you talking about? Mostly all we see is bushes and trees."

"Today was different. I was flying a VR mission over by the Parrot's Beak at daybreak. You know how it's kind of swampy and open over there? Well, anyway, my LOH had only begun his VR when a couple of hundred gooks got up out of the swamp and started to beat feet for the border. They must have been on their way back from some night exercises and they didn't quite make it. We were only a hundred meters from the border, and they must have thought running was their best chance."

"What'd you do?"

"At first, I hesitated. The sight of so many bad guys overwhelmed me. Then I told the LOH to head east and orbit. I had the front-seater try the minigun and grenade launcher first, but they jammed. I rolled in and used the rockets as best I could, but the little bastards were pretty spread out, so they didn't make good rocket targets. Too bad I wasn't loaded with flechettes. Man, I never thought I'd see people run so fast through the muck. The whole thing was over in a flash."

B.J. was right about having needed flechettes. They were the modern equivalent of grapeshot. Each flechette rocket warhead was packed with two thousand three-inch-long one-sixteenth-inch-diameter aluminum nails. Each nail was crimped at the back to make it fly pointed-end first. The rocket warhead was built to explode a certain distance out from the ship. The nails would blossom out and scream down on the ground, peppering an area the size of a football field. The ground troops had similar rounds for their tanks and artillery. They were called beehive rounds. We'd heard about the grunts finding enemy soldiers nailed to trees after they'd been taken under fire with beehives.

"I bet nothing like that ever happens again. You'll be the only one in the outfit with that kind of an experience."

"You're probably right. In a way that's good. Shooting at trees and bushes is a lot less personal."

"Yeah, but it's a hell of a lot more frustrating not knowing if you're really doing any good or not."

"True. Guess we can't have everything. We can have a drink, though."

I took the drink from B.J. and gave a toast I'd coined as an answer whenever anyone asked how I was: "I'm still here." The toast carried multiple meanings, which everyone understood. It was good to still be alive, and bad to still be where we were.

★ CHAPTER 24 ★

Trading Places

A couple of interesting things happened when the squadron had a change of command. First, the ground troop area of operations for the three-quarter Cav shrank. Second, our unit was directed to fly at least three hunter/killer teams for nine hours of VR per day each. Orders were to fly whether or not there was any enemy activity or special needs for VR. Nine hours per day was a heck of a lot of flying, for both the pilots and the ships. In the 1700s, the Prussian general who taught the American revolutionaries close order drill said that you can tell a European to do something and he'll do it, but to get Americans to do something you have to tell them *why*. Nobody told us why nine hours was a magic number. At least no official rationale was provided. The rumor mill had it that the new division commander had a bet going with the commander of the 9th Infantry Division. Occasionally, we'd fly our nine hours by merely filling in the logbooks to that effect. That was the only way not to drive the whole unit into the ground, literally.

Sometimes we flew VR in conjunction with 1st Air Cavalry operations in the Tay Ninh area. We got to know one grunt platoon leader, Steve Parker, pretty well. I planned several missions with him, and then flew my hunter/killer team in support of his troops. One night, in the officers' club, Steve started talking about how he'd like to go on a VR mission so he could see what it was like from our viewpoint. He felt it might help him be more effective somehow.

"Why don't you fly with me tomorrow?" I asked. "The mission we're on isn't too ambitious. I'll leave my copilot here to enjoy the air-conditioning, and you can fly up front with me."

"Gee, that'd be great. Let's do it."

"Okay, meet me at the ship tomorrow at oh-nine-hundred. I'll give you a short briefing and we'll be on our way."

Steve came out to the ship a little early. He was anxious to go. I hadn't finished my preflight, and I took the opportunity to explain some of the inner workings of the ship to Steve as I finished up. I told him how to get into the ship and helped him get onboard. I climbed up on his boarding step, leaned in, and buckled his shoulder harness and seat belt.

"Boy, this is real luxury," said Steve. "In the slicks we just sit on the floor. I used to worry about falling out, but everyone gets used to it after several dozen troop insertions."

"Sometimes, the way we fly, the belts are a necessity. By the way, if you have to get out real fast for some reason, you just pull up on this one lever. It holds the belts together. Also, if we should roll over on our left side and your canopy hatch can't be opened, reach back and get this breakout knife." I tapped the knife to show Steve where it was. "Use the knife to pound on the canopy. The canopy is designed to break away in pieces from the force."

"What the hell do you mean, 'If we should roll over'?"

"Don't get excited. It's better to be prepared than not, that's all. If I thought we were going to crash, I wouldn't be getting in myself."

I showed Steve the turret sight, but instructed him to leave it stowed. Of course, I offered the mandatory general observation, "Don't touch anything I don't tell you to."

I took off and, with the LOH, flew to the assigned VR area. As we neared the subject location, I saw there was an FAC orbiting overhead.

"FAC on station, this is Centaur 4-4."

"Four-four, this is FAC-10. Go ahead."

"We're supposed to do a VR here. You got something working already?"

"Nope. I was just cruising, looking for bad guys. This seemed a likely spot. You guys go ahead. I'll stay out of the way."

"Roger that. . . . One-eight, this is 4-4. The FAC says we can have the area to ourselves. Get busy, will you?" I said.

Once the LOH was low-level, I started to orbit around him. He started calling up signs of fresh activity. Then the raised, stressed voice of the LOH pilot exploded in my headset: "Receiving fire!"

I threw the Cobra into an attack run, the LOH straightened his flight path, and, with as much speed as he could muster, headed out of the area to the right. I fired five pairs of rockets and stopped at the last possible moment, breaking out purposefully low to skim the treetops. The LOH called as I pulled up hard, made a pedal turn, and rolled back in on the target, "Four-four, 1-8's been hit." Now I had to divert my attention to finding and helping the LOH in case he went into the jungle.

"One-eight, 4-4. Say your position."

"We're back to altitude and headed to Tay Ninh due south of the contact area."

I broke off my attack and looked around to find the LOH. He was at my two o'clock high position. I pulled in more power and dropped the nose to catch up to him.

"FAC-10, this is 4-4. Be advised, my LOH took fire. If you can put some ordnance down there it would be most appreciated."

"Four-four, 10. I heard. Air strike's already on the way."

"Four-four out. One-eight, hold steady, I'm coming up on your right rear to take a look." I maneuvered the Cobra to within ten feet below the LOH and looked it over. There were several holes forward of the engine compartment. "One-eight, this is 4-4. You got several holes immediately forward of the engine compartment. I don't see anything leaking, though. You gonna be able to make it back to the base?"

"Four-four, 1-8. As far as we can tell we're okay. No abnormal instrument indications, and the ship's flying fine. Stay with me, though, just in case something develops."

"So, Steve," I said, "I bet you didn't expect the LOH to take fire today, did you?"

"What are you talking about?"

"Didn't you hear the LOH call 'Receiving fire'?"

"No. Is that what was going on? I thought you guys were putting on a show!"

"Sorry to disappoint you, Steve ol' buddy. That was the real stuff. So, what do you think about our end of the business?"

"You can keep it. I wouldn't trade places for all the tea in China."

"How come?"

"At least when I'm in the bush, Charlie has as hard a time seeing me as I do seeing him. Up here, you guys got no place to hide. Yes sir. You can keep it."

Steve's comment was very interesting. I'd never thought about it quite that way.

The Tay Ninh POL was located on the western side of the base. That was the side away from the city and closest to Cambodia. I guess being a couple of miles closer to Cambodia didn't really make any difference, but it seemed to. It did mean we got to the refueling point faster whenever we ran missions in the Elephant Ear. It sure seemed to make a difference one bright, sunny, and surprisingly mild day as I called to my LOH partner, "One-four, this is 4-4. I'm bingo on fuel. Time to head back."

"Four-four, roger that. We're on our way up," said the LOH.

While my gunner watched the LOH intently, I took the time to look around at the landscape. The Elephant Ear was strikingly lush in its dark green jungle tint. If the area hadn't been so generally dangerous, it would have been pleasant to sight-see over it.

We approached the base from the west and landed at the POL. The POL had been covered with tar, like the Corral, in order to keep down the dust. It partly worked. When the heavy-lift, twin main rotor CH-47 Chinooks landed for their giant gulps of nourishment, they still blew up dirt. They also blew our LOHs around on the refueling pad. At the bottom of their landing approach, the Chinooks would rear back, noses high in the air, looking like some strange stallion on its hind legs. One group of Chinooks was even named the "muleskinners." I always wondered if their refueling approaches were necessary or if they were just pilot antics. This time into the base it was my turn to get the fuel. I climbed down, picked up the refueling nozzle, got back up on the skid step, opened the fuel tank cap, and started pumping in the juice.

Wham! Wham!

The nearby explosions of 122-millimeter rockets sent concussions through my body! All I could think of was being in the POL with all that jet fuel. If the attack was successful, there was going to be a gigantic fireball with me in the middle of it. I threw down the refueling nozzle, jammed on the fuel cap, jumped into my seat, and took off to the west. There was no time for niceties, like getting a takeoff clearance. The front-seater struggled to close his hatch. There were several more explosions to our rear. When the concussions reached us, I could feel them in the ship's controls. Finally, we were a half mile from the edge of the base camp. I wasn't plugged into the ship's radios, so I yelled to my copilot, "You take the aircraft."

"I got it," he yelled back.

Now that we were clear of the potential conflagration, I took time to close my own hatch, strap myself in, and hook up to the radios. I contacted the base. "Tay Ninh TOC, this is

Centaur 4-4. We're just off Tay Ninh. Can we be of assistance with counterattack fire?"

The Army's countermortar squads were a little-understood group. It was their job to run out and measure the craters left by incoming artillery. As I understood it, this got done during the attacks! By analyzing the shape of the craters, it was possible to trace backward to where the incoming shells had originated. Normally, our own artillery would then pound the origination area. Getting a Cobra or two into the act sometimes worked better. Unlike artillery shells, once we got to the suspected location we could see. If there were targets in the area, we could engage them specifically, rather than generally.

"Four-four, that's affirm. Proceed to grid 352621."

Flying as fast as I could, I arrived at the designated location quickly and saw where the rockets had been launched. The ground showed fresh burns but no other sign of bad guys. That in itself wasn't too unusual. Charlie set up his rockets to fire using time-delay devices. That way, counterbattery artillery didn't pose much of a threat to him.

"TOC, this is 4-4. We found the launch site. No bad guys in sight. Request permission to fire."

"Permission to fire granted."

I emptied my rockets into the area between the launch site and the Cambodian border, which was only 200 meters to the west. Then we flew back and started the refuel, rearm sequence all over again. There was no way to know if we'd done any good, but it was satisfying to shoot back after having come so close to being hit by those damn rockets.

During a close air support mission in the Boi Loi woods, our fire team temporarily orbited around the ground troops we were supporting. We were at 1,500 feet.

"God, that smells terrible," exclaimed my copilot. "Did you fart?"

"Wasn't me. Besides, you know the airflow in this beast is

from front to rear. I'm the one who gets gassed from your bad habits, not the other way around."

"I give up, then. Don't you smell what I'm talking about? It's sickening sweet."

"Oh, that. Guess this is your first time. That's the smell of cooked people. That last napalm air strike must've been effective. The ground guys will have an easier time now. Just watch."

"How can they stand that smell without throwing up? It's so strong up here, it must be terrible down there."

"I guess they get used to it, same as you will. Hell, if you think that smells bad, wait until you get a whiff of that rotten gook fish paste, *nuoc mam*, that they eat. There's a *nuoc mam* factory by the river east of the base. On a hot day, I've smelled it at two thousand feet. In a different way, I think it's worse than this. Why, one time last year, I used the smell of *nuoc mam* to home in on the base when it was fogged in!"

I don't know if the new guy believed me or not, but I did succeed in getting him to concentrate on something other than the fried-body smell, which really was sickening.

There actually was a VR mission on which I located something by smell. I was orbiting the LOH in our standard manner but was at only 1,000 feet due to cloud cover. The LOH was moving generally northward and I was at a point in my orbit to his east when some God-awful smell enveloped the cockpit.

"One-three, this is 4-4. I think we flew over something to your east. How about working your way over and taking a look?"

The LOH acknowledged with two clicks of his microphone. Then he altered his search pattern to the east. Two or three minutes later, he called up with what he'd found.

"Four-four, this is 1-3. We got three bodies here. They've been staked out and look like they were skinned alive."

"One-three, 4-4. Understand, three skinned bodies?"

"Four-four, that's a roge'."

I radioed the information about the grisly find back to the base. Later, ground troops were inserted at the site and the bodies were recovered. I never heard whose bodies we had found. They could have been local villagers, ARVN, or even U.S. soldiers. It didn't really matter much. All bodies smelled the same when they rotted.

Since my first experiences with antiaircraft units, we'd improved our tactics. Whenever we knew there might be antiaircraft in an area we were to attack, we used a heavy-fire team: three Cobras, rather than the normal two. The third Cobra loaded up with flechette rockets. Enemy antiaircraft positions consisted of a circular trench, like a doughnut, with a mound of dirt left in the middle. The heavy machine gun would be mounted on a large tripod set on the middle mound. While the gunners remained dug in the trench, the guns could be angled upward to engage us in any direction. Using normal rockets, it took a direct hit for us to take out a position. Using flechettes and a steep dive from high altitude, the third Cobra would nail the bad guys into their own trenches. Normally, it took only one pass. But even using these tactics, taking out antiaircraft positions using helicopters was a tricky enterprise.

One night, I was scrambled out as a wingman on the number-two gun team. The number-one team had already done its part for a ground troop unit that had come under attack in its night defensive position. The way the troops formed a circle of APCs and tanks for the evening reminded me of a wagon train in a western movie. As we passed the number-one team flying in the opposite direction, its fire-team leader warned us to watch for one antiaircraft position that had become active on their last attack run.

"Four-four, this is 4-1. I don't think we have time to get a third Cobra up here," said my fire-team leader. "What do you think?"

"I concur. It's only one site. We can handle it ourselves."

As we flew on toward the contact, we saw one small burst of .51-caliber tracers arc upward. We tuned our radios in to the command-and-control ship frequency. There was a bit of a weird conversation going on. The command-and-control ship, trying to guide the action, was calling Dean Priest, who was out on a "Nighthawk" mission. As far as I could tell, Dean had invented the Nighthawk mission. Along with a powerful zeon searchlight, Dean had mounted a minigun in the side of his slick. Each night, he'd fly around, mostly single-ship and in free-fire zones, looking for bad guys with the searchlight. When he found some, he'd zap 'em with the minigun. The tactic was a valuable addition to our efforts.

"Centaur 2-8, this is Fox-6."

There was no answer.

"Centaur 2-8, this is Fox-6."

"Ah . . . Fox-6, go ahead."

"We took some fire from a fifty-one a few minutes ago. The snakes had to leave. How about coming down here and locating the position with your searchlight?"

There was a long dead-air pause on the radio. What the C & C ship was asking for could be considered close to suicide. The searchlight on Dean's ship didn't do much good from a high altitude. That fact, combined with the relative slowness of the slick, made the risk extreme.

"Six, this is 2-8. Please confirm. You want us to look for an antiaircraft position?"

"That's affirmative."

Another long pause ensued before the radio crackled with Dean's answer: "Bite my ass!"

The C & C ship gave Dean a chance to change his mind— or, at least, his reply.

"Two-eight, say again. You're breaking up."

Dean had decided that discretion was indeed the better part of valor and obviously didn't give a shit who knew. Dean confirmed his last transmission even more emphatically.

"I said, 'Bite my ass!' I'm heading back to refuel. Two-eight out."

The next day, Dean told me he had been reprimanded for this tactless way of letting the man in charge know how stupid his request was, but that was the extent of Dean's punishment. Dean was doing so well with his Nighthawk missions that it paid to let him have some rope.

Attacking antiaircraft positions with a slick was about as smart as expecting fully loaded Cobras to operate in confined areas. In a way, that's what one of my missions called for. I was to run a VR in an area of known enemy contact. We were to get our final briefing at an artillery fire support base. Fire support bases normally only had a small clearing inside their perimeter defenses to allow "ass and trash" missions to and from their location. The particular base we were landing at wasn't far from Cu Chi, and it had once been manned by the French, back before they gave up their colonial fight. This last fact made the base "interesting" in that no one knew where all the land mines around it were. There was one road into the base, and the helipad. The rest of the perimeter was no-man's-land. I flew around the fire support base and decided that I could probably risk landing, although the helipad was surrounded by barbed wire on three sides and a defensive dirt wall on the fourth. My LOH and I made careful approaches and landed on the 100-by-50-foot helipad without incident and went in to get briefed. On the way out to our ships after the briefing, the LOH copilot chatted with me.

"How about I switch with your copilot for this mission?" he asked. "I've never been in a Cobra before."

"It's okay with me as long as Howard and my copilot don't care," I said. "It's up to them."

"How about it, guys? Any problem?"

"Not for me," said Howard.

"It's okay with me also," said my copilot.

This was actually good news to me. My assigned copilot was a hefty guy. He weighed close to 200 pounds. The LOH copilot was very slender and probably tipped the scales at around 130 pounds. Our ships were still at max weight, since we hadn't flown far, and the takeoff out of the little helipad would be doable but marginal. The weight difference between copilots would help.

I cranked the Cobra and contacted Howard.

"One-four, this is 4-4. You up?"

"Roger that."

Our ships were parked with the LOH in front and me in the rear. I told Howard the plan for our takeoffs.

"Right. I'll pull back as far as I can. That should give you enough room to get off."

Howard clicked his microphone twice.

I lifted to a low hover and pulled the cyclic back slightly. The Cobra drifted back very slowly. I moved the tail a little to one side and then the other so I could look back and make sure it didn't get caught up in the five-foot-high perimeter barbed wire.

"One-four's on his way."

I watched as the LOH took off over the roadway leading into the base. Once he was clear, I made preparations for my own departure. I figured I had just enough room to get into translational lift before I got to the perimeter wire in front of me. To get all the length I could from the small area, I pulled in some more collective and backed up the ship, putting its tail over the perimeter wire behind me. Then I gently nudged the cyclic forward and the ship responded with forward movement. When I was sure my tail was clear, I increased the forward cyclic. The ship was accelerating to its translational lift speed. I was doing okay. The takeoff was going to work out fine. Then, out of nowhere, an armored personnel carrier (APC) pulled out on the road in front of me. It looked huge and filled my forward vision! There was no time to stop. There was no room to the right. The APC had a twenty-foot whip radio antenna, and worse yet, several grunts riding on top of it. The ship barely began to sink as it entered translational lift. I pulled in as much collective as I dared to try to climb over the APC. No good. Rotor rpm began to bleed off. I slid the Cobra left to put its fuselage between the APC and the dirt berm wall of the base. As I reached the APC, I moved the cyclic left to lift the rotor over the heads of the guys on the APC. The rotor wash buffeted the APC's deck and the men on top as the rotor flew low over their heads. One of the guys looked right at me as we inched by. The expression on his face said, "Holy shit! We're all gonna die." The ship squeezed by the back end of the APC, but I had asked too much of the engine. As we cleared the road, the master caution aural warning whooped and the light flashed in my eye, telling me the rotor rpm was below its operating range. The Cobra settled toward the ground. It came down in between two rows of barbed wire fence that circled the perimeter. Visions of the Cobra crashing in the middle of the mine field and exploding flashed through my mind. I struggled to guide the ship in a circular path between the barbed wire fences by very tenderly and minutely moving the controls to use as little power as possible. Finally, after we'd covered about fifty yards, and miraculously hadn't caused an explosion or crashed outright, the caution warnings stopped and the ship flew itself into normal climbing flight.

"That was damn close, wasn't it?" exclaimed my temporary copilot. "I'm not sure I like this shit."

I took a breath. "I want to thank you."

"What for?"

"For being small and wanting to ride. If we hadn't traded copilots, I don't think I would have made it through that."

"You know, you're probably right. . . . I guess you're welcome after all."

CHAPTER 25

Change of Scenery

One of the best things about putting a ship into maintenance for one of its regularly scheduled inspections was that we had to disarm it. The easiest way to disarm a Cobra was to shoot off all the ordnance. We'd go out to a free-fire zone and ripple-fire all the rockets, which was very satisfying. It was something we never did on actual missions because tactics demanded that we spend more than a few minutes on station with the ground troops. The knob on the rocket pair selector worked like the channel selector on an old-fashioned television. It could be set to one pair, two pair, five pair, all the way up to "ripple-fire." With each push of the rocket-firing button, the designated number of rockets would be sent on their way. One of my VR missions in the Elephant Ear had come to an end, and the ship I was flying was due back at Cu Chi for maintenance. I decided to do something I'd been shown as a copilot many months before. I climbed the ship to 6,000 feet, reached up to the instrument panel with my left hand, and set the rocket pair selector to ripple-fire. I turned the Cobra to a due west heading and entered a dive to gain some airspeed. I pulled in some extra power with the collective pitch, and when I reached 170 knots, I pulled into a nose-high climb. When the ship's nose reached a forty-five-degree angle above the horizon, I pressed the rocket-firing button. One right after the other, each of my fifty-two rockets fired into a ballistic trajectory, arcing their way westward to explode in heavy jungle too far away for me to see them. The rockets took no notice when they crossed the Cambodian border. It felt good to think I might have disturbed Chucks making their way down the Ho Chi Minh trail with ammo destined to be shot at me or my friends.

Back at Cu Chi, I entered the final approach for the Corral. I was headed east and flying to the right side of the road that ran between our hootches and our sister troops' area. As I passed over the operations shack, I reduced power to start my descent. I saw a Cobra back out of its revetment on the left side of the Corral. The Cobra's pilot hadn't contacted the tower, so his intentions were unclear. The pilot pivoted the ship to the right, putting it into the wind, and then set the Cobra down close to the revetment line. I figured the pilot was getting ready to call the tower but was waiting for a second ship, which hadn't yet cranked. I continued my approach. As I passed the maintenance hangar I jigged my ship to the left, lining up with the center of the Corral. I began the slow transition to hovering flight by bleeding off airspeed through the application of rear cyclic. I was now committed to land. That's when the idling Cobra on the side decided to pick up to a fifty-foot hover. It leapt into the air right in front of me! The rotor wash from the hovering bird made my main rotor begin to lose lift. I started settling to the ground with an increased rate of descent. I slid the Cobra to the right as far as I dared and pulled in more collective, but it didn't help much. I was going to hit hard. I pulled the cyclic back to make sure all my forward speed was gone. Just before we struck the ground, I pulled in all the collective pitch I could. The rear of the skids hit first. We bounced up a little. I fought to keep the ship level. We came down again and I lowered the collective pitch. The ship rocked and then was stationary.

"Cheated death again," I told my copilot.

"Yep. Like they say, 'Any landing you can walk away from . . .'"

"That's affirm!"

A minute later the other Cobra came down and pivoted around to hover back to his revetment. We were almost nose to nose. I thought I knew who the pilot of the offending ship was. I switched my radio to troop frequency.

"Hey, there. Is that 4-3?" I asked.

"Yes. That you, 4-4?"

"That's right. You surprised to see me?"

"Why?"

"I was on short final when you did your hover stunt, that's why! How about tuning in the tower next time you're going to come into the Corral?"

"Oh. Sorry about that. Point well taken. You done for today?"

"Sure 'nuff. I'm bringing this bird in for maintenance. You almost made it need a lot more maintenance than was planned on."

"Okay, don't hold a grudge. Let's go get a beer. I'll buy."

"Damn straight you will."

We met in the O-club. I sat at the bar and Popov got me one of his beers. He leaned on the bar opposite me and took a big swallow.

"So, Spalding. You ready to go to Vung Tau?"

"What for?"

"I heard the old man needs to assign a new Cobra platoon armament officer and you're going to be it. The armament school's in Vung Tau."

"Well, I'm not crazy about the extra duty, but I could use a short trip. Guess I'll talk myself into liking it."

Popov had been right. I was assigned extra duty as armament officer. That meant it was my responsibility to see that all the Cobra weapons functioned the way they were supposed to. The school at Vung Tau was required. Vung Tau was a seaside city south of Saigon rumored to be a place for rest and relaxation (R & R) for both sides, ours and the enemy's.

One of our slicks flew me down. They'd spend a couple of hours in town and then go back to Cu Chi. I was going to be there for a week. The slick crew and I got on an Army bus that went to the officers' quarters in town where I would be staying. We had the bus all to ourselves. As we approached the camp gate, I noticed a group of people up ahead standing on an APC and looking off into the distance. Some of them had binoculars and were pointing excitedly. The bus stopped when we got to the group and we off-loaded to see what was happening.

The bus driver queried a sergeant standing nearby, "What's up?"

"There's an air strike going on out there, that's what!"

I felt no concussions and couldn't see anything that looked to me like an air strike. "Where is it?" I asked, thinking I must be blind.

"It's right out there," the sergeant said, pointing, "about ten klicks. If you stand on top of the bus, you'll be able to see it."

Ten klicks! These people were excited to be seeing the real war "as close" as ten kilometers away. Us Centaurs looked at each other in disbelief. The slick pilot walked over to the bus driver.

"Let's go. We'd rather see town. We see enough of this kind of stuff every day and it's a hell of a lot closer than this."

The bus driver looked disappointed but answered respectfully, "Whatever you say, sir."

The slick crew had been to town before, and they wanted to get off before my destination. When the bus stopped to let them off, twenty or so Vietnamese kids ranging in age from seven up to fourteen crowded outside the door.

"Ignore these kids," the driver told the slick crew. "They're looking for handouts. Push your way clear once I open the door. Keep an eye on your watches and wallets, too. Some of these little guys are more than beggars."

The door was opened and the kids pushed each other to try

to be the closest to the GIs getting off. The slick's crewmen actually had to push their way through.

The officers' quarters in town turned out to be an old French hotel with very high ceilings and overhead fans. It wasn't cool, but it beat the devil out of being out in the sun. I was assigned a room with Bret Foxthorn, a pilot from a different unit who was also going to armament school. The bathroom had running water, from rain collection cisterns, and a toilet. Compared to hootch living, this was paradise.

Bret and I met with a group of three other pilots and we headed outside the compound to tour the area. It felt very strange to me to be walking around, unarmed, surrounded by so many Vietnamese. Naturally, we had to pay a visit to some of the bars. It was 1400 so the main business day for the bars didn't start for several hours. In fact, we were their only customers. Each bar we walked into was dimly lit and, since it was so bright outside, we couldn't see for a minute. As we entered the first bar, numerous baby-san bargirls instantly congregated around us, enveloping our party. They were shoving each other to get one of the new customers to themselves. Soon, our little group was packed tightly within the mass of groping women. The top of the women's heads reached only to my chest. I felt as if I were in a horror film, surrounded by zombies who were pawing me. We couldn't move freely either toward the bar or back outside. Politeness didn't work. I felt myself getting mad, like when I got shot at, and started pushing back, sometimes hard. That seemed to work. The bargirls got the message and left me alone. I led the way out of the bar with the others following. We repeated this spectacle in two other bars.

The fourth bar we picked was a bit off the beaten path. It was light inside, and we made it to a table without being attacked. Of course, as soon as we sat down, four bargirls came over. Their game was well known anywhere there were "rich" American servicemen. The girls were very friendly. There was little doubt that services beyond lap sitting would be available to those who might wish them. A waiter came over to the table and the girls all ordered whiskey. We all ordered beer. The drinks that arrived for the girls were served in a kind of shot glass. Most times the glass contained tea. The cost for the girls' drinks was astronomical.

The girl who had claimed me wore a tight-fitting halter top and pants that looked like they were painted on her. She climbed onto my lap without my asking and made small talk in broken English, asking where I was from and other questions. She was the first female I'd been close to since I left home, but my reaction was not what I had expected. At best, my emotions and desires were neutral. At worst, they were hostile.

The baby-san made short work of the tea. Her glass was empty in a flash. The waiter reappeared instantly.

"I have whiskey," she told the waiter.

Jesus! What a racket, I thought to myself. Talking to the girl was a little like playing a slot machine. Pay money—watch the tea drain—pay more money. I reached down, turned the shot glass upside down, and said, "No."

"What's the matter, GI? You no like me?"

"You're okay. That's not it."

The girl reached down and turned the shot glass right side up. "Bring whiskey," she said.

I repeated my refusal more strongly. "No!"

The girl whispered her plea in my ear while she stroked my hair with her left hand and placed her right hand on my crotch, "I beaucoup like you. Please buy whiskey. Be numbah-one GI. I be numbah-one girl."

I shook my head no again and moved the little hand away from my gonads. The girl looked at the waiter and shrugged her shoulders. She got down off my lap and walked away. The other guys bought their girls a couple of more teas until they had time to finish their beers. Then we left.

"Hey, Dan," piped one of my new acquaintances, "what

was the problem with that baby-san? She looked cute to me. You real particular, or what?"

"Hell, I don't really know. I guess I'd rather kill 'em than fuck 'em. Besides, I'm really cheap. Paying good dough for that crappy tea pissed me off."

"Speaking of cheap," interjected Bret, "I hear we ought to visit Market Street. Word is, there are some real bargains over there."

We all agreed and set out for Market Street. One of the locals explained that the street we were on ran perpendicular to Market Street and all we needed to do was to keep heading the way we were going to intersect with it. The closer we got to Market Street, the more people there were. Apparently, Market Street was the hub of the community. We allowed ourselves to go with the flow of the pedestrian traffic, figuring they knew where they were going. Soon we turned right and started up Market Street. Contrary to my conception, the street wasn't named "Market Street." It was actually an open-air market where foodstuffs and dry goods were offered for sale on both sides of the street. Open-air shops were placed one right next to the other, and butchered animals were hanging out in the sun. The stench from the hanging meat made the smell of burned bodies seem like perfume. I couldn't stand it. We'd only walked ten yards up the street when we agreed to forget about it. We turned around and quickly retreated from the noxious odors. We didn't go back.

Armament school was interesting. We learned how all the systems worked, including how to troubleshoot electro-hydraulic problems with the weapons turrets. A Marine major in our class seemed to be a regular guy, but compared to us he was an old man. I was curious about the major's motivations.

"Major, how come you're in armament school? Surely

someone of a lower rank will be doing the detail work in your unit."

"That's right. I'm taking this school before Cobra flight school. I want to know the systems well before I start transition training."

"You mean you're not Cobra qualified?"

"That's correct."

"What have you been flying?"

"A-4s."

The A-4 was a fixed-wing jet attack/fighter. I'd certainly have preferred flying it over any helicopter. Incredulous, I had to ask, "Why in the world would you be transitioning into the Cobra?"

"Well, you know how fast jets are. We don't get very intimate with the battle. I want to get closer to the action. I figure the Cobra is a way to do it."

The major was, after all, a real Marine. "You're right about that, sir. I hope you'll be happy with your choice." I suspected he didn't fully understand what he was getting into, but that would be his problem.

School settled into a routine. Bus over to the camp for classes during the day. Bus back to the hotel for dinner. There was a USO-sponsored show each night in the hotel. I'd have a couple of drinks, watch the show, and hit the sack at around 2200. It was a lot less intense than front-line duty, and it was over too soon.

Arriving back at Cu Chi, I went to see the enlisted armament troops who, in theory, worked for me. These guys were older enlisted men who had grown up around helicopter armament, and they really knew their business. I told them if they needed any help with anything to let me know, and then basically left them alone. A couple of weeks later, a Stateside-trained Cobra armament specialist fourth class was assigned to the unit. This guy was well qualified, but he had a problem: He was trying hard to be the CMFIC (chief motherfucker in charge), and I was starting to get complaints from the other troopers. I took some time before a flight to counsel the new specialist about not being such a hard-ass, but I don't think he listened. Two weeks later I came in from a VR mission and was told the new specialist, Green, was dead.

"What happened?" I asked the operations officer.

"Near as we can tell, Sergeant Topsan was working on a jammed grenade launcher. He was holding the hammer back with a screwdriver. The new guy was standing in front of the ship, supervising. Apparently, Topsan told Green to get out of the way, but he didn't listen. The screwdriver slipped, and the grenade fired. The round didn't travel far enough to arm, but the forty-millimeter projectile took out a large part of Green's upper abdomen. He died instantly."

How dumb! Why would anyone, especially an armament specialist, stand in front of a weapon when someone was working on it? There was no answer.

We operated for the rest of my tour without a Cobra armament specialist.

Bill Molnar was an Australian who had been going to school in the United States and, through some means I never quite comprehended, had been drafted into our Army. Not many people seemed to know about it in the States, but the Aussies had their own contingent of troops in Vietnam. Periodically, Bill would somehow get a special shipment of beer from his countrymen, an Aussie Care package. The carton would have the normal markings of an American brewing company on it, but inside would be cans of Australian beer. Bill wouldn't drink American beer. He called it pommie piss.

Bill had taken a lesson from Dean Priest. Bill had a minigun mounted in his LOH's left side. Not the fixed-mount forward-firing kind, this one was mounted so it stuck out the side and could be swiveled in all directions. The utility of the arrangement proved itself over and over, such as when Bill and I were flying a VR mission ten kilometers northwest of Nui Ba Dinh. Bill had been on the deck for twenty minutes and had found several signs of fresh enemy activity before calling with a startling announcement: "Four-four, we just flew over an antiaircraft position! It's fresh, but not manned. We're going back for another look."

I watched the LOH make a large circle to the left and come back over the area he had recently covered, but from the opposite direction. Bill called, "Receiving fire."

Suddenly, pieces of trees and brush were being thrown into the air as Bill's minigunner chewed up the jungle. My copilot opened up with his minigun, adding to the volume of fire concentrated on the emplacement. I rolled into an attack run and launched several pairs of rockets. Bill didn't break off his attack right away. He let his gunner hammer the position before he broke off to the right.

"One-five, 4-4. You okay?"

"Yeah. They never touched us. I'm going back in to see what's left."

Smoke was drifting up through the trees where my rockets had hit. Bill must've figured the sight was obliterated. He headed straight for the emplacement.

"Taking fire!" yelled Bill. Bill rarely yelled. Facing a .51 at point-blank range would have unnerved most anyone.

I banked the Cobra hard right and into a fifty-degree dive angle. I rolled so fast my copilot didn't have time to engage the minigun. Seven or eight pairs of rockets later, I broke out of the run by skimming the treetops.

"One-five, this is 4-4. Where are you?"

"We're over here, two klicks west."

"Roge'. I'm on my way back up to altitude. Think that's enough for one day?"

"Right-o. Let me know when you've got me in sight and I'll join you."

Bill rendezvoused on me and we headed back to Tay Ninh to refuel, rearm, and inspect for damage. We gave the antiaircraft machine-gun position a wide berth on the way back.

Bill flew a few more missions with his souped-up LOH, but he soon made a mistake. At least it was a mistake as far as his flying career went. Bill went to see the flight surgeon about some very infrequent but annoying dizzy spells he'd been having. The flight surgeon didn't think having dizzy pilots up in the air was such a great idea, and Bill was grounded. Not being able to fly was very frustrating for Bill. He never seemed to be his jolly Aussie self after that. Of course, becoming armament pit officer might have had more to do with Bill's attitude than just not flying. It was hard to tell.

★ CHAPTER 26 ★

Bluffing

I stopped in Operations and picked up a Coke to drink on my way to the flight line. By now, my copilot would have finished repreflighting the ship we'd flown the night before. I was going out to do my normal double check on the ship's condition but I met my copilot walking back to Ops from the flight line.

"What's up?" I asked.

"May as well turn around," he said. "We need another ship."

"How come?"

"Actually, it'd be better for you to see why for yourself. I didn't believe it. Go take a look at the forward section of the tail boom on 727."

I walked down the left side of the Corral to the ship and around to the left side of the tail boom. The underside of the boom had one bullet hole in it. The half-tube sheet metal cover for the tail rotor driveshaft was blossomed out the top where the bullet had passed through from bottom to top. I twisted the quick-disconnect fasteners to the left and opened the cover. The tail rotor driveshaft wasn't one long two-inch-diameter tube. It was made of several sections of tube coupled together. The bullet had come through the ship where two sections joined together. The nut on the section connection clamp bolt had one of its sides shaved off. I could see the bolt threads inside what was left of the nut. Remembering that the tail rotor shaft was spinning while the Cobra was in flight, considering the Cobra's speed, the fact that its last mission was at night, and the comparatively minute size of the bullet as well as the coupling nut, the odds of this having happened were astronomical. If the bullet had been a quarter of an inch closer to the center of the bolt, the Cobra would have lost tail rotor thrust for sure. Depending on how the severed driveshaft would have flailed around, things could have gotten even worse than that. Were we unlucky to have been hit, or lucky the drive-shaft hadn't severed? Maybe the answer was both. My copilot came over to the ship just then.

"We've drawn 825," he said.

"Guess it wasn't our time to go last night," I said.

"I think fate merely wanted to give us a scare," he said.

We both preflighted our new ship, looking carefully for stray bullet holes.

To my surprise and elation, the troop designated me as a qualified fire-team leader. I had noticed that, within the Centaurs, that level of responsibility had normally been reserved for the commissioned officers—and captains at that. During field operations, the fire-team leader was air mission commander. Although the new responsibility weighed on my subconscious, I resolved to do my duties with as much skill as I could muster. One of the things dif-

ferent about being fire-team leader was that I got to deter-
mine tactics for each situation. The wingman provided support as directed, but the fire-team leader made the decisions
about how and when to employ the weaponry at his dis-
posal. My Vung Tau roommate, Bret, had introduced me to
a tactic his unit used.

"We take two Cobras and a slick with a zeon searchlight
to look for bad guys. The slick orbits at altitude and illu-
minates the ground. One of the two Cobras, the mouse,
flies around inside the light. He looks for bad guys, but, of
course, they can see him quite readily, too. The other
Cobra orbits outside the light at an altitude between the
slick and the mouse. If the mouse finds anything worth
shooting, or gets shot at, the second Cobra provides the
response firepower."

"We don't do anything like that," I said. "In fact, I'm sure
if we did, we'd lose a Cobra each night we went out. Either
the terrain or Charlie would be sure to get 'em."

"That's peculiar. Even though it makes me nervous as
hell, the tactic works great for us."

"I guess the way we have to fly to survive is as different
from region to region as the regions themselves are."

That was all the tactics Bret and I ever discussed, but there
was a valuable lesson even in that one brief exchange: Use
what works and screw anything else.

Sometimes tactical doctrine had to give way to the situation. That's what happened one day when I was the fire-team
leader and some LRRPs called for extraction. I had been the
team leader that inserted the LRRPs on their mission two
days before. I scrambled out of the Corral and headed to the
landing zone with my wingman close behind and the extraction slicks right behind us. I called to the LRRPs as we got
within range.

"Fox 3-5, this is Centaur 4-4 en route your location."

A barely audible voice whispered over the radio, "Four-
four, this is 3-5. We're at the same drop-off location from

yesterday. Be advised, bad guys very close, but they don't know we're here."

I flew on a few more minutes until we were almost on station. The LRRP keyed his microphone and I could hear shooting in the background. There was no whispering now. "Four-four, 3-5. Need help! We've been detected. Had to pop our claymores already."

There was very little time to take action. Since I remembered exactly where the LRRPs were to have dug in, I decided to risk shooting without having them identify their location. "Three-five, where do you want rockets?"

"Four-four, 3-5. Put 'em ten meters north. Hurry. We're having trouble holding them back."

This was a dicey proposition. Ten meters was the theoretical kill radius for our rockets. The LRRPs were calling down fire virtually on top of themselves. "Three-five, confirm. Only ten meters north?"

"That's affirm. Do it!"

"Four-five, this is 4-4. Runs will be west to east with left breaks. I'll be taking it down lower than normal. Keep your fire twenty meters to the north of mine."

"Four-four, 4-5's got you covered."

I rolled the ship right and into a steep dive. I lined up on the large tree I remembered as having been next to the LRRPs. Then I made a small correction to the left. I waited until I was down to 1,100 feet before I fired the first pair of rockets. They leapt for the ground and exploded close to where I had aimed. I waited a few seconds with my heart in my throat before firing the next pair. But there was no "Cease fire" call from the LRRPs, so I fired several more pairs. At 500 feet I broke hard left. My gunner opened up on the area below us, and my wingman's rockets impacted under us as I coaxed the Cobra to grab altitude. The next time the LRRP called, he seemed to be under a little less stress: "Good job, 4-4. Put the next series ten meters more to the north and west."

I was exhilarated. I'd done what the grunts needed. It was one of the most satisfying experiences I ever had while flying.

There was a briefing for all Cobra pilots that evening. It was called and conducted by the CO. "Settle down, gentlemen," he said. "I know you've already put in a long day, so I'll keep this as brief as possible. Simply put, we've got a problem. From now on, if you're on a VR, don't fire more than two pairs of rockets. Any questions?"

Someone in the back of the room wanted clarification to this basically illogical order. "Sir?"

"Yes, go ahead."

"Does this mean even if the LOH takes fire?"

"That's affirmative."

"I don't get it," said someone else. "How are we expected to do the job right with that kind of restriction?"

"Don't ask me," said the CO. "I'm passing down orders the way I received them, but I can tell you this. There seems to be a shortage of rockets. If we use them up on VRs, then when some outfit is in heavy contact we'll not be able to support them. Do the best you can with this. That's all."

Grumbling broke out in the small crowd. The CO scanned the audience for any more questions and, finding none, dismissed us. Privately, I resolved that I'd use whatever rockets were necessary if a LOH took fire. There was no way I expected a LOH crew to take the risks they took without committing to as much support as they might need. I did, however, operate my VRs without using rockets except in the case where the LOH took fire. My LOH pilot partners thought the compromise was wise.

Compromise wasn't one of Dean Priest's operating modes, and somehow my own fate seemed to become intertwined with Dean's for a period of time. My fire team had been scrambled to support a ground unit south of Tay Ninh. The grunts had run into a fairly heavy concentration of the enemy.

"Fox 3-8, this is Centaur 4-4, on station."

"Roger, 4-4. We're taking fire from our west, about one hundred meters out. See what you can do."

I led the team in two rocket attack runs and was rolling into a third when the ground troops changed their minds. "Four-four, this is 3-8. Now we're getting fire from the north and south."

I looked at the troops in their defensive lines. Bullet strikes could be seen hitting the ground around some of them. The firing seemed intense. There was no way my one fire team was going to take care of all the area surrounding the troops for very long. I changed radio transmitters.

"Centaur Ops, this is 4-4," I said.

"Go ahead, 4-4."

"Better scramble the number-two team. We'll be out of ammo here in short order and I don't think Fox 3-8 will be done needing support."

"Wilco, 4-4. Out."

Switching back to talk to the troops, I called to them: "Three-eight, I've got plenty of ordnance left. What target is priority?"

"I don't know what to say. I think we're surrou—"

Three explosions sounded over the keyed radio microphone. I looked down. Black smoke was rising from inside the troop perimeter.

"Four-four, we're taking mortars from our east now. Do something!"

I called my wingman. "Four-two, you fly east on the south side of the troops and circle left. I'll start on the north side and circle right. Hose down any likely hiding places with the miniguns and grenade launchers. Join up with me on the eastern side of the troops."

"Wilco, 4-4."

"Ready, break."

As the ground troops passed by my three o'clock position, and my gunner was tearing up the area, I looked over to find

4-2. He was at my exact opposite position, and a trail of grenade bursts was exploding underneath his flight path. On the other side of the troops, 4-2 fell in behind me. "Follow me, 4-2," I said. I dove and launched a rocket attack on the troops' eastern side, allowing the rockets to spread along my flight path. When I broke off the run I pulled up but didn't turn left or right. My gunner hosed down the area with the minigun, and my wingman copied my strike. As he began his break, I rolled left onto an attack on the north side of the troops. I continued this "pull-up, turn left, and hit the next flank" sequence, until we were out of rockets. Then we worked the area over with grenades and minigun fire until we were out of ammo for them, too. That's when Dean Priest called.

"Centaur 4-4, this is 2-8."

"Go ahead, 2-8."

"I'm inbound your position on a medevac extraction. How about some cover?"

The ground troops must have called for the medevac on a different radio frequency. It would have been nice to know a medevac was going to happen before we had expended all our ordnance! I checked to see the status of the number-two team. "Number two Centaurs, you up yet?"

"That's a roge', 4-4. Four-one ETA your location fifteen minutes."

Fifteen minutes might be an eternity for somebody wounded on the ground. "Fox 3-8, this is 4-4. You still taking fire and can your wounded wait fifteen minutes?"

"Affirmative on the fire, but it's lessened considerably. Negative on the waiting. We got two hurt real bad."

That's what I had been afraid of.

"Two-eight, this is 4-4. You been listening to the troops?"

"Four-four, that's affirm."

"Four-four's team is out of ammo. If you're willing to try, we'll escort you into the LZ with low passes, or you can wait fifteen minutes for 4-1. It's your call."

Dean didn't even hesitate. "Let's do it now," he said.

I took the empty Cobra fire team toward the south, where I saw Dean already starting to go low-level, which would minimize his exposure.

"Fox 3-8, pop smoke," Dean called.

Thirty seconds later he identified the location. "Two-eight's got yellow smoke."

"Affirm, yellow," called the troopers.

"Four-two, 4-4. You take the right side, I'll take the left. Roll in a few seconds behind me." Four-two clicked his microphone twice.

When Dean was within 100 yards of the LZ, I rolled in, pretending I had rockets. The gooks didn't know we were empty. At least, I hoped they didn't know.

"Two-eight's taking fire," Dean called calmly.

I held the dive until the last minute and broke out in a left turn, skimming over the trees. As the ship turned through ninety degrees, I looked back over my left shoulder and saw 4-2 reaching the bottom of his run. I didn't climb, but rather made one big circle to the left, keeping up my speed. I figured the noise might keep Chuck's head down. Then, as I turned through a northerly heading, I made a maximum-effort climb. I had reached 1,000 feet when Dean called.

"Two-eight's coming out the same way we came in."

I clicked the microphone twice and rolled the ship hard right and into a pretend run. I caught up to Dean at the bottom of my run. As I flew past him, I circled my ship to the right. By the time I'd made a full circle, Dean was out of the danger zone. Two severely wounded soldiers were on their way to the hospital.

Back at the base, I ran into Dean in the ops shack. "Thanks for the assist today," he said.

"Glad it worked out for both of us."

"Yeah, me too. You know, I have to fly a Nighthawk mission tonight, and my normal copilot has flown too many hours. I think I'll request you to fly with me."

I thought Dean was pulling my leg. I didn't have the slightest desire to accompany him as his copilot on one of his nightly outings. "Yeah, right," I said mockingly. "I'd make a terrific copilot for you. I haven't even been in a slick for seven months."

Dean hadn't been kidding. The Cobra platoon leader came to visit me in my hootch.

"Spalding, you're off number one as of now. Priest needs a copilot tonight, and he wants you. Go see how the other half lives."

I hoped my lack of enthusiasm wasn't too obvious when I answered, "Yes, sir."

I met Dean at his ship as the sun was setting. We climbed in and took off. Dean sat on the left side of the ship, rather than the right side, as would be normal. Since the minigun and the searchlight were on the left, Dean said he could do a better job of flying and spotting targets that way.

"You want to fly?" Dean asked.

"Sure."

"Okay, you got the aircraft. Try not to crash."

I took the controls and continued to climb out. Compared to the Cobra, the ship felt extremely slow and the controls were real sloppy, but it wasn't long before I was flying tolerably.

"Where are we headed, Dean?"

"Tay Ninh."

"Oh, great. One of my favorite places."

I shot an approach to the POL. It wasn't precise, but it was safe. After we refueled, Dean flew us around to the VIP pad and shut down the aircraft.

"We're supposed to pick up a cover ship here," he explained.

"A cover ship? I thought you worked by yourself on these missions."

"Most of the time that's true, but tonight we're going up into the Elephant Ear. I thought some cover might be a good idea."

I agreed wholeheartedly. Dean was a bit of a wildman, but he wasn't totally crazy. This thought was a little comforting, considering where we were going and what we were going to do that night. We met the pilot and copilot of the 1st Air Cavalry's Blue Max Cobra in the TOC. The aircraft commander was a warrant officer. He had a dark complexion, a heavy shadow beard, and a flattop haircut. He seemed to be an okay guy, but, to me, he moved slowly for a Cobra jock. We briefed ourselves on what the plan was going to be, went out to the ships, cranked up, and took off for the Elephant Ear.

"Dan, you've got one overriding assignment if we take fire. See the circuit breaker with the safety ring over your left shoulder?"

I looked up and touched the jerry rigged ring of silver metal running through the circuit breaker. On the Nighthawk ship, a lot of things were nonstandard. The silver ring was just one of them. "Yes, I see it."

"If we take fire, pull the breaker, pronto."

"Sure will. What's it control?"

"That's the nav position lights."

"You mean we're going to cruise around with our lights on?"

"Yep. Doesn't matter, really. The zeon light makes us a great target anyway, and the position lights help the Cobra keep us in sight."

The operation was sounding more harebrained to me all the time. When we got into the pitch-black area that was the Elephant Ear, Dean and his crew went into their routine. Dean lowered the ship to within 100 feet of the trees, slowed down to twenty knots, and circled over the woods with the light on. We were sitting ducks! It was hard to believe Dean got away with this night after night. Looking past Dean to the jungle, it was amazing how well things could be seen in the brilliance of the searchlight. The crew could widen or narrow the beam at their discretion. We'd been looking things over for five or ten minutes when our Blue Max cover called to us matter-of-factly, "You're taking fire from your rear."

Quickly, I reached up and pulled the position lights circuit breaker. The crewman on the searchlight doused it immediately. Dean rolled right out of his left turn, put the nose down, and pulled in a lot of collective pitch to exit the area as fast as the slick would go. Behind us, the explosions of Blue Max's rockets sent concussions through the floorboards.

Thirty seconds later, the Cobra driver called us, "I'm back to altitude and I've got you in sight." Now, I knew a little about how LOH crews felt about their cover ships. I was real glad he was up there behind us.

"Roge'," called Dean. "I'm going back in to see what we got." Dean maneuvered back into the area. As soon as the light was turned on, we took fire. This time we could see the sparkling muzzle flashes ourselves. Dean ran the slick out fast. Dean was a savvy pilot. He knew the limitations of the ship he was flying. In "Indian country," Dean let the Cobra do the work.

"So, Spalding. What do you think?"

"I don't think I'm right for this mission. That's what."

"How so?"

"You know how you instinctively move in the right direction to keep from getting shot up?"

"Yeahhh?"

"My instinct isn't to turn off the lights and beat feet. My instinct is to roll in on the target. I think that would get us killed."

"Probably would, at that, probably would."

One of the slick's crew members chimed in. "Let's hope Mr. Priest doesn't get hit tonight. I don't think we want Mr. Spalding flying the mission."

"Roger that!" said the other gunner.

A week later I ran into Popov in the mess hall. We sat down to eat lunch together.

"You hear what happened on Dean's mission last night?" Popov asked.

"No. What?"

"He was flying in the Elephant Ear again. The Blue Max Cobra he'd been working with all this time called him in the middle of the mission and said he thought his tail rotor had come off the ship. They crashed in a big fireball. Dean and his crew tried to get to them, but there was no place to land. Both pilots died. They pulled them out this morning. There wasn't much left."

"That's too bad. I met the Cobra guys once. They seemed okay. You know, that's the third time I've heard of someone losing the tail rotor on a Cobra since I've been in-country. I read about a problem with them before I ever enlisted in the Army. I think it had something to do with our missions overstressing the tail rotor gearbox. What I heard was, if the tail rotor comes completely off, the center of gravity moves so far forward that the nose drops way down and the main rotor breaks off the ship. Then you're a streamlined rock."

"I've heard that, too. I spend a good deal of time checking the tail rotor on my preflights in the hope that whatever the problem is it would be noticeable."

I'd always thought that whatever was going wrong would show up on a preflight, but the more I reflected on Popov's idea that it might not, the more sense it made. It made no sense to think that all the guys who were buying the farm didn't know how to do a preflight. Still, I redoubled my own inspection efforts.

A month after the Blue Max Cobra plowed into the ground, the bad guys attacked the fort on top of Nui Ba Dinh. This happened occasionally. Our listening post on the top of the highest terrain around was a real thorn in the enemy's side. Every so often he'd try to do something about it. My fire team was called out to provide support for troops pursuing the enemy on the mountain. I arrived on station and located the troops. A group of tanks was lined abreast at the base of the mountain. A company of infantry were scaling the mountain. They were about 1,000 feet up. Several weeks earlier, during some previous enemy attacks, B-52 raids had been made on the mountain's western and northern faces. The raids had turned this part of the mountain into a giant, slate-gray gravel pile. Of course, what looked to me at my altitude like gravel was really quite large granite boulders. It was slow going for the troops, and the boulders provided plenty of cover for the enemy.

When I talked to the ground troops, their problem became evident. The tanks could no longer elevate their guns enough to provide direct-fire support. The troops were taking sporadic fire and were preparing to assault a set of cave entrances 100 meters above them.

"Four-four, be advised," said Fox 3-2, "gooks got a single fifty-one up above us somewhere, too. They took some shots at the C & C ship."

"Three-two, this is 4-4. Thanks for the warning."

I called to my wingman, "Four-seven, this is 4-4. I've never known anyone who made runs on this mountain, but here's the way we're going to do it. A normal dive attack would be ineffective for trying to get at the caves. I'll fly level toward the caves, you stay one thousand feet over and behind me. I'll get close to the mountain. You hang back at a greater distance."

"Sounds okay to me," said 4-7. "But how are you going to break off the run? You won't have much speed, and as you turn away from the mountain, you'll be a sitting duck."

I started my attack run. "Just watch," I said. "Hold your fire," I told my copilot. "If you shoot, all the brass will fall on our troops. We'll be directly over them."

Firing rockets from a level attitude was different. My

first pair struck low from my aim point. I made a little climb and tried again. That did it. My rockets were going where they were supposed to. The explosions looked puny compared to nature's huge creation. Whether or not the rockets had any effect on the surrounding granite was a matter for a debate I didn't have time for. I fired several more pairs until the mountainside filled my entire field of vision. I began to see the small cave entrances clearly. I fired several more pairs trying unsuccessfully to get them to fly into the caves.

My copilot's normal attack dive duties of calling out knots of speed or feet of altitude were inappropriate, but as the mountain loomed he improvised. "Aren't we getting too close?" he asked.

I rolled the Cobra hard left until it was partly inverted. Then I pulled the nose under and added a lot of collective to keep positive-g on the ship. The Cobra arced down through the air. The lower part of the mountain filled my area of vision out of the canopy and, in relation to our screaming dive, apparently rose rapidly to meet us. The ship continued through the back side of the loop. We shot past the ground troops and then the tanks. We were fifty feet over their heads. The tankers, standing in their hatches, looked up at us as we zipped by. One of them waved, and one gave us a thumbs-up. As I got away from the mountain, I started my climb back for another run.

Reassuringly, the radio crackled, "Four-four, 4-7's got you in sight."

"Four-four's on the way back to altitude for another run. What'd you think?"

"I can cover you okay, but don't get so close. For a second, I thought you were going to crash."

"So did I," quipped my copilot.

I ignored my wingman's advice. It was necessary to get in close to do any good for the grunts. My copilot, like me before him, had no choice but to go along for the ride.

★ CHAPTER 27 ★

Rest, Relaxation—Explosion

It was time for R & R. My wife and I were going to Hawaii. JoAnn had made reservations for us at the Hilton Hawaiian Village. We were able to get reduced rates because of my military status. While I was winging my way east, JoAnn was on her way west. It was her first trip on airplanes. One of the stewardesses stopped to chat.

"I really like your outfit."

"Thanks."

"You meeting someone in Hawaii?"

"Yes, my husband. He's getting R & R from Vietnam."

"I thought that might be it. These days, we're carrying a lot of people who are doing the same thing. In fact, this trip is probably made up of a lot of women just like you."

"I need to visit the ladies' room. Where is it?"

"Walk back to the rear of the plane. You'll see it back there."

JoAnn stood up and walked unsteadily down the aisle toward the rear of the plane. She'd had a couple of drinks. That, combined with the altitude, made her tipsy. JoAnn felt good. She was wearing a tight fitting orange-red minidress complemented by leg-hugging white patent leather go-go boots. People couldn't help but watch her shaky trip to the rear of the plane.

Two thirds of the way back, JoAnn found what looked to her like the bathroom door. She stepped to her right, turned to face the door, and began to try to turn the handle. It didn't budge. Continuing to pull on the handle, she turned her head over her right shoulder and cheerily asked the man in the seat opposite the door, "Hey, mister, can you give me a hand with this?" Looking over to see what was going on, the man opened his eyes wide and pulled his head back in surprise. JoAnn was pulling on the emergency door handle! The man didn't say anything but excitedly waved for a stewardess.

"What are you doing, ma'am?" asked the stew.

"I'm trying to get into the bathroom."

The stew grinned broadly. "Well, if you get that door open I think you may have a bigger problem than using the bathroom. That's the way to the outside, not to the toilet."

Suddenly scared, JoAnn quit pulling and stepped back briskly. "If I'd gotten that thing open, would I have been sucked out?" she asked.

"Don't worry, hon. You couldn't get it open. The bathroom's further back. It's marked 'Lavatory.' "

R & R was a blur. At the airport, we were briefed that there were a lot of spies all around the islands and we should keep our mouths shut about operational details. Then we boarded buses for the trip to the receiving station. I was the first person off the bus. I was walking briskly up a wide ramp, heading for a couple of large double doors, when someone "attacked" me from my right. JoAnn threw her arms around me and gave me a big kiss. The other guys were walking by us looking for their own spouses. In the cab, on the way to the hotel, it felt like we were strangers, but that was soon rectified. The first few days we called room service a lot. There was a horrendous amount of lovemaking going on. I spent ten days in Hawaii and never even put a toe in the Pacific Ocean. In later years, I'd relate to our friends that no woman could have survived the experience without getting pregnant. JoAnn was no exception.

On the next to the last day we flew to the Big Island, Hawaii. We drove around the island to see Volcano

National Park. At the national park boundary the road became deserted. I wound my way along the seven miles of two-lane road that snaked up to the volcano. At the top, we found out why there weren't any other cars. The road was blocked by a black, crunchy-looking lava flow that was still cooling off.

The plane trip back to Oahu was rough. We flew in a Convair 880 propjet and got bumped around a lot. That's when I found out JoAnn was terrified to fly. Until we landed she busied herself by holding on tight, crying, and jumping with each turbulent bounce of the plane. I knew a lot of pilots who were married to women who were afraid to fly. A strange coincidence.

I made reservations to eat in a rotating restaurant at the top of a skyscraper. It was supposed to be very romantic. It was very civilized. Not at all the kind of place Cobra pilots from Vietnam were accustomed to. The waiter was dressed in a tuxedo.

"What can I do for you this evening, sir?" he asked.

"I'd like to start with a Mai Tai. What do you want, hon?"

"I'll have a Bloody Mary, please."

"I'm sorry," said the waiter, looking at JoAnn, "but I'll need to see your ID before I can serve you."

To me, this request had an unreal quality to it. In only a few hours I was going to be back on a plane headed for the risks of war, and this guy wanted to see our IDs.

"Look," I said, "I'm twenty. My wife's birthday was two days ago. She's nineteen. I'm on my way back to Vietnam tomorrow. What's the problem?"

"Well, sir, the problem is, the drinking age in Hawaii is twenty. I can't serve your wife. I'm sure you under—"

I was starting to get angry, like it was time to kill someone. "No, I don't—"

JoAnn grasped my hand, squeezed it to bring me closer to

the real world, and interjected, "That's okay, babe. Don't worry about it. Bring me a Virgin Mary."

"Yes, ma'am. That will do fine. Thank you."

The next day was difficult for both of us. We tried pretending the time for my departure wouldn't arrive. We made love one last time. I rested for an hour and then it was time. JoAnn stayed in the bed. We thought it would be easier for her not to see me off at the airport. She started crying and didn't seem to be able to stop. Continuing to get ready to go while JoAnn was having such a hard time was emotionally trying, but I had no choice. JoAnn was still crying when I closed the hotel door behind me for the last time.

My flight back stopped in Guam for refueling. We stretched our legs for an hour. Guam was the huge Air Force base where the B-52s that supported us were based. Their large camouflaged triangular tails stuck up from behind the fence that separated them from our side of the base. There seemed to be hundreds of them.

"Look down at the end of the runway," said one of the guys. "What kind of a plane is that?"

Peering into the distance, I could barely make out a shape I'd never seen except in artistic renditions. The plane sat low to the ground, was black, had a very pointed nose, and the vertical tail surfaces were inclined inward toward the center of the plane.

"That's the YF-12A," I said. "It's the fastest airplane in the world. They use it for reconnaissance."

"I think it's been redesignated the SR-71," someone else said.

"Sure hope it takes off before we have to leave."

The plane sat there for a long time. We saw the Blackbird's jets start. Soon the plane was speeding down the runway on its takeoff roll. The nose of the ship came up and it lifted into the air. The pilot smoothly pulled the nose up into what looked like at least a sixty-degree climb. The roar of the engines rumbled across the field to us. Twenty seconds later, the plane was out of sight.

"All the waiting must have been to get everyone out of the way," I quipped.

We boarded the DC-8 for the last leg of the trip to "Disneyland East." I was sitting in a window seat two rows behind the leading edge of the wing. The pilot turned onto the runway at its very end. Power was added to the engines in a smooth but deliberate fashion, and the big plane began to lumber down the runway. We were very full of fuel, troops, and baggage. The plane accelerated slowly. I watched the side of the runway moving to our rear at increasing speed. Then the left inboard engine caught fire! The whole compressor section flew out the front of the engine compartment! A piece slammed into the fuselage between my window and the window in front of me. The compressor struck the ground, throwing off pieces. The remains darted off the left side of the runway like a wheel that had come off a car at high speed. Flames leapt from the engine cowling and licked upward. The pilot applied heavy braking, throwing us forward in our seats. The plane stopped. I heard the firebell ring loudly in the cockpit. I couldn't help thinking of the irony. I was going to burn up on a pleasure trip. I wished I had on my flight suit. I stood up to start for the door. The flight engineer came running back, telling everyone to sit down. They had the fire out. We were to wait patiently. After being towed back to the ramp and off-loading, the officers were taken to the bachelor officers' quarters. At first, we were told that we'd be leaving the next day after they flew in a replacement engine, but it turned out that all four engines were damaged in the incident. Then the plan became to fly us out on another flight the second day. It rained, and rained, and rained some more. The runway flooded and the relief ship couldn't land until the third day. As the three days passed slowly, we tried to amuse ourselves. It took only an hour to drive around the whole island. We spent some of the time figuring out what a person from Guam might rightly be called. Guamites, Guamitos, Guamanians, Guamies, and Guamos were all suggested. Naturally, I arrived at my unit three days late. I walked into the operations shack to check in.

"Where the hell have you been?" asked the ops officer. "We were thinking about filing an AWOL report on you."

"Gee, thanks for the vote of confidence. Weren't you guys notified by MATS about our little trouble on Guam?"

"Nobody told us anything."

"They said they were notifying our units. Guess they lied. Anyway, the left main engine on our jet had a catastrophic turbine failure on takeoff. We spent three extra days in Guam. The engine blowing up was the only exciting thing that happened in those three days. Hope I don't ever get to see another one, though. It was spectacular. Flames and pieces of engine flew everywhere."

"I'll tell the old man. He may want to check it out further."

"Be my guest. Anything new around here?"

"Not really. Same old shit."

"I'm beat. See you later."

I walked to my hootch, unpacked my bags, and got dressed in my fatigues. Then I walked back to Operations to check the duty roster. It hadn't taken them long. I was number-one gun team leader that night. Hawaii quickly became a dim remembrance. In fact, to do my job, it was important to forget about it.

★ CHAPTER 28 ★

Business as Usual

I stripped off my flight suit and hung it across my chair. Next, I unlaced my heavy combat boots, took them off, and stored them under my bunk. I was off duty for the afternoon, and I planned to take full advantage of the precious time by relaxing in the shade of the hootch with a fan blowing air over me. Because of the unrelenting humidity, removing my flight suit didn't exactly make me cool. Nevertheless, it did feel good to leave my shirt off, put on a pair of cutoff jungle fatigues, and slip some flip-flops on my feet. My hootch-mates were apparently all on missions. Except for me, the hootch was empty. The relative quiet worked like a tonic to help me wind down from the day's tension. I walked into our hootch common area and opened the refrigerator to get a soda. There were none. Maybe hootch-5 had some. I walked through the doorway to cross the twenty feet between the two hootches. The sun baked into my back as soon as I cleared the door. My flip-flops clippity-clopped on my heels as I made my way over the boardwalk to the midpoint between the hootches. *Whoooosh!*

The loud gravel-grating sound of a rocket flying low and directly over my head snapped me out of my relaxation! I dropped onto the boardwalk, hitting my chin. I fought off the adrenaline-primed urge to get up and run. Unfortunately, there was nothing I could do about the pounding of my heart. Almost immediately, there was a huge explosion fifty yards to my left. I waited for more explosions, hoping

they would be at least as far away as the last one. Lying
prone, I still felt like I was a target with a bull's-eye painted
on it. If I could, I would have pressed my body down harder
and physically merged it into the boardwalk. Thirty seconds
of slow-motion time passed like molasses flowing in January. There were no more explosions. My heart rate began to
return to normal. I stood up, brushed the dirt off my bare
front, and strolled into hootch-5. A lone occupant was sitting in the shadows of the hootch's far corner. "You got a
soda I can have?" I asked.

"Sure," said Charlie Riggs, motioning to his refrigerator.
"Help yourself. That one was kind of close, wasn't it?"

I took the few steps to the refrigerator, opened its door,
bent forward, and peered in to find a drink. "Damn straight!"
I said. "I think they were aiming for my head."

Charlie didn't seem to me to be properly sympathetic.
"Better you than me," he said.

I closed the refrigerator and started out of the hootch. Had
our roles been reversed I might had said the same thing.
Riggs intuitively knew that. "Screw you, Riggs. By the way,
thanks for the soda."

The next time I saw Riggs, we were walking in opposite
directions. I was on my way to the flight line for a VR mission and Riggs was on his way to Ops.

"Where you headed, Spalding?" he asked.

"I'm on my way out to Parrot's Beak for a VR. Where's
727 parked?"

"It's on the north side, two revetments down. I flew it this
morning. There was something wrong with it. I turned it in
to Maintenance. Guess they got it fixed."

"Yeah. What was the 'something' you thought was wrong
with it, anyway?"

"I couldn't put a precise name to it. It felt like it had some
kind of intermittent vibration, but it was faint and elusive. Be
a little wary with it."

I turned and started for the flight line. "Sure will. See you later. Thanks for the update."

Charlie waved and started off in the opposite direction. My copilot had completed his preflight of 727. I spot-checked the tail rotor and the main rotor. Everything seemed to be okay. The logbook showed Maintenance's entry from Riggs's gig that morning. It read "No problem found." That in itself wasn't too unusual. Some problems seemed to hide from us. As soon as they were reported to the maintenance crews, they'd go away. We started the ship and I took off behind our assigned hunter LOH. We climbed out straight ahead and then turned left out of the traffic pattern. As I applied right cyclic to roll to a level attitude, the ship shook with a vertical vibration that was in sync with the main rotor rpm. It wasn't subtle. It felt a little like riding on a hobby horse. I called the LOH: "Centaur 1-5, this is 4-4. I may have a problem."

"Roge', 4-4. We'll swing around to keep you in sight."

"I got a significant vibration when I rolled right. I want to play with the ship a little before we get too far away."

"Roger that."

It was comforting to be close to the base and to have 1-5 watching. If we went down, at least we'd be picked up. I tried rolling left, fast. No problem. However, no matter how fast or slowly I rolled to the right, the phantom lopping would occur. There seemed to be no correlation with forward speed or power setting. After some time experimenting, the mere knowledge of the vibration's character made it seem less threatening. "One-five, 4-4. I think we're okay."

"You sure?"

"Not really, but Maintenance already looked at this bird this morning and couldn't find anything wrong. If we don't go now, it'll get too late for the mission. Let's do it."

"You're the boss."

I flew 727 a few more times on my tour. The phantom

problem reappeared so I only made left turns. It wasn't convenient, but it seemed to be the prudent thing to do.

A week or so later, Riggs and I were playing poker with three new guys. We were crowded around our three-foot-square coffee table. Water condensed from the air rapidly onto our cool drinks. We had to keep mopping up the water to keep the cards from getting wet. It was an hour after sunset, and the daytime heat was beginning to wane. The oscillating fan in the corner opposite my seat was aimed to blow air directly on each of us. Each small burst of air was a relief. I was sitting in a chair with my back to the hootch door, which was a couple of feet away. The door squeaked and someone stepped into the hootch. I didn't hear the door close. Before I could look up to see who it was, a hand shot by my right cheek. The hand reached the table corner closest to me and set down an old-fashioned pineapple-style hand grenade. All poker action immediately stopped. I watched in shocked disbelief as the hand released its grip on the lethal ball. With its characteristic *ping*, the spring-loaded safety handle flew up and off. Immediately, as the primer fuse lit, the loud sound of a match being struck filled the now ghostly quiet room. We had five seconds before the explosion. I yelled "Grenade!" Contrary to Hollywood style, none of us jumped on the compact spheroid of steel and explosive that would blow us apart. We all scrambled to get the hell out of range! I took three giant steps into my room, dove under my bunk, crawled through the hole in the wall into my bunker, covered my head, and waited for the concussion that was sure to follow. It never came. The grenade was a dummy. Someone had played a combat joke on us. We never found out who. It was a good thing for the jokester.

Like Cu Chi, Tay Ninh had a runway for fixed-wing airplanes. Tay Ninh's runway was quite long and could accommodate fighters. Normally, we never used runways. We made our landing approaches to various helipads located throughout the bases. Because the VIP pad at Tay Ninh was only thirty yards from the TOC, we used it a lot. The VIP pad was located one hundred yards to the north of the runway. When we were parked facing south, we had a good view of any airplanes that were landing or taking off.

One day, I was landing my fire team at the VIP pad after several hours of providing close air support to some ground troops in a convoy that had been ambushed. Having flown a lot the night before, we were all a little groggy. Actually, "numb" would be a better description.

My earphones crackled with an inbound radio call: "Tay Ninh tower, this is Ramrod 4. Request fly-by permission."

"Ramrod 4, say aircraft type."

"Ah . . . we're an F-4."

"Ramrod 4 is clear for a low pass."

Some Air Force guy was all worked up over the great mission he'd just flown. We were fifty feet in the air and my approach was going smoothly. I figured my copilot might like to see the little show that was about to happen. "Joe, watch off to our right over the runway," I said.

"What for?"

"I think you'll enjoy it. Some jet jock's going to make a low pass. There's usually more to it than that, but they never request 'Permission to show off.' "

I saw the smoke from the F-4's two engines headed our way. In a flash, the ship was skimming over the runway. Then it pulled up slightly and into a victory roll. The roll was followed by a loop. The thunder from the jet's engines could be felt inside our own cockpit. It was spectacular. What power they had compared to us! I had reached the VIP pad and was hovering over it to park.

"Ramrod 4, you're clear to land," called the tower. "Thanks for the show."

I pedal-turned the ship to face the runway and set it down.

I let the engine run and left the radio on. The F-4 was now on short final for landing on the runway.

"Joe, I'm going to check this F-4 driver's situational awareness," I said.

The F-4 touched down at the end of the runway. Its nose-wheel touched, and the pilot was braking hard as he reached a position exactly opposite our nose. I keyed the microphone and growled, sounding as much like a minigun as I could, "BRAAAAAP."

Instantly the F-4 pilot answered, "Got me that time, Centaurs. Guess I'm dead now."

The tower chimed in, trying to be serious, but I could hear the guys laughing in the background. "Now, now, boys. Let's not tie up the airways with useless chitchat."

Later, another mission completed, I landed in the Corral. I hovered the ship into its revetment and shut down the engine. After the rotor stopped, I tried to cycle the collective pitch lever through its full range of travel. The Cobra's hydraulic accumulator was our last-chance emergency backup device for retaining collective pitch control in the event of hydraulic pump failures. After each flight, we'd move the collective up and down to check accumulator operations. Five full strokes of the collective indicated a properly operating accumulator. When I pulled up on the collective this time, it wouldn't budge. "Joe, this bird's got an accumulator failure," I said. "Mark it in the log and tell Maintenance."

"Roger that," said Joe.

I grabbed my gear and headed for Operations to fill out the after-action reports.

I told the Ops officer that 725 was down. "I think it's got an accumulator failure."

"Okay." The Ops officer took out a grease pencil and made a red *X* in the aircraft status box. "You've got a VR mission to fly in an hour. I'll get you another ship."

"Thanks. When Joe comes in, let him know what ship you're giving us, will you?"

"You bet."

I walked to the hootch, plopped onto the common room's sofa, watched half an hour of television, and drank some ice tea. Then it was time to get back to it. I walked to the flight line, looking for Joe, who would no doubt be preflighting our newly assigned ship. I saw some very strange activity around 725. The pitch change links, which provided all control to the main rotor, were disconnected from the rotor pitch change horns. A ten-foot-long pry bar was angled between the top of one of the rotor pitch change horns and the underside of the main rotor hinge plate. A mechanic was hanging from the bar at its farthest point from the rotor hub. Fifteen feet in the air, the mechanic did some jerky half pull-ups. Never having seen this procedure before, I went over to see what the crew were up to.

"Hi, guys. What's going on?"

"Nothing wrong with the accumulator on this bird, Mr. Spalding."

"Really?"

"Yeah, the problem's a whole hell of a lot worse than that. The main rotor bearings are frozen."

"Frozen, like in 'won't move at all'?"

"That's right. Look at Frank up there. He can't get them to budge even with all that leverage. We've never seen anything like it before. Guess we'll replace the whole rotor system. Good thing you landed when you did. If these things had frozen while you were flying, you'd be dead for sure."

I turned and walked to my newly assigned ship, while I dwelled on fate and said a little thank-you prayer. "How's the ship look?" I asked Joe.

"Just fine. Say, what are they doing to 725?"

"They're working on the rotor bearings. They froze up."

"No shit?"

"That's right. You ready to crank? We're going to have a good mission."

"What makes you think so?"

"I feel lucky. That's all."

★ CHAPTER 29 ★

Friendly Fire

Coincident with his call sign, Centaur 1-8 had turned eighteen halfway through his tour. One-eight was the youngest guy in the unit, and he made the perfect LOH pilot—he was short and had a small build—but he had an elegant quickness, like a featherweight boxer.

I was working a VR mission with 1-8 as my low ship just south of the Vam Co Dong River near Tay Ninh. The area was very sparsely populated but not a free-fire zone. The way this area was used by the populace, it was like the opposite of a no-man's-land. Everyone used it equally. Due to the area's proximity to Cambodia, Charlie used it for infiltration. The local Vietnamese used it for farming. On this particular mission, I spotted a herd of water buffalo. The enemy sometimes used water buffalo as transport for supplies. Whenever the opportunity presented itself in the right locations, we looked over water buffalo herds carefully.

"One-eight, this is 4-4. There's a small herd of water buffalo two klicks north of your current position. How about taking a look?"

"Wilco, 4-4."

The LOH straightened out its flight path and headed north. When it flew over the herd, the buffalo hardly took notice. They were used to helicopters. One-eight began to circle the herd.

"Four-four, 1-8. I've got a gook with these animals."

I told my copilot, "Be ready."

"This guy is real fidgety," said 1-8. "He's motioning us away. I'm going to get him to show some ID."

The LOH circled the man from ten feet away. The man pivoted his body, keeping the LOH in sight at all times. This went on for a couple of minutes and then the LOH called with its report. "Four-four, this guy's acting real strange and he won't show any ID. I think this is a VC buffalo herd. I'm going to shoot one of the buffalo and see what happens."

The LOH broke away from circling the man and flew 100 yards south to where a single buffalo stood. The LOH hovered close to the animal. Suddenly, the buffalo fell to its knees and rolled over on its side. The radio crackled with 1-8's update: "I sure wouldn't have believed it! My gunner took that buffalo out with one shot from a forty-five to the— Uh oh, our suspect's beating feet to the west. I'm going to head him off."

The LOH headed for the now rapidly running man, but before it got to him the man dove behind a rice paddy dike. A second later, the call I was expecting came over the radio.

"Oh, shit. He's got an AK," said 1-8. "We're taking fire!" The LOH rolled hard left. My gunner opened up with the minigun, and I rolled in toward the defiant but stupid cattle watcher. Before I could fire my first rockets, the man seemed to fall to the ground. I broke off my attack.

"One-eight, this is 4-4. I think my gunner got the guy. I've got you in sight."

"Roge'. We'll take a look."

The LOH flew toward the prone body from the west. When it came within fifty yards, the man suddenly sat straight up, pointing his rifle at the LOH. One-eight called excitedly, "Taking fire! Taking fire!"

We couldn't fire at the man because the LOH would have

flown into our own ordnance. The LOH turned left abruptly and I saw tracers from its M-60 striking around the lone enemy. He fell to the ground again. I called to see what had happened: "One-eight, 4-4. You okay?"

"Yep. I think we got the little bastard for sure that time!"

The man was lying on his back with his legs spread wide open.

"You want me to make sure?" I asked.

"That's a big negative! We'll take care of it. I'm going to have the guys drop a grenade right between the creep's legs. That way we'll be damn sure he's dead."

The LOH hovered sideways, keeping its gun trained on the body. The LOH stopped directly over the body for a moment. The nose dropped as the LOH accelerated out of the area before the grenade explosion. As soon as the explosion occurred, the LOH re-entered the area and the gunner put one .45 round in each animal's head. Those buffalo wouldn't be carrying any rockets across the border that night.

Dawn was about to burst upon us. One-eight and I were flying circles five miles south of the Elephant Ear. We were waiting for a B-52 carpet bombing strike. The command-and-control Huey, which was carrying the general who ordered the raid, was with us. The thought that we might not be far enough away from the target crossed my mind more than once. What if the bombardiers screwed up? There'd be little pieces of Cobra spread all over the countryside before we could do anything about it. We knew the enemy feared these raids greatly. Part of the reason the B-52s were so feared was that, flying at 30,000 feet, they were not detectable. One minute everything would be peaceful. Then, without any warning whatsoever, the whole world would explode. It was ten seconds to strike time. I turned the Cobra north to see the action. There it was. Seemingly hundreds of bombs burst in the jungle, one immediately after the other. Huge fireballs blossomed against the early morning twilight sky only to fall back into themselves, leaving smoke where jungle had once stood. The bombs fell and exploded for what seemed like a full minute. Now it was our turn to go into action. We were there to give the general instant bomb damage assessment (BDA) so he could tell how effective the tremendously expensive raid had been.

"One-eight, this is 4-4. You ready?"

"Roge'. Let's do it. I'm on my way down."

"Got you covered," I said. I called to the command-and-control slick: "Two-seven, this is 4-4."

"Go ahead, 4-4."

"How about you staying at two thousand. I'll be working at fifteen hundred. Wouldn't want to run into you."

"Two-seven, wilco."

I followed 1-8 due north into the smoking ruin of the forest. The bombs had cut a rectangular swath from the jungle that measured 1,000 meters long and 200 meters wide. From my altitude, it looked as if God had taken a safety razor and cut an area out of the earth's beard. We were all somewhat tense. There was supposed to be a large concentration of the enemy at the target location. That's why the raid had been ordered in the first place. One-eight worked the area in silence for a couple of minutes.

"Four-four, 1-8."

"What have you got?"

"We killed a lot of trees."

I had expected my VR partner to be shot at. At the very least I expected he would be calling up lots of destroyed bunkers or huge body counts. Incredulous, I asked for confirmation. "Say again."

"I said, 'We killed a lot of trees.' "

On my VHF radio I got a call from the C & C ship. "Four-four, this is 2-7. The headman's getting antsy. What have you guys got?"

"Wait one, 2-7."

"One-eight, understand trees and nothing else?"

"That's affirm, 4-4."

One-eight's tone was matter-of-fact and I-told-you-so all at the same time. He'd complained bitterly about having to get up two hours before dawn for a stupid BDA that wouldn't be worth anything. His theory had been that even if something had been where the raid struck, the terrible pounding would erase any signs of activity he might otherwise have been able to find. He seemed to have been right.

"Two-seven, 4-4. I think it would be best if you let Six listen in to the LOH directly. Come up two three zero point one zero."

The radio crackled with the general's voice. It seemed brimming with anticipation of a great success. "One-eight, this is Six. What have we bagged down there, son?"

A little diplomacy would now be in order, but diplomacy wasn't in 1-8's bag of tricks. "We killed a lot of trees," he said.

There was dead silence on the radio for fifteen seconds. "One-eight, this is Six. I can't believe that. Take a closer look. Intelligence indicates you should concentrate on the northeastern end of the strike."

Obligingly, the LOH headed to the far end of the bombed-out jungle. He flew around in silence for a minute and then called up with a new report.

"Six, this is 1-8. We killed more trees up here. Could be the remains of a small old bunker complex, but mostly we just killed trees."

The answer from the general was uncharacteristically low in volume. It dripped with disappointment. "Roger. Understand. Guess that terminates your mission. Thanks for the help."

The next time I used 1-8 as a hunter we were assigned to an area close to LOH Alley. The border of the area we were to VR actually butted up against our no-low-level restricted area.

"Four-four, this is 1-8. We've got fresh bunkers."

My copilot marked the position on the canopy and then picked up the turret sight and began to track behind 1-8, who called with another update. "Fresh activity on this trail. We're going to follow it."

"Activate the turret," I told my copilot.

As I'd expected, the yelling started right after that. "Receiving fire! Receiving fire! Receiving fire!"

I slammed the cyclic left and forward to roll in behind 1-8's position. The LOH stopped its zigzag and dumped its nose to pick up speed. He was heading from my left to my right at a forty-five-degree angle from our flight path. My copilot didn't fire the minigun. Urgently, I maneuvered to put my sight pipper behind 1-8. That did it. I was lined up. I glanced at the slip/skid ball. I was way out of trim to the right. Simultaneously, I looked up, jammed in all the right pedal I had to correct my trim, and pushed the rocket-firing button. The rockets accelerated away from my ship. Two arrows of death and destruction were loosed into the wild blue. I was horrified to see the rockets heading to the right of where I had been aiming. Things began to move in slow motion. My brain calculated that the rockets were going to hit 1-8! Unconsciously, I held my breath and mentally urged 1-8 to get the hell out of the way. Miraculously, the two rockets hit somewhat behind the fleeing LOH, but not by much.

"I'm hit! I'm hit!" 1-8 called.

I concentrated on putting the next several pairs of rockets where they were supposed to go and broke out of my dive to skim above the treetops. I pulled up hard into a climbing right turn.

"Sing out if you see the LOH," I told the copilot.

There was no sign of 1-8.

"One-eight. Where are you?"

No answer. I strained my eyes in a westerly direction, which is where 1-8 should have headed if he hadn't crashed. "One-eight, 4-4." No answer. "One-eight, 4-4." Still no response. The depression of having shot down my own LOH began to sink in. I switched the radio to our troop frequency.

"Centaur Ops, this is 4-4. We've lost 1-8."

"Roger, 4-4, we've got a rescue ship en route to him already. He called in a minute ago. He's down at the ARVN compound in Trung Lap Village."

I was partially relieved. At least the LOH hadn't crashed. "Ops, 4-4. We're heading over there to see if they need us. Four-four out."

I flew the ten klicks to Trung Lap. The LOH was in one piece, and there was a crowd of ARVN around it. At least there was no danger that the LOH crew would be captured by Charlie. I could only hope I hadn't hurt them too badly. I flew back to Cu Chi, rearmed, refueled, and parked in the Corral. I walked to my room and lay down to rest. I didn't mention my fear of having nailed my own LOH to anyone. I let it eat at my insides. Two hours after I got back, Conners stuck his head in my door.

"Hey, Spalding, they dumped what's left of 1-8's LOH up at the maintenance hangar. You want to see? They say it's full of holes."

I sat up and swung my legs over the edge of my bunk to begin putting on my boots. "Guess I'll go up with you."

Conners and I walked past Ops to the maintenance hangar. "Anyone hear how the crew's doing?" I asked.

"All of them took some shrapnel, but no one is seriously injured."

I looked over the LOH. It had three bullet holes in the Plexiglas and one in the doghouse sheet metal. There were numerous not-round shrapnel holes in the right front Plexiglas and the right side of the ship. Bloodstains were spattered all over the inside of the ship. When the wind blew around in an open helicopter with wounded men in it, blood spattered everywhere. I leaned into the ship's doorway to get a better view of the holes in the Plexiglas. I wanted to see if they had been caused by shrapnel moving from the rear or the front of the ship.

"Kind of beat to hell, ain't it?" said a new voice.

I looked around and saw 1-8 standing five feet behind me. Both his legs were bandaged, as was his right arm, which was in a sling.

"Sure is," I said. "You supposed to be up and around?"

"They told me at the hospital I was free to go. Won't be flying for a while, but overall I'm not too bad off."

"How's the rest of the crew?"

"They're okay. They took less shrapnel than I did. Right now they're back at the barracks having a drink and telling war stories."

"You know what?" I began. "Except for the bullets, I think I'm the one that shot you. I feel terrible about it. I'm really sorry."

"Don't be sorry. You didn't do it. I saw an RPG go by underneath us. It exploded off to my right front. I kind of flew into the outside of the explosion."

"You sure? Seems to me I must have done some of this. My first pair of rockets couldn't have hit more than ten meters or so behind you."

"Hell, that's great! Quit worrying. From where I was sitting that's right where I needed some rockets. You couldn't have done better if you'd tried."

I was relieved by 1-8's revelations. He had no reason I could imagine for not accepting my error as the cause of his misfortune, but somehow I couldn't completely shake my concern over the incident. Maybe it was because of the intense sinking feeling in the bottom of my stomach that I had experienced when I "knew" I was going to hit the LOH with that first pair of rockets. No matter what caused my latent concern, I had to learn to live with it. There were more missions to fly, like the one where I figured out how to best put the automatic grenade launcher to work.

*   *   *

During that mission, I orbited around my LOH as he inspected the VR area for signs of bad guys. The LOH had been low-level for twenty minutes and hadn't found very much activity. We were looking over what used to be a village. Over many years, the various bombardments and artillery strikes had almost made the remains of the village indistinguishable from the surrounding terrain. There was a single structure remaining in the whole area—a small but substantial house. It was full of holes, and pieces were missing from its stucco-like sides, but it was still standing, tin roof mostly intact. The LOH began to spend a lot of time around the house.

"Four-four, 1-3. This house looks like it's being used by Charlie for shelter. There are some cooking utensils, and soot marks where fires have been made inside the house. The trails leading to the house aren't very fresh, but they're definitely there."

"One-three, 4-4. I'm going to be bingo on fuel in another fifteen minutes. How about coming up to altitude and I'll take care of the hut?"

One-three clicked the microphone twice and started up to altitude. I watched the LOH climb and decided this would be a good time to try out a theory I had about using the automatic grenade launcher. My copilot was not exactly a new guy, but he'd only been in-country for a couple of months. Enemy action had died off during that time, and the copilot hadn't gotten much chance to show his stuff. We were in a free-fire zone, and this was a perfect opportunity to let him get some exercise.

"Tim," I said, "how'd you like to see what you can do with the grenade launcher against that house?"

"Gee, that'd be great. Why don't you want to use rockets?"

"It's real hot today. I don't feel like reloading them back at the rearm point. Besides, I think it would be good for you to get some practice."

There was no turbulence to speak of that day, and the

wind was steady out of the west. The LOH reached our altitude. "One-three, 4-4. Orbit where you are. I'll be right back. Keep an eye on the house. We'll see how good my front-seater is today."

"One-three, wilco."

I descended to 1,000 feet, within the effective range of bad guy small arms fire. Since the LOH hadn't found any indications of fresh activity, I felt it wasn't too foolish a thing to do. I flew to the south side of the house, turned left, and headed north. This made our flight path such that we would pass 100 meters to the right of the house.

I instructed the copilot, "Don't fire until I tell you."

"Okay."

I flew north and initiated a further descent. When the house was at our nine o'clock position, I eased the cyclic back and pulled in more collective power to bring the fuel-lightened Cobra to a hover at 800 feet.

"Okay, Tim. See what you can do with the grenades."

Tim pressed the firing buttons, and the grenade launcher worked without jamming. I felt the jolt from each round that fired. Puffs of smoke rose where each grenade landed. Tim was able to keep almost all the grenades inside the area of the house. It was amazing what being at a hover did for the accuracy of the notoriously inaccurate turret weapon. In short order, there was so much smoke and dust that we couldn't see the house very well. Tim pumped in the rounds until the weapon emptied itself of all 350 rounds. It took a minute. When the launcher quit firing, I accelerated and climbed up to 1,500 feet. We flew around for five minutes until the smoke and dust cleared. The house was completely gone!

"What do you think, 1-3?" I asked.

"I think I'm glad I'm on your side. That's what. I never saw anything like that before. I'll buy you guys a beer tonight."

"Thanks. I'll have to pass, though. I'm number-two gun team wingman tonight. See you at the base."

At the rearm point, I gave Tim a hand reloading the grenades. We took the end of the grenade belt, fed it into the input end of the eighteen-inch-diameter, four-foot-long, silver grenade drum. Tim went around to the other end of the drum and began to turn the crank that rotated the inside of the drum and "sucked" in the grenades.

"You know," said Tim, "that's the first time I've been allowed to use the grenade launcher over here. It seemed to work great. How come the other aircraft commanders don't let me fire them?"

"I don't really know, but a lot of the guys don't want to bother reloading this contraption. If they're reloading rockets, this just slows everything down. Besides, you won't see me doing what I did today very often, either."

"Why's that?"

"In case you hadn't noticed, we were hovering at 800 feet. I can't think of a better way to make myself into a target. If there were any bad guys around we'd get our asses blown off. Trouble is, if we don't slow way down and get low, the grenades go everywhere."

"Oh. I hadn't thought about the trade-offs before."

"Well, son, if you don't want to get your ass blown off over here, then I suggest you start thinking about such things more deliberately."

My assignment to the number-two gun team that night held, as I'd expected it would. Sometimes assignments were changed at the last minute, but normally they weren't. Since the enemy action had died down from the levels of the start of my tour, I didn't fly as much at night as once was the case. There was still plenty of opportunity, but the action was nowhere near as intense as it had been. However, this particular evening we got scrambled to do something unusual. We cleared the base perimeter and the lead ship made a turn to the right. The southerly direction wasn't unheard of for us, but it was a little out of the ordinary.

"Four-seven, 4-4. Where are we headed?" I asked.

"We're on our way toward Can Tho."

The area in question was at the north end of the Mekong Delta and pretty far away from the Cambodian border and any major cities. The enemy didn't have much reason to occupy that territory, and because the terrain was so open, when he tried, he usually got wiped out by our superior fire-power. Thus, the area was normally pretty quiet. I'd only made two other trips down that way before. We approached the area for contacting the ground forces that had requested us, and the lead ship went into our close air support routine.

"Fox 4, this is Centaur 4-7."

"Four-seven, Fox 4. What's your ETA?"

"Be there in five minutes, 4."

"Roger that. I can hear you approaching now. I'll tell you when you're overhead."

"Four-seven, roger."

"Four-seven, this is Cu Chi TOC."

"Go ahead, TOC."

"We're up on this freq. Wanted to let you know we're listening."

"Understand."

The guys in the TOC must not have had much going on. They almost never listened to what was happening to a given unit we were working with. Normally the TOC would have been busy processing the next emergency. Of course, the possibility existed that we were on a special operations mission for which we had not yet been fully briefed, but that was not likely. We continued toward the rendezvous point. The night air was still and the flight was very smooth. There was only a half-moon. I could make out some features on the ground, but the blue-tinted canopy made it difficult to be precise about what I was seeing.

"Four-seven, this is Fox 4. You're overhead now."

The lead ship set up a wide orbit and I followed him around while we got briefed. There was no sign of life from the good guys.

"Fox 4, we do not see your position," said 4-7.

"We're not showing a light. Be advised, we have sighted a heavy squad of infantry moving along a dike. They're a hundred meters out on azimuth one two zero and headed our way. We want you to take them out for us."

"Fox 4, this is 4-7. We have no-joy on the infantry squad. It's too dark to see 'em. Please show a strobe for our reference."

"Negative, 4-7. We don't want to be seen."

We flew a few more orbits while 4-7 tried to locate the dike and the enemy to no avail. The lead ship pilot had decided enough was enough. "Four, this is 4-7. I still don't see the target. We're going to abort this mission unless you show us some light."

At the prospect of a mission abort, the TOC spoke up. "Four-seven, Cu Chi TOC. Be advised. Fox 4 is a lone adviser with a group of ARVN trainees."

Terrific, I thought. On-the-job training for new ARVN soldiers! No wonder Fox 4 didn't want to give away his position. He was feeling very alone right then. In a firefight with only raw recruits on your side things could go to hell in a handbasket real quick.

The lead ship called me. "Four-four, can you make out where they want us to fire?"

"I think I see the dike. Can't see any troops, though."

"Okay. Seeing the dike is better than nothing. You take the lead. I'll be your wingman. At least we can try to do these guys some good."

"Wilco," I acknowledged.

I slowed my Cobra to 100 knots, while 4-7 flew a wide left circle to come up in my wingman's position. I searched the ground carefully to locate the dike I thought the grunts were referring to. I rolled into a medium-steep dive and fired the first pair of rockets. As usual, the trail of fire from the rocket motors temporarily blinded us. The rockets hit the ground and exploded in short-lived fireballs. I fired several more pairs and broke off the run while 4-7 covered us with his own rockets. I looked back over my left shoulder to the ground, hoping to see some fires. The little fires sometimes started by our rockets could be used as aiming point references at night. This night there were no fires.

"Fox 4, this is Centaur 4-4. How was the placement on those rounds?" I asked.

"That was pretty good. You might even have got a couple of bad guys. They're running like hell now. Move the next run to the south by fifty yards."

I came to the attack run initiation point, slowed the Cobra to 40 knots, and rolled over and down into the attack. I aimed slightly more to the south. I fired four or five pairs of rockets in quick succession. The last pair left the ship before the first pair hit the ground and then they started to explode one pair right behind the other.

"Cease fire! Cease fire! Cease fire!" The panicked screaming in my ears made me jerk my head back. Immediately my emotions transitioned from aggressive attack into shock and despair. I pulled out of the attack and climbed back to altitude. Four-seven didn't fire a single round in the second attack run, but continued to fly as wingman. I must have picked an incorrect aiming point. It was so dark. I had a foreboding about further communication with the grunts, but it was necessary.

"Fox 4, this is Centaur 4-4. What's your status?"

The grunts were busy tending to the situation. "Centaur 4-4, wait one."

We flew two large orbits of the area. There was still no way to make out any sign of life in the flat blackness of the ground below.

"Four-four, this is Cu Chi TOC. You got a problem?"

"Cu Chi, 4-4. I'm not sure. I think maybe my rounds were misplaced. I may have killed some friendlies. Will advise."

The radio silence and darkness enveloped me. In a way, I felt mad at the ground troops. Why couldn't they have marked their position for us? Why?

"Four-four, Fox 4. Be advised, we've called for dustoff. We have five casualties from enemy mortar fire. You're released to base."

I didn't buy the mortar fire story. I suspected the grunt team leader was doing himself, my fire-team leader, and me a favor. I guess he figured there was nothing that could be undone about the situation. Why get into some kind of bureaucratic snafu about how it was I shot up a bunch of friendly troops when it could be blamed on the enemy? Anyway, it was his call. I let it go at that.

"Roger, 4. You want us to hang around for dustoff cover?"

"Negative. I said, 'You're released to base.' Out."

I didn't blame him. If it'd been me I wouldn't have wanted us around either. We flew back to the Corral and landed. If I could have slinked past Operations I would have. I thought real bad news would be waiting for us, but we never heard anything more about the incident.

On a night mission several months later, I was fire-team leader and we were orbiting overhead waiting for the command-and-control ship to decide how to best use us. There was a hell of a fight on the ground. I could see lots of muzzle flashes from both the night defensive perimeter of good guys as well as from the surrounding fields and tree lines. It looked as if the grunts might get overrun. The grunt commander in the C & C ship seemed not to know what to do. He was talking to ground, demanding status.

"Fox 5, this is 6. How far from the perimeter is the enemy on the north side?" asked the commander.

The grunt's microphone clicked on. We could hear shots and some explosions in the background.

"About fifty meters. Oh, shit! We're taking mortars now. Can't you ge—"

"Calm down, son. Calm down. Don't panic or we'll never get you out of there. How much room is there on the eastern side of the perimeter?"

The grunt's voice was urgent. It snapped with briskness. "I'd say there's one hundred met—*Ayyyaaaah!*"

I cringed as the grunt's bloodcurdling scream sent shivers up and down my spine. I saw a fireball blossom and die right in the middle of the night defensive camp. The commander, flying 2,000 feet over the action, reacted by demanding more status.

"What's wrong, 5?"

No answer.

"What's wrong, 5?"

Still no answer.

"Damn it, 5! What the hell's going on?!"

I clicked on the intercom and spoke to my copilot, "Seems to me it's obvious what's wrong. Fox 5's been hit."

The ground radio came back to life. "Hello, anybody there?"

"This is 6, who's on the radio? Put 5 back on."

"This is Corporal Smith. I can't put the lieutenant back on. Both his legs are blown off. We need dustoff in a hurry. He's losing a lot of blood. What do we do now?"

The rest of that mission is a blur of nonmemories, but the primal scream of the wounded soldier lingers insidiously in the dim recesses of my personal being.

★ CHAPTER 30 ★

Anomalies

I pulled out of an attack with the g's pressing me into the seat. The heavily laden Cobra strained like an overburdened weight lifter under the load I was imposing on it. I pulled in a little more collective pitch to get the maximum allowable torque from the engine. The Cobra shuddered. The engine rpm suddenly began alternately surging above and falling below its normal operating range. Even after over a thousand hours of combat flying in Cobras, this shudder, vibration, and noise were completely new and unexpected. The instant I took to decide what to do seemed like hours. It felt like the ship was going to shake itself apart. Tentatively, I lowered the collective pitch with the intention of entering auto-rotation. Better to be "gliding" when the engine finally blew, I thought. To my welcome surprise, the surging stopped almost as soon as I decreased the power setting. I decided the risk of continuing the mission was worth it, but I flew by keeping my power settings as low as possible. After rearming and refueling, the takeoff power required to fly back to the Corral caused the ship to shake violently again. When we shut down, I had the copilot red-X the ship. I walked toward the maintenance hangar and spotted the master sergeant in charge of the Cobra crews.

"Hey, Sergeant," I said, "who's responsible for 825?"

"That'd be Jefferson, Mr. Spalding." The sergeant motioned toward the far corner of the hangar.

I twisted and turned between the disabled ships in the

hangar as I walked over to the ship Jefferson was working on. He was up at the top of the main rotor mast screwing on the single four-inch-diameter "Jesus Nut" that kept the rotor connected to the drive shaft. (If the nut came off in flight the only emergency procedure available was to yell "Oh, Jesus!")

"Jefferson, can I talk to you a second?" I yelled above the clamor of the hangar work.

Jefferson climbed down onto the wing stub and crouched down so we could talk. "What's up, sir?"

"I'm flying 825 today. I red-Xed it. We were getting gross engine surges at high power settings. I've never felt anything like it before."

"Sounds like it might be the variable air inlet guide vanes. I'll take a look as soon as I'm done here. Thanks for letting me know."

"Anytime, Jefferson. Just take care of my ships so I can feel nice and safe."

"Yeah, right."

Over the next several weeks the maintenance crews replaced everything they could think of that might cause the surge problem. Guide vane controllers, fuel controllers, override clutches, and the like were all changed. None of this had any effect on the symptoms we pilots were experiencing in 825. Then two other ships began to exhibit the same characteristics. Since Maintenance had run out of things to replace, we weren't allowed to ground the ships. We flew them every day and tried to mitigate the problem with judicious power control.

"Isn't there something else we can try to get rid of this problem?" I asked the maintenance platoon leader.

"Nothing I know of. You know what, though, maybe you could get the engine manufacturer's technical representative to take a ride with you. Maybe he could isolate some probable combination of causes."

I set up an appointment with the rep for the next morning.

I was finishing up the preflight when I saw a civilian walking across the runway toward the Corral. I could tell this guy had been around awhile. He was in his mid-forties and had graying temples and a beer belly.

"You Spalding?" he asked as he approached the Cobra.

"Yeah. You the engine tech rep?"

"That's right. You about ready to go?"

"Sure. Let me button everything up and we'll get to it."

"I understand you think you're getting engine surges."

This was a nice approach for a company rep. Pretend the pilot doesn't know what he's talking about. I managed to ignore the offhanded slur. "That's right," I said. "They occur most violently when we pull out of our attacks, but we also get them sometimes when we're taking off or hovering with a load."

"Okay. Let's go out and you can demonstrate to me what happens."

We climbed in and buckled up. I cranked the Cobra and called the tower for takeoff clearance. Because of light early morning traffic, the clearance was instantly granted. I pivoted the ship to head into the wind and gently pressed the cyclic forward to start the takeoff. As we reached translational lift speed the ship did its normal glancing blow off the ground and I added a little power to initiate the climb up out of the Corral. As I rolled slightly to the right, the ship's engine did its surge trick a little.

"Take me back," said the rep.

We were still inside the base camp perimeter and the guy was already begging to get back on the ground. "What do you mean, 'Take me back'?" I asked. "I haven't shown you the problem yet."

"I felt the problem just now, didn't I?"

"Hell, that was just barely noticeable! What I'm talking about is maybe ten times that bad. Don't you want to see the real problem?"

"No. I've felt enough. Take me back."

"Okay. Whatever you say."

I called the tower and got clearance to stay in the traffic pattern. I landed and parked the ship. We both got out. I walked around to the front of the ship to discuss the situation with the rep. "So, what do you think it is?" I asked.

"I don't have any idea. It's nothing I ever experienced before. All I know is that I won't fly in any chopper exhibiting that kind of symptom."

"Look," I said, almost pleading, "maybe you don't understand our situation. If you can't tell us what's the matter, we're going to have to keep flying these things. You were kind of our last hope for fixing the problem or at least directing that the ships be grounded."

"I can't order a grounding. That's beyond my authority, and I can't help you fix 'em because I don't know what's wrong. Sorry."

The rep waved good-bye as he headed back across the runway toward the aviation assault battalion headquarters area. We kept flying the ships, but for the rest of my tour I tried hard not to be assigned to one of the surgers.

Six months later, Stateside, I ran into one of my copilots. We chatted about "old times."

"Do you know what happened to those ships that had the engine surges?" I asked.

"Sure do. Shortly after you left the unit they blew up, one after the other. One exploded at the bottom of an attack run. One came apart when picking up to a hover in the Corral, and the last one blew up during takeoff coming out of the POL."

"Anybody get hurt?"

"The two guys in the first ship to blow were both killed. The other four made it out okay."

"Too bad we couldn't figure out what was wrong."

"Yeah, but you know that's just the breaks."

I wasn't so sure, but what else there was to say about it I didn't know.

*   *   *

Our LRRP insertion was going like clockwork. I had the slicks inbound for the LZ in the Boi Loi woods, and my wingman, 4-2, was in position behind me. The LZ was a good one. It was very wide and had lots of room, but it was surrounded by tall woods on three sides. The slicks were approaching from the south—the LZ's open end.

"One hundred meters," I called for the slicks. "Start your deceleration. . . . Seventy-five meters . . . Fifty meters . . . Twenty meters. You're there."

The slicks touched down as we flew past the LZ at altitude. I saw the LRRPs jump out and head for the tree line on the right.

"Gooks in the LZ!" screamed the lead slick pilot. "We're taking fire! The LRRPs are under fire!"

This was an air mission commander's nightmare: chaos in an LZ with no established ground position. It was like the bad guys had been waiting for us. "Two-five, get the LRRPs back on board," I commanded. "Don't leave without them. Four-two, hold your fire until I open up."

I could see people running around in the LZ. For us, it was impossible to tell the good guys from the bad guys. We didn't dare fire for fear of killing our own men. I saw the slicks' machine gunners open up, and the LRRPs began to run back to them. Finally, the slick called, "LRRPs on board. Heavy fire from the north and east! We're coming out south!"

I rolled in from the west and walked rockets around the north and east sides while the slicks pivoted in the LZ and headed out to the south. Two LRRPs and a door gunner were wounded. There was no way to tell how many bad guys were taken out.

Artillery fire mission spotting was usually boring. One such mission proved different. I was assigned to spot for an artillery barrage on what was left of an isolated and supposedly abandoned village. I took a LOH along with me to do an artillery damage assessment after the barrage. I'd called in many spur-of-the-moment artillery fire missions during my tour, but being assigned this type of mission was not routine. One thing that made me look a little positively at this particular mission was that I knew most times the artillery units worked their asses off and never got any word about how good or bad they were doing. Whenever we gave them instant damage assessment, they were glad to have the information.

My LOH and I arrived over the village at the appointed time. I contacted the artillery unit and called in the strike. We were using 105-millimeter howitzers. They were the smallest of the guns used by the artillery units, so once they were zeroed in on the target area, I let them pound it for ten minutes. There wasn't much left when they were done. That is, there wasn't much left on the surface. I was sure Charlie would have his normal quota of tunnels and underground bunkers. Artillery didn't do much to them. I put the LOH low-level and he began working the area, which was maybe 300 meters square. It didn't take long for the LOH to call with a report.

"Four-four, 1-2. We got fresh signs of enemy activity here."

The LOH was crossing from my right front to my left rear. He overflew the remains of a hootch. As soon as he cleared the hootch, I saw a gook make a run from under the remains of the tin roof.

"Break right!" I shouted at the LOH. "I'm in hot."

I rolled the Cobra hard left and down. Because of the proximity of the LOH, I didn't want to use rockets. With my left hand, I reached up to the weapon-select knob and turned it to the inboard pods, which were loaded with self-contained miniguns. We were headed down and picking up speed fast since I hadn't taken time to slow the ship before entering the attack. As soon as the pipper was close to the wildly running gook I pulled the trigger on the front of the cyclic. The *braaaap* of the wing-mounted guns was more deep-throated than that of the turret weapons, and the tracers spewed out at twice the rate. Bullets struck all around my target, but he was crafty. He ran toward me and zigzagged at the same time. I had to steepen my dive and work the tail from side to side to try to nail this guy. The hail of lead seemed to splash all around my target, but he ducked under some wreckage where I couldn't see him. I broke off the attack and made a climbing right turn.

"One-two, you clear?" I asked.

"Roge', 4-4. We're at altitude to the west."

I selected the outboard pods and started to roll in on where the man had taken refuge. I hoped that the probable tunnel he was headed for had been caved in by the artillery. I was into the attack and the sight pipper was right where I wanted it. I started to press the rocket-firing button. Then my radio crackled with an urgent voice. "Cobra over Ban Rang Village, cease fire! Cease fire!"

I broke off the attack.

"This is Centaur 4-4, over Ban Rang."

"This is Cu Chi TOC. Cease fire, 4-4. Do not fire on the village."

"What the hell are you talking about, Cu Chi? We just finished dumping a hundred rounds of 105 artillery in here. I've got a gook in sight. Why can't I fire?"

"We have our orders. Your orders are to finish the artillery damage assessment and return to base. Acknowledge."

This was strange as all get out, and it more than a little annoyed me. The LOH crew was equally exasperated. The LOH called me with a lamebrained idea that was worthy of our Nighthawk pilot.

"Four-four, this is 1-2. You got any problem if we retrieve the man you spotted? If we can capture him, maybe he could at least provide some intelligence under interrogation at the base."

"What is it you propose, 1-2?"

"My crew has volunteered to go in and locate the guy. I'll

land with your cover, and they'll pull the man out of his hiding place."

"It's your asses, guys. If you're game, count me in."

I flew some low passes over the LOH while he landed twenty meters east of the last place I saw the running man. I saw the two LOH crew members get out. One carried his M-60 machine gun and the other carried an M-16. They walked over to the debris, then momentarily disappeared under it before emerging with the guy we were after. They half walked and half dragged the prisoner over to the LOH, loaded him in, and took off. I was very surprised it had gone so uneventfully. I never did find out what the hang-up was with my firing into the bombardment area.

A ground unit was making a sweep over by the Van Co Dong River. My hunter/killer team was assigned to work with them. We arrived overhead and called in to the C & C ship that was running the show.

"Fox 6, this is Centaur 4-4. We're overhead at fifteen hundred feet."

"Ah . . . roger, 4-4. The grunts' call sign is Fox 2. They're north of the stream that runs west to the river and they're making their way toward the house at the southwest corner of the rice paddies."

I looked down and saw a combat line of troops moving slowly toward what surely used to be a French plantation house. The house was at the apex of where the river and the stream came together. It had a faded orange tile roof. The grunts were advancing from the east and north. Anybody in front of the advancing infantry was trapped by the river and the stream.

"Roger, 6. We've got the grunts in sight. What do you want us to do?"

"Right now we're bingo on fuel. How about playing shepherd until I can get back?"

"Wilco, 6. Fox 2, this is Centaur 4-4. How do you hear?"

"Fox 2 reads you loud and clear, 4-4."

"Fox 6, we have contact with the ground troops."

"Roger, 4-4. See you soon. Out."

The Huey, flying 500 feet over my own altitude, turned and flew toward a forward refueling point. In a way it was nice to see the C & C ship leave. Sometimes the presence of a commander "in charge of everything" could get in the way of effective mission accomplishment. I much preferred working directly with the troops on the ground. We flew wide circles, watching the troops getting closer to the building. Suddenly, the line of troops dove behind the last rice paddy dike between them and the house and bullet ricochets hit the rice paddy dike as the grunt radioman's excited voice filled my earphones. "Four-four, we're taking automatic weapons fire from the house!"

If the C & C ship had been around it would have been necessary for him to coordinate the next set of actions. However, as things stood, I was in position to do something right away. The troops were only about twenty meters from the house. The short distance made the term "close air support" a reality, but I was in perfect firing position and the troops were behind the paddy dikes. I rolled hard left and down toward the house while I told my copilot, "I'll break out real low. You fire off to the right toward the river when I stop firing." He clicked his floor mike twice. I rolled the ship right and stabilized the pipper on the roof of the house. I waited until I was down to 1,000 feet before firing the first pair of rockets. They headed right for the target. The copilot announced, "Five hundred feet." I pushed the firing button twice more. The first pair of rockets blew a hole in the roof. The second and third pairs went in through the hole. We were down to 300 feet, and I started my break straight ahead. The copilot fired the minigun. A huge ball of smoke, fire, and debris from a secondary explosion inside the house filled my vision. There was no way to avoid it. I flew the Cobra straight through the fireball! I could hear and feel pieces of stuff hitting the ship. The controls were buffeted by the turbulence. As I shot through the other side of the smoke, I was down to only three feet over the trees. The copilot's minigun firing stopped right when we needed it the most. I broke into a hard climbing left turn. I strained to look back and down over my left shoulder to get lined up for the next run. The entire house was gone! There wasn't anything left except a dirt area outlined by some very low remnants of the walls. There was a crater in the center.

"Fox 2, this is 4-4. Are you still taking fire?"

"Negative, 4-4. That was great! Do it again!"

How was I supposed to do that? There wasn't any target left. Oh, well, it was worth one more run to be sure, but I didn't have to be so urgent about it. I climbed to a higher altitude and circled to make a run in the same direction as before.

"Did the minigun jam?" I asked the copilot. The gun hadn't sounded like it was jammed, and I was annoyed by the lack of covering fire from the copilot. Frustrated, I said, "I wanted you to keep firing until we got back up out of the dead man's zone."

"No jam, sir," he said. "There's a bunch of civilian farmers on the west side of the river. You didn't want me to hit them, did you?"

My voice softened to allow an apology. "Oh. I didn't see them. Of course, you did the right thing. Thanks."

We made another run and then the troops went in and mopped up. They found the remains of what was apparently a whole squad of bad guys. We didn't lose a man, but the Cobra had a few new holes and dents in it.

★ CHAPTER 31 ★

Holidays

The LOH slowed to 60 knots as it began circling a tree line–checkered area 100 meters south of the village. The new-to-the-unit pilot called up excitedly, "I've got a gook by this tree!"

The LOH made another circle.

"This guy's keeping the tree between me and him. I can't see him well enough to ID him."

Concentrating on the lone man, the LOH circled again, but as it came around to the east side of the tree a fusillade of automatic weapon fire erupted from the adjoining tree line.

"I'm hit! I'm hit! I'm hit!" the pilot screamed.

The LOH hesitated in midair, straightened its flight path, and headed west. I rolled in on the tree line and fired four pairs of rockets. As I broke into a climbing right turn, I strained to see the LOH. What I saw wasn't comforting. The LOH had landed in a marshy area only 200 meters from the enemy.

"One-one, this is 4-4. What's your situation?"

The voice that answered strained for breath. "We're shot up pretty bad, 4-4."

Tracers spewed out of the woodline toward the stationary LOH. I rolled in on where I thought the fire was coming from and loosed several more pairs of rockets. On my breakout, I switched the radio from our working frequency to the international distress frequency, the "guard."

"Mayday, mayday, mayday. This is Centaur 4-4, five

278

miles west of Cu Chi. I've got a downed LOH. Any slick in the area, please respond."

"Hey, look at that," said my copilot. "The gunner's gotten out of the LOH and is firing back into the tree line."

"Centaur 4-4, this is Hornet 2-1. We'll be at your location in five minutes."

"Roger, Hornet. Come up frequency two five two point five."

I changed back to our working frequency. "One-one, 4-4," I called. I let a few seconds pass, but there was no answer. "One-one, 4-4. Acknowledge." Still no answer. "Hornet, how do you read 4-4?"

"You're loud and clear, 4-4."

I wondered what the hell was happening. With no radio contact to 1-1, all I could do was guess at the help my comrades might need. I made another rocket run, hoping I was doing some good. Unexpectedly, the gunner got back into the LOH, it picked up to a wobbly hover, and it took off to the southwest. The LOH was losing fluid from its underside. Thoughts of leaking fuel and flames flashed in my mind!

Urgently I called, "One-one, 4-4. You're losing fuel! Put the ship down." No answer. Hurriedly, I clicked the radio transmit switch to guard frequency. It was worth a try.

"Centaur 1-1, this is 4-4. Set the ship down. You're losing fuel."

There was still no answer. I felt helpless following along, waiting for the conflagration, not knowing where the LOH was going or even if it knew where it was going. Finally the LOH crossed a dirt trail on top of some heavy rice paddy dikes. It landed.

"Four-four, Hornet 2-1's still with you."

"Roger, 2-1. How about picking up the crew?"

"We're on final approach one mile to the east."

As it turned out, the reason I hadn't been able to communicate with the LOH was because the pilot had switched channels to talk to Operations. He was trying to coordinate his own rescue! In the pilot's hospital room, we had a little talk about how that wasn't such a great idea. However, his skill at overcoming adversity couldn't be questioned. He'd been shot through the left arm. In order to fly the LOH, the observer had controlled the collective pitch and the wounded pilot had done the rest.

The Centaurs were different from the troop assault helicopter battalions in more than one way, but one particular difference made us a little jealous. Every so often the troop assault battalions would get a maintenance stand-down for a week or so. The affected unit wouldn't fly for that week so that they could spend extra time on maintenance of their ships and the deleterious effects of continuous combat flying could be mitigated. Of course, during a stand-down, the pilots had some extra free time to relax and unwind. The aviation battalions seemed to have a stand-down every other month, but during my year's tour, the Centaurs had only one stand-down, and it was in effect for only twenty-four hours.

We set up a barbecue outside the maintenance hangar. Everyone in the troop got as much down-home barbecued pork as he could eat. After all the Regular Army chow and the C rations we were used to, the taste of a barbecue sandwich was best described as scrumptious. There was a beer bash afterward. The evening hours passed with idle talk. Along with everyone else, I drank enough beer to get pretty tipsy. I wasn't falling-down drunk, but the next thing on my list was getting back to my hootch and going to sleep. The mere thought of sleeping through the night without being scrambled and getting to sleep late the next morning was a very relaxing prospect.

"You know, Tom, I really wish they'd promote someone else to be a fire-team leader. With just you and me being qualified, we have to fly way too much."

"I'm for that. Maybe you and I ought to talk to the CO about it?"

"Maybe we should, at that. Recently, I flew forty-five days straight, had one day off, and then flew another thirty days in a row. I was in my one-and-only Nomex flight suit all the time, so it didn't get washed. Hell, if I'd crashed and burned the flight suit probably wouldn't have helped me. It would have burned up from the impregnated body oils!"

Tom chuckled. "What time is it anyway?" he asked. "I think I'm drunk enough to go sleep for a year."

I glanced at the large illuminated dial of my watch and discovered that in my inebriated condition I had to stare at it for a second or two to focus. "It's twenty hundred hours, I think."

Just then the scramble horn sounded the alarm for the number-one gun team. During the stand-down, no gun teams existed. We were officially unavailable. Tom and I looked at each other briefly in the semidarkness outside the light emanating from the maintenance hangar. Then we ran as best we could to the operations shack. We burst into Operations.

"What the hell's going on? You guys know we're in a stand-down," I said.

"I can't help that," said the night duty officer. "A ground troop on the far side of the river is in contact and there's no one else available to help. Our unit's the only one available."

I looked at Tom. "I'm drunk, but I guess I could try it."

"Me, too, I guess. Most of the other guys are way far more gone than us. We can make up a fire-team together."

"Who leads?"

"Since we're both equally incapacitated, I don't think it makes much difference. Let's draw straws. Short straw loses and has to lead."

"Right."

Tom drew the long straw. I had the honor of being lead. We selected two Cobras that, according to the ops status board, were in flying condition, raced back to the Corral, drafted two more-drunk-than-us copilots, and cranked for our departure. I tried to be extra careful with the starting checklist, but my brain was obviously operating with a hindrance. I picked the ship up to a low hover and started to inch out of the revetment. The world seemed to swim around the outside of the canopy. The sensation began to make me motion sick. Nausea flushed through me and I thought I would vomit, but somehow I managed to call the tower and take off. Once we were higher in the air, things seemed to be less disorienting. At least there wasn't anything to crash into. I felt I was doing pretty well, until I looked at the airspeed and altitude a few times. They were both fluctuating over a large range. I was overcontrolling—a lot. We were approaching the contact area.

"Fox 7, this is Centaur 4-4. We're five minutes from your position. Show a light."

"Four-four, 7. Roger that."

Ten seconds went by and then the brilliant white flashing of a strobe light could be seen as a beacon in the middle of the black void.

"Seven, 4-4. I've got your light."

The swimming sensation came back. If these guys needed serious close-in assistance we might not be able to give it to them without the risk of killing some of the friendlies. I thought it would be best to let them know our limitations.

"Seven, be advised. We're not sober tonight. If you can use us at least one hundred meters out from your positions that would be best."

"Roger, 4-4. Understand. No problem here. We need fire three hundred meters to our south."

Some of the anxiety flushed from my system. Even drunkards could avoid the good guys at that kind of range. We did, and went back to base with the grunts happy to have done business with us. My landing approach into the rearm point was none too pretty to watch. At the bottom, I didn't quite come to a hover and the ship hit the ground with a little right forward movement. I bottomed the collective to keep from dragging us over and breathed a sigh of relief when the ship quit quivering and stabilized on both skids.

Christmas at Cu Chi included a Bob Hope show. I never saw it. It was my privilege to fly five hours that day to provide cover for Mr. Hope. There was a truce with the enemy. I was directed to take a full hunter/killer team even though, because of the truce, we were not to go below 1,500 feet. Talk about rat-fuck missions. This was the king of 'em.

I spent New Year's Eve in the LRRP bunker at Tay Ninh. Well, most of the night, anyway. When midnight struck, I was sound asleep. I was startled awake by the tremendous noise of hundreds of small arms and machine guns being fired into the air! I stumbled up and out of the bunker to see the spectacle. Tracers were everywhere. A ring of bullets streaked upward all around the base. That's when I got the first whiff of tear gas. Someone was up to his old tricks. What better way to celebrate New Year's than by gassing people? I didn't have my gas mask. In the pitch-black night, I rapidly walked crosswind, hoping to get out of the way of the gas, but I had to take a couple of breaths. The gas burned my eyes and throat, but I missed getting too large a dose. It didn't matter. The combination of the gas, what I'd eaten that day, and the malaria pills I'd taken the day before did its work. I had to take a crap, right then. I ran for the latrine, but couldn't make it. At the last possible moment, I stopped and pulled down my pants in one motion. Hurriedly, I squatted, like the locals, and put my butt over the edge of the board-walk. A huge quantity of watery feces shot from my body. The effects of the gas made me want to vomit at the same time, but somehow I managed not to. I cleaned myself with my underwear, gave the gas time to dissipate, threw the underwear in a trash barrel, walked back, and went to sleep.

"Spalding, we need to talk," said the new Cobra platoon leader, Captain Billings.

I was finishing putting on my flight suit in preparation for a flight to Tay Ninh to do a VR. As I shrugged on the shirt, I told the captain to come in.

"Thought I'd catch you before you took off," said Billings. "You have an R & R in Australia coming up in two weeks, right?"

"That's right, sir. I've waited till now so that I wouldn't have long in-country when I got back."

"Well, I'm sorry, but you can't go."

"Why the hell not?"

"You know you're one of only two fire-team leaders in the unit. We can't spare you."

"Shit! Why didn't you think of this when I applied?" Billings stepped toward the door, opened it, turned around to face me, and said, "It didn't occur to me then, that's all. Sorry."

I was very disappointed. Slots for Australia were hard to get. I'd had to wait a very long time for the one I'd secured. My plan had been to take the Australia R & R, fly missions for one more month, and then take the normal three weeks off that guys took before going home. Of course, it didn't do any good to cry about the situation. I resigned myself to my fate and went about my missions. Two weeks went by. I crossed paths with Tom on my way out to preflight a ship.

"You hear who went to Australia today?" asked Tom.

"No. The only thing that matters is that it wasn't me."

"Oh, yeah? Think so? Well, it was Billings that hopped a ride to Saigon today! What do you think about that?"

My temper flared, but the guy to vent it on was already on his way to Australia. "I think they don't make platoon leaders like they used to," I said. "There's no doubt we can't trust this one. Watch your ass after I'm out of here."

I walked out of Ops into the burning sunlight and headed for the Corral and my assigned ship. I had a new copilot that day. He'd been in-country for about a month, but this was my first trip with him. As I approached the ship, he waved at me and smiled in a friendly sort of way.

"Ship's in fine shape, Mr. Spalding. No gigs in the logbook."

"Great. Let's go."

I walked around and climbed into my seat. I noticed the copilot wasn't wearing a chicken plate.

"You better get Ops to issue you a chicken plate, son," I said.

"Oh, they already did."

"Really? So how come you're not wearing it?"

"I don't like them. They're too hot and heavy."

I boiled. First a scheming platoon leader and now a stupid copilot.

"You dumb shit! You will never ever fly with me without a chicken plate. Do you read me on this?"

The copilot's attitude was casual. "Sure, I hear you. How come nobody else I've flown with cares? It's my ass, isn't it?"

"I don't give a crap about you, mister. Fact is, that chicken plate's only real good for thirty-caliber stuff, and sometimes we duke it out with fifty-ones. In an attack, you're in front of me. For them to get to me head-on, a round first has to go through the ship's nose, then through you, then through my instrument panel, and then through my own chicken plate. If this happens, you're dead meat no matter what, but if you're wearing a chicken plate, maybe I'll make it. Now shut up and do what I tell you."

I didn't quite stop the forward movement of the Cobra as I landed in the Corral. The ship's assigned revetment was at the far end of the area, so I let it drift forward. For the whole mission, I'd noted the continuous very high frequency vibration in the floorboards that characterized this particular fairly new Cobra. The mechanics couldn't find anything wrong with the ship, so we pilots had taken to ignoring the vibration as an idiosyncrasy. The vibration did play in the back of our minds, though. Flying the ship was a little like turning the crank of a jack-in-the-box as a little kid. You knew something was going to happen and you knew it would be scary, but you didn't know when it was going to happen and, in this case, you didn't know what it would be. There was a group of four LOH pilots walking along the left side of the Corral. They were going to be in front of my revetment at about the time I'd try to enter it. A little harassment was in order.

"Watch this," I told my copilot.

I worked on getting close to the group of walking pilots. The rotor wash buffeted them and their clothes whipped in the wind. I concentrated on a point where I would pull in a lot of collective pitch. I planned to create enough rotor wash to blow off their caps. One of them looked back over his right shoulder at me and grimaced. I started to pull in the collective when there was a loud *pop* behind my head. Visions of burst oil lines or exploding jet engine turbine sections flashed before me. I quickly twisted the throttle to the right, rolling off the power, added right pedal, pulled back on the cyclic to stop my forward movement, and did a hovering autorotation. As soon as the ship touched the ground, my copilot leapt out with the fire extinguisher. I'd never seen anyone exit a Cobra so fast. The rotor began to slow, and there was no sign of fire. I sat there shutting off the electrical systems. One of the LOH pilots walked over to my side of the ship and climbed up on the skid to talk.

"What's wrong, Spalding? Did the fire go out?"

"I don't know what happened. There was a big pop behind my head. I shut everything down."

The maintenance officer came to see me later that afternoon. "Got a Coke I can have?" he asked as he plopped down, shirtless, on the couch.

"Sure." I retrieved a cold Coke from the refrigerator and handed it to him.

"Boy, you got some strong wrist, I tell you that."

"What are you talking about?"

"That pop you heard turned out to be the ventilation fan

coming apart. It turns at a real high rpm. That's what you guys have been feeling for the last month. It must have been out of balance. Anyway, it disintegrated. Pieces of fan went all over the engine compartment, but the damage from that is minor compared to what you did. Didn't you push the flight idle stop release button when you shut off the engine?"

"Yeah, I did."

"Then you must have done it when you autorotated."

"Done what?"

"You twisted the throttle so hard that you bent the flight idle stop mechanism. We have to replace the whole thing."

"You know, I'm real sorry about that, but I was a little excited at the time. I guess the adrenaline did what it was supposed to."

Billings came to see me after his R & R.

"Spalding, you ready to stop flying?"

"Not really. I'd rather stay busy. I'd like to keep going till two weeks before my DEROS [date of return from overseas]."

Billings seemed perturbed by my answer. I guess he was hoping I was ready to quit.

"Oh, well, I can't let you do that. I need a night operations officer, and you're it. You start tomorrow."

After a few nights of being operations officer I was dog tired. I took over at 1700 hours and was relieved each morning at 0800. I was working fifteen-hour shifts! Besides the long hours, it was damn hard to sleep in the heat of the day. The job was boring in the extreme. Except, that is, when we had to scramble fire teams or medevac missions. Of course, there was one moment of terror breaking the weeks of sheer boredom.

It was 0200 and a burst of automatic weapons fire reached our ears. It sounded like it came from among the hootches.

"That was an AK," said the sergeant.

"Yeah, I know," I said. "Somebody better check it out."

I waited for either of the enlisted men to volunteer, but it became obvious I'd have to wait until hell froze over.

"Okay. I'll do it. If I'm not back in thirty minutes, scramble the troop."

I picked up my rifle and walked out of the building toward the sound we had heard. As I moved away from Operations, the pale light escaping from the windows was slowly left behind me and I was surrounded by the dark. What would I do if the shots had been fired by some drunken trooper? What if he didn't like officers? What if the shots had come from an enemy sapper who was the lead for an attack? The even deeper darkness between the hootches seemed to be a trap waiting to be sprung, but I had to search it. I moved as quietly as I could and went around the corner of each hootch by first looking around it. The night's silence worked to exaggerate the tension. It was like I was point man, but there was no squad or platoon backing me up. I searched the whole compound, found nothing, and returned to Operations.

"What'd you find, Spalding?"

"Nothing. Not a damn thing."

The war situation was getting politically sensitive. We received orders that we couldn't call the Vietnamese "gooks," not even the bad ones. The bad guys were getting more sophisticated. The pilots had to use an SOI (signal operating instructions), a two-by-three-inch square booklet that contained sets of code words to be used in radio transmission, for communication. The guys told me that using the code words was a giant pain in the ass. The SOIs were also something else to remember to destroy if a pilot got shot down. The pilots didn't need these kinds of complications. In some ways I was glad to not be flying.

The night before I was to leave for Saigon on a dawn flight, one of my former copilots, now a pilot-in-command, walked into the hootch to see me.

"Got a drink for someone who saved your ass tonight?" he said.

"Now what'd you get into?" I asked sarcastically.

"You don't want to know."

"Sure I do. Don't you think you owe me for all those safe flights you had with me?"

"Okay, but it's going to make you nervous. We were on a one-mile final to the base when my copilot looked down and saw an antiaircraft trench being built. Guess the gooks thought it was dark enough not to be seen. Anyway, I rolled in and nailed 'em."

There hadn't been any significant enemy activity in over a month and now they were setting up antiaircraft positions off the end of the runway the night before I was to leave.

"Damn!" I said. "I swear to God, those bastards are after me personally!"

"Guess you could look at it that way. Let's hope there were no more positions put in place during the night." As he turned and walked out he said, "Sleep well. Good luck, and have a good trip home."

The trip home on a chartered 707 was long, crowded, and uneventful. San Francisco was cold and windy. While I waited in the airport for my plane to the East Coast, I looked at all the people coming and going. Twenty-four hours before, I'd been in a combat zone wondering if my ass was going to get blown off before I could get home. These people had no idea about where I'd been, what it was like, or how lucky they were not to have had to be there. It was an eerie feeling. There were no comrades in arms with me. It was lonely.

When I reported for duty at Hunter, in Savannah, five of us recently returned combat vets were in the colonel's office to receive our assignments.

"We're short of fixed-wing instructors," began the colonel. "Anyone fixed-wing rated?"

The irony was too much. I laughed a little.

"What's so funny, Mr. Spalding?"

"I'm a civilian rated fixed-wing instructor and I've been looking to get into fixed-wing since I joined the Army. That's all, sir. After my combat tours in the Cobra I'm probably a little rusty, though."

"No problem. I think they need ground instructors. You interested?"

"Sure am."

So I did nine months as a fixed-wing ground instructor. On the basis of my experience and achievements, I was offered a direct commission to first lieutenant. If I accepted the commission, I would have had to add a year to my prior enlistment commitment. I was flattered, but my wife, with our Hawaii-child on the way, wouldn't even consider it. I turned down the commission. During my time teaching in the fixed-wing school, another Huey pilot with similar civilian background and I went through a prototype Army fixed-wing transition course. After ten or so flight hours, we were rated Army fixed-wing pilots. It had taken about as much time as I'd expected when I first entered the Army and asked for fixed-wing school.

The Army decided it had too many pilots, especially warrant officer pilots. I volunteered to receive my discharge one year earlier than planned. The airlines weren't hiring, but my dad did manage to get me in to talk to the chief pilot at Eastern. The man was glad to talk to me, liked the fact that I had short hair, said he had no openings, and showed me a computer printout that contained the names of two thousand pilots looking for a job with Eastern. A lot of them had heavy jet time. Besides, the major airlines had adopted a policy that you had to have a college degree to fly for them.

Disappointed, I decided to go back to college on the GI bill. At least the GI bill was there. After all the things I'd been through, it did prove to be a useful benefit. My dad said he'd help out with finances, and I planned to work at what I could to make ends meet. The first thing I did when I got to the school was to go to the local airport.

"May I talk to the chief instructor about a job?" I asked the girl behind the operations counter.

"Sure. You looking for an instructor position?"

"Yeah. Here's my résumé."

I had almost 1,800 flight hours; 1,200 of them were combat hours gained in one year. I had been awarded four Distinguished Flying Crosses (DFC). After World War II, my dad, who had accumulated 900 hours over five years and received two DFCs, walked into a job with a major airline. Seemed to me I ought to be a serious candidate for employment.

The chief pilot came out of his office, still reading over my résumé. He studied it for a minute longer while I waited. Finally, he looked up.

"Can't use you," he said. "Even if I could, I wouldn't hire you. I'd rather hire one of my students who just got his license."

He handed me my résumé, turned, and began to walk back into his office. His comment had shocked me.

"How come?" I asked.

"At least I know they can fly," he said.

He closed the door.

RELUCTANT WARRIOR
A MARINE'S TRUE STORY OF
DUTY AND HEROISM IN VIETNAM

by Michael C. Hodgins

Published by Fawcett Books

Read on for a glimpse
into the heart and courage
of a reluctant warrior . . .

Stranger, bear this message to the Spartans,
"That we lie here obedient to their laws."
Epitaph, Thermopylae, 430 B.C.

Twenty-six years have passed since I served in Vietnam. Many books have been written by and about the young men who served in that tragic endeavor. In the minds of the public, stereotypes have been created, lessons have been taught, wisdom instilled. Yet the angst of the entire episode is only vaguely familiar to most Americans now living, summarized in the media as "The Vietnam Experience." But, Vietnam was not an experience; it was a place. Many Americans, as young men, had formative experiences in that place sometime during the ten years that our servicemen fought there. Each was unique. *Reluctant Warrior* attempts to share with the reader the essence of one experience, mine, circa 1970. It is not a war story. It is not even about Vietnam, although the events recounted occurred there. Rather, this is a story about how things were when I was young and my Country was at war. It is a story about ordinary young men who did extraordinary things, together. It is a story about duty, about honor, about leadership. It is a story about moral courage, glory, and luck. It is a story about Marines.

As the title *Reluctant Warrior* suggests, I went to Vietnam with few illusions. Having served several years as an enlisted Marine, I well understood the undercurrents in the ranks. Upon reporting to OCS, I joined several hundred other young men seeking greater responsibility. We were volunteers, recruited from college campuses across the country and from the enlisted ranks. The Marine Corps made each of us a promise: If you accept a commission in the United States Marines, we will shave your head and send you to Vietnam. Since one Marine in three was stationed in Vietnam at the time, it was a promise the Corps had no difficulty in fulfilling. Upon acceptance of the offer of a commission, each candidate took an oath to "preserve and protect" the United States of America from all enemies, "foreign and domestic." We then commenced an arduous training program designed first to test our resolve and then to instill the knowledge we would need to succeed. Each young man embarked on what became, for those who survived, the most formative experience of his life. And we were challenged, literally, by enemies "foreign and domestic." By 1970, a lieutenant of infantry stood an eighty percent chance of being wounded by enemy action before he finished his tour in "the bush," and the Corps, like the other armed services, was confronting a deterioration of discipline in the ranks. At the Basic School, my instructors, with few exceptions, wore Purple Hearts among their decorations. Many were outpatients from Bethesda Naval Hospital, recovering from wounds so horrible that we made jokes to ease the tension of their presence among us. The statistics for "friendly forces" were no more encouraging. In Vietnam, "Demeaning labor, boredom and bitterness led to drinking, drug abuse and fights in the rear, while in the bush arduous small unit activities were at once traumatizing and devoid of measurable success." In the words of one Marine general, "It [the bush] appeared to sap the souls and the spirit of the men." "In some strife torn units, officers faced the daily threat of assassination. It was not enough simply to be vested with the authority of rank. The small unit leader had to earn the respect of his troops merely to survive."* And no one, officer or enlisted, wanted to be the last unfortunate son to die in Vietnam.

But the violence of the late sixties was not confined to the battlefields of Vietnam. It was rampant on the streets of our Republic as well. The period 1965–75 was one of the most tumultuous in our Nation's history. With the advent of television news, the war became a "media event." Everyone was involved, made to feel at risk, vulnerable to tragedy. People took to the streets all across the Country demanding an end to compulsory military service. "Hell no! We won't go!" and "Ho, Ho, Ho Chi Minh!" became mantras of the era, "people's wars" the avant-garde movement of the time.

*U.S. Marines in Vietnam, 1970–71, pp 344–69.

Liberalism's heroes were such men as Che Guevarra, Fidel Castro, Mao Tse-tung and Ho Chi Minh, leaders of the enemy camp. Protests in the United States and around the world were led by student activists from the nations' universities, the same universities that spawned the young leaders of the Armed Forces upon whom the scorn of the nation was heaped. In fact, the most vexing moral question confronting the graduating college seniors of the day was to serve or not to serve in the Armed Forces of the United States. The decision, once confronted, became the comprehensive final exam in moral courage for young men of the sixties. It was a question of core values, patriotism, and moral courage. The system was there, riddled with loopholes for any who took the time or had the intelligence to investigate. In many quarters, it was considered smart to avoid, evade, even cheat the system. Most simply let fate deal their hand, as the system intended.

The decision changed us, those who served and those who did not. After twenty years, the moral issue is blurred in the body politic, but there is still a dichotomy. Those who chose not to serve did no wrong, for the law of the land did not require them to go in harm's way. They had only to take their chance and do their duty if they were called. In fact, of the thirty-five million or so young men eligible for the draft during the war years, only about ten percent (3,500,000) actually endured the experience in any branch of service. But for each principled young man who chose to avoid or evade his duty, another, perhaps less privileged, went in his place. And while the vast majority of the young people who were called, by patriotism, economic necessity, or the draft, to serve in the Armed Forces during these years never saw an enemy or fired a round in anger, some did. Some died. Many were maimed. All returned to a Country devoid of empathy, changed forever by their experience.

Today, it is common for men who stepped aside when faced with the call to arms in the sixties to set themselves out as the "right choice" to lead America into the next century. They seek the trappings and power of political office with the same self-righteous conviction and deceit with which they sought to avoid the hazards of military service in their youth. The self-serving conviction that enabled them to shirk their responsibility and circumvent the law of the land in the sixties still permeates their values today. The success of such men on the contemporary political stage suggests that we, as a society, have learned nothing from our sacrifice. I hope that this is not so. I hope that America will choose its next generation of leaders from among those reluctant warriors of the sixties who in the tradition of their Nation's forefathers went forward toward the sound of the guns when they were called. They are men who know the value of freedom, a value captured in a piece of graffiti scraped in charcoal letters above the entrance to a bunker I inhabited briefly in the Que Sons:

> For those who have fought for it, freedom has a flavor the protected never know.

Semper Fidelis!

RELUCTANT WARRIOR
by Michael C. Hodgins

Available now in hardcover from Fawcett Books